LA

Celebration Breads

Recipes, Tales, and Traditions

BETSY OPPENNEER

ILLUSTRATIONS BY JOHN BURGOYNE

SIMON & SCHUSTER

NEW YORK LONDON TORONTO SYDNEY SINGAPORE

SIMON & SCHUSTER
Rockefeller Center
1230 Avenue of the Americas
New York, NY 10020

For information about special discounts for bulk purchases,
please contact Simon & Schuster Special Sales: 1-800-456-6798 or
business@simonandschuster.com

Designed by Joel Avirom and Jason Snyder
Design assistant: Meghan Day Healey

Manufactured in the United States of America

10 9 8 7 6 5 4 3 2 1

Library of Congress Cataloging-in-Publication Data

Oppenneer, Betsy.
    Celebration breads : recipes, tales, and traditions / Betsy Oppenneer
        p. cm.
        1. Bread. I. Title.
    TX769.O686 2003
    641.8'15—dc21   2003054367

ISBN 0-7432-2483-3

To my love, my best friend, my strength,
my supporter, my playmate, my most honest critic,
my traveling companion, my everything—my husband, Keith

———————

Acknowledgments

As a food professional, I hate buying cookbooks with recipes that don't work. I strive to ensure that my recipes are well tested by enlisting family, friends, and other bread enthusiasts so that each recipe is tested at least twice (sometimes three times).

Each of my testers deserves a giant thank you. They not only baked a lot of bread but also answered a questionnaire on each recipe telling me what they thought of the taste, ease of preparation, how attractive the bread was, and whether they would make it again. Their comments were invaluable and without them *Celebration Breads* would not be what it is.

Here are my wonderful testers: my dear friend Barb Knepper—who took my bread class when we both lived in Fürth, Germany—not only tested the largest share of recipes for this book but also tested recipes for one of my previous books *The Bread Book*. Last year my wonderful brother-in-law, Lowell Franks, decided on a whim that he wanted to make bread. He watched my video, walked into the kitchen, started making wonderful bread, and hasn't stopped since. I'm so proud of him!

Our friend and neighbor Ernie Schori loves to bake and tested quite a few recipes. Ernie is from Switzerland, has baked professionally, and is a storehouse of information on both baking and Western Europe. He even emailed his sister, Charlotte Fischer, in Switzerland for information. Another close friend and professional "foodie," Bill Dollard, baked a bunch of breads that he shared with his neighbors—boy, do they love him!

Our oldest son, Erik Oppenneer, who was weaned on bread and loves to bake when time permits, tested recipes too.

I met and recruited Joanne Sawyer, Jay Lofstead, Karen Plomp, Debbie Fortin, Bonni Brown, Vicki Soule, Diana Warshay, Pedro Arellano, Dick Cosler, Pat Kleinberg, Sue Benbow, Debra Widera, and Kathy Matuszewski from a bread chat group on the Internet. I've never met these wonderful people face to face, but I feel they're truly good friends.

Other people have helped with *Celebration Breads,* one of whom is my wonderful husband, Keith. He's helped with research, sorted out which testers had what recipes, and collated their return comments during the testing phase—not to mention his doing the dishes and laundry and countless other tasks so I could keep working. His support has made my life easier, and his love keeps my spirits high.

My mother has typed, and typed, and typed until I'm certain her fingers are at least an inch shorter than when I started this project. The research has been long and involved, and she has helped keep me organized. I've sent many packages from New Hampshire to Georgia so she could type numerous tidbits of information and email them back to me. She's been extremely tenacious, never stopping until finished. Whoever says that people in their mid-eighties aren't useful hasn't met my mother! Carolyn Barney also volunteered to type and help keep my mountains of research organized.

My son Mark, an outstanding wordsmith, helped edit the first draft manuscript. He can take my words and make them sound better and much clearer.

As a member of The International Association of Culinary Professionals, I've also had many people I could call for information or verification. Many thanks to Elizabeth Baird, Naomi Duguid, and Pam Collacott from Canada, and Kathie Alex from France. Elizabeth Andoh from Japan furnished wonderful information that I tried to find a way to use, but most Japanese people don't use their breads for celebrations. Gerard Reijmer and Pat van den Wall Bake-Thompson from the Netherlands, and Scott Givot (who also forwarded information from Ingrid Espelid Hovig and Astri Riddervold, a noted Norwegian ethnologist and culinary historian), and Aase Dotterud from Norway were also a great help. Thanks to Susan Slack, Kitty Morse, and Barbara Tropp from the United States. Sadly, Barbara died within a week after making her contributions.

Lee Crawford of the Burleson County Czech Heritage Museum, Helen Zemek Baine, and Helene Baine Cincebeau were extremely gracious and shared their knowledge of Czech information and lore.

Many thanks to the following embassies and governments that furnished information: Bulgarian Embassy Culture Counsel, Chinese Information and Culture Center in New York, Cyprus Tourism Organisation, Government of Cyprus, German Embassy, Embassy of Japan, Republic of Lithuania Ministry of Culture, Embassy of the Republic of Slovenia, Embassy of Sweden, and Cultural Ministry of Taiwan.

When I requested information from the various foreign governments and tourist councils, the Embassy of the Republic of Slovenia put my request for information on their chat website. I received a most informative message from Anja Hajdinjak, who not only shared her customs and recipes but also sent a picture of her grandson in his traditional *kurent* costume so that I would know what it should look like.

For many years I have admired the illustrations of John Burgoyne. His drawings bring food to life, and I find his work much more alive than many photographs. I was more than thrilled when he agreed to illustrate my book both inside and on the jacket. You're the greatest, John. Thanks.

I also want to thank my very good friend and agent, Judith Weber, and my new friend and editor, Sydny Miner. Without them *Celebration Breads* would not be.

Contents

Introduction

*B*read has been my passion since I won a cooking contest when I was a Brownie scout in the third grade. At first I just enjoyed getting my hands in the dough and "playing." As I got older, I became interested in the history of bread and the customs pertaining to bread from other countries. *Celebration Breads* marks the culmination of a lifetime of learning about bread.

No food has had a greater influence on religion, culture, history, or our lives than bread; it has been a sacred symbol for years. Bread was a vital part of many pagan rites. There are at least 250 references to bread in the Bible, most of which are celebratory. Christians celebrate Holy Communion with bread to signify the body of Christ. Jews commemorate the release of the Children of Israel from slavery in Egypt with unleavened bread. Not only do Christians and Jews regard bread with reverence, but Muslims also show their respect for bread as the staff of life. Should a piece of bread or a loaf fall to the ground, it is picked up, kissed, and put to the forehead three times.

People around the world have different beliefs, practices, attitudes, histories—so many things seem to separate us. *Celebration Breads* acknowledges our cross-cultural reverence for bread as one of the few things that bring us together, that make us one. Whether we are breaking the bread, giving it as a gift, decorating a temple with it, or wearing it on our heads, we use it to bring people together for all manner of celebrations.

This book also acknowledges our quickly changing world. As we begin the new millennium, many of our traditions and celebrations are at risk of being left behind. We live in a fast-paced time that doesn't seem interested in older things. How many times have you heard that none of Grandmother's recipes were written down, or that she took them to the grave with her? What a great loss that so many wonderful bread recipes are not being passed on to younger generations!

I was heartened as I worked on this book to hear the comments of my recipe testers. They told me things like "My mother used to make this" or "I shared this bread with a friend who said their grandmother (or aunt, or someone from "the old country") made something similar to this bread." *Celebration Breads* is part of the answer to the question of how to preserve the disappearing culinary traditions of our cultures.

My research for this book presented some interesting challenges. For example, it is almost impossible to find the "true" or exact recipe for many of the breads in this book. Over the years bakers have personalized their versions of a recipe so that no two recipes for the same bread are identical. Recipes passed from mother to daughter or to daughter-in-law may never have been written down. Not only did the ingredients for the same bread vary tremendously but also the shapes. My technique for resolving these challenges was to find as many recipes as I could for the same bread, compare and synthesize them, and then rewrite the recipes to fit modern preparation techniques using mixers, food processors, and bread machines. The recipes in *Celebration Breads* are in many ways a bridge from the fading past to a future of renewed traditions. The breads you will produce are traditional at heart, but modern in technique.

Another challenge I faced was authenticating source countries for many traditions. Several recipes, especially those of Eastern Europe and Russia, can be found in all the neighboring countries. When I was able to determine beyond a reasonable doubt that a recipe began in a particular country, I list it by that country rather than by all the countries that also claim it.

This sampling of celebration breads—with their histories, tales, and traditions—is not by any means the only one that should be remembered and passed along to our children, but it is a start. Celebrate, rejoice, and bake bread.

1

Ingredients

Yeast

Yeast is an amazing living fungus that hangs in suspension until warm water activates it. Once activated, like any living thing, it requires food and nourishment, such as flour and other bread ingredients. Yeast feeds on the natural sugar in the flour and creates carbon dioxide. The kneading process helps fill the gluten meshwork with gas bubbles, which in turn make the bread rise. Yeast is commercially available in three forms:

ACTIVE DRY YEAST is available at the grocery store in small ¼-ounce foil packages or in 4-ounce jars. You can also buy yeast in bulk at some specialty food stores or through mail-order catalogs. If you use bulk yeast, this conversion formula is helpful: For each package of active dry yeast called for in a recipe, use one scant tablespoon—not quite a full spoon— of yeast.

Of the two major yeast companies in America, one specifies that a scant tablespoon equals a small packet of yeast, while the other says to use 2½ teaspoons yeast for a packet. Both ways of measuring equal the same amount. Like all perishable products, yeast packages are stamped with an expiration date. Most yeast remains good past that date, but you should "proof" it to be sure. See page 22 for detailed instructions on proofing and activating yeast.

COMPRESSED OR FRESH YEAST is available at some grocery and health food stores in the refrigerated section, and from some bakeries. The packages are approximately an inch square and ½-inch thick. Fresh yeast is becoming harder and harder to find because it is more perishable than active dry yeast. Also fresh yeast is easy to damage when defrosting it from its frozen state. However, bought fresh from a reliable source, it produces outstanding breads with a wonderfully intense flavor and a smooth texture. Many bakers, especially in European countries, feel that fresh yeast gives much more flavor to their breads than dry yeast.

FAST-RISING OR QUICK-RISING YEAST comes in foil packets or small jars just like active dry yeast. This is a different strain of yeast developed to give quick results. With rare exceptions, this type of yeast is activated by the *rapid or quick method of activating yeast* (see page 23). To substitute fast- or quick-rising yeast for active dry yeast, use a scant tablespoon for each package called for in the recipe. Just remember to cut the rising time in half for each rising period. Do not use this type of yeast if you're letting the dough rise for an extended period of time. Do not let the dough double in size before it goes into the oven or it will deflate. Watch it carefully and put it in the oven just before it has doubled.

Flour and Meal

The natural sugar in flour feeds the yeast and gives a "carbo-boost," much like the lift humans get from sugar. When mixed with liquids and beaten, flour forms a gluten meshwork that gives bread its structure and texture. It is important to use hard-wheat flour—not soft-wheat flour—when making yeast breads. Soft-wheat flour does not contain enough protein to form gluten, which means that the bread won't rise very high. Only hard-wheat flour—or a mixture of hard and soft wheat, as in all-purpose flour—provides yeast breads enough protein to form a strong gluten meshwork. Flour comes in many varieties, but in the interest of simplicity, only the types used in this book are described below.

WHEAT FLOUR

ALL-PURPOSE FLOUR, a mixture of hard and soft wheat, can be used for all types of baking, from light cakes to hearty breads. As its name implies, it is designed to be all purpose. It comes bleached as well as unbleached.

> *Bleached.* Although this flour contains hard wheat, it is not good for making yeast breads. The bleach shortens the gluten strands, which keeps the bread from rising properly. Short gluten strands make short, dense loaves.

> *Unbleached.* I use unbleached flour with no bromates or chemical additives for most of my baking. It is versatile and dependable, and produces loaves with full volume and texture. I know I can expect good results.

BREAD FLOUR is made with hard wheat and works well for yeast breads, but only if it is free of chemicals and bromates. I get the same results from unbleached all-purpose flour, which is often less expensive. Most bread flours require kneading the dough again for almost half as much time you would normally be kneading; that is, if you normally knead for 10 minutes, you will have to knead bread flour for almost 15 minutes.

Whole-Wheat Flour is available as hard-wheat and soft-wheat flour. The hard-whole-wheat flour is higher in protein than all-purpose flour, but the germ and bran will produce a denser loaf. For a lighter loaf, I use a finely ground whole-wheat flour or mix my whole-wheat flour with unbleached all-purpose flour. You can make a good 100 percent whole-wheat bread as long as you keep the dough extremely moist and don't add too much flour.

Soft-Wheat Flour is available in several varieties: cake flour, pastry flour, and self-rising flour. Each kind does a great job for its purpose *but does not work well in yeast breads.* Most soft-wheat flours are bleached, but because of popular demand many millers are beginning to offer their soft-wheat flours unbleached.

Semolina Flour is made from the coarsely ground endosperm of durum wheat. Semolina flour is used mainly in Europe, Russia, and Middle Eastern countries. Semolina is known best as the flour used to make pasta. It is high in protein, has a wholesome nutty flavor, and gives a rich golden color to baked goods. When using semolina, keep the dough as soft as possible, since too much of this flour makes the bread heavy. Semolina flour doesn't have a very long shelf life and will produce dry breads if it isn't fresh. **Durum flour** is a by-product of semolina flour. It's the bran and germ from durum wheat with just a small portion of the endosperm. You can make 100 percent semolina breads, but durum flour should be mixed with wheat flour; otherwise the loaf will be extremely heavy and almost inedible.

RYE FLOUR

Rye has an earthy, sweet-and-sour flavor and can be cracked or made into meal, flakes, or flour. There are three types of rye flour available.

Light (or White) Rye is finely ground and milled from only the endosperm. It contains very few vitamins, minerals, or oils from the germ and bran. It is most often used by commercial bakers.

Medium Rye is the most readily available rye flour in grocery stores. It is a midrange flour that can make anything from a light rye bread to a very heavy dark rye bread. The grain for medium rye flour is ground after the bran is removed.

DARK RYE OR PUMPERNICKEL is milled from the whole grain with the bran and germ intact. This flour produces a hearty, bold-tasting loaf. It is favored in many parts of Scandinavia, Europe, and Russia—as well as my kitchen!

CORNMEAL

Cornmeal is made from ground yellow or white corn and is available as stone-ground or enriched degerminated.

STONE-GROUND CORNMEAL is more nutritious than enriched degerminated cornmeal. It is made from dried whole kernels of corn. The kernels are slowly ground on large stones, a process that prevents the meal from overheating during the grinding. This method of milling produces a rich, intense, sweet corn flavor, and the meal feels oily to the touch. Because it still contains the germ, stone-ground cornmeal should be stored in an airtight container in the refrigerator or freezer for no longer than four months.

I grew up with Nora Mill stone-ground cornmeal from the Sautee-Nacoochee Valley where I was raised (see page 331). The true corn flavor of this robust and hearty cornmeal makes for some of the tastiest corn bread in the world.

ENRICHED DEGERMINATED (OR BOLTED) CORNMEAL is also made from dried whole kernels of corn, but it is ground through a series of steel rollers. To extend the shelf life of the meal, the fiber and germ are removed, and then vitamins and minerals are added to the meal. Enriched degerminated cornmeal is available in all grocery stores. It keeps for up to nine months in an airtight container at room temperature. Breads made with this kind of cornmeal tend to be dry and crumbly, which is why I prefer stone-ground cornmeal.

BUCKWHEAT

Buckwheat flour or Saracen corn is not a grain but the edible fruit of the buckwheat plant and a kissing cousin to rhubarb and sorrel. The nutritional value is similar to that of wheat. Buckwheat flourishes in cool climates and is a staple of middle and northern European countries as well as parts of Maine and Canada. It has a strong, pungent flavor. Flour from dark buckwheat tastes stronger than that from light-colored buckwheat. Since buckwheat is not a true grain and does not contain the necessary proteins to make yeast breads, it must be mixed with at least 50 percent or more wheat flour. Most Europeans use buckwheat for various types of pancakes or flatbreads.

Liquids

Liquids activate yeast, stimulate gluten formation, and cause yeast to ferment during rising. They also affect other qualities of bread. For example, milk adds nutrition, aids in browning the crust, and extends the bread's keeping quality. Breads made with water have an earthy flavor and a crisp crust. Potato water—water in which potatoes have been boiled—gives bread more volume and a velvety texture.

Sweeteners

Sweeteners activate yeast, aid in browning the crust, and bring out the flavors of other ingredients. Each sweetener also adds its own special taste to bread. Granulated, brown, and raw sugars are interchangeable in equal measurements. You can substitute honey, molasses, or syrup—corn, cane, or maple—for sugar. Because liquid sweeteners are more concentrated, you can use less in your recipe. The dough may require extra flour, since these sweeteners are liquid.

Powdered and confectioners' sugar are pulverized forms of granulated sugar. They contain cornstarch, which prevents the sugar from clumping together. I do not use either of these sugars in bread dough but do use them for icings and glazes. *Pärlsocker,* or pearl sugar, is an unusual alternative to icing breads. These large granules of sugar are slightly larger than pretzel salt and remain soft and bright white during baking.

Salt

Salt controls fermentation, slows down the rising time, and adds its own flavor to breads while bringing out the flavors of other ingredients. It is best not to dissolve the salt in the liquid used to soften yeast because salt inhibits the growth of the yeast during the early phases of development. Add it with the dry ingredients.

I use a scant teaspoon of salt for every package of yeast in a recipe. If the recipe calls for more salt than that, you can safely reduce the amount without affecting the flavor. Table salt contains anticaking agents that add a slight chemical taste to baked goods and interfere with rising. I prefer to use kosher or sea salt because each has a clean, pure salt taste and doesn't leave a chemical aftertaste.

Fat

Fat—lard, shortening, butter, and oil—improves the keeping qualities of bread, produces a lighter, more tender texture, and makes slicing easier. It also lubricates the gluten meshwork of the dough, which helps the dough rise better. I do not use margarine when I bake because no two margarine products are alike. Many contain water or chemicals, which makes margarine unreliable as a cooking fat.

LARD is used to make the tenderest of all baked goods. Many people cringe at the thought of using lard—rendered pork fat—but if you consider the small amount you ingest per serving, it isn't nearly as frightening as you might think. Use it occasionally for those special breads. I cut lard into cubes measuring about a tablespoon each, put them in freezer zip-style bags, and store them in the freezer for up to nine months. I can use as little or as much as I wish this way.

VEGETABLE SHORTENING produces the second tenderest baked goods. It is made from saturated and polyunsaturated oil and contains no cholesterol. Shortening is packaged in wide-mouthed cans or cubes that are just a little larger than a stick of butter. Although shortening is stable and can be stored at room temperature for up to a year after opening, I often keep shortening in the refrigerator because it is easier to cut into flour if it is cold.

BUTTER, long prized for its flavor, produces the third tenderest baked goods. I use unsalted butter in most of my recipes. The salt in salted butter is added to extend the shelf life and can mask the flavor of butter that is going bad. Old or improperly stored butter turns rancid and can ruin baked goods. Never use butter that has an odd smell or taste, since both intensify during baking. Using unsalted butter allows me to control the amount of salt in my breads.

OIL (PURE OR REFINED) is made from nuts, grains, fruits, or vegetables. Pure oils are extracted from a single source, such as olives or sunflower seeds. They are not processed further after extraction and have a relatively short shelf life after opening. They have a distinctive flavor and should be used in recipes where that flavor is desirable. Refined oils are mixtures of extremely stable vegetable oils, which are processed or refined to extend the shelf life. They have no flavor or odor and cannot be detected in baked goods.

Eggs

Eggs add flavor and color and contribute to the leavening process, making the loaves rise higher. Egg breads generally have a delicate texture and more tender crust.

2

Equipment

BAKER'S PEEL OR PADDLE. These large wooden paddles have a tapered front edge and a handle. Some of them are made of metal. They are used to slide pizza and large freestanding loaves—or any bread for that matter—in and out of the oven. My favorite peel works on the same principle as the professional loaders for commercial ovens. A piece of parchment paper or canvas wrapped around the surface of the paddle works like a conveyor belt, sliding the dough on and off the peel slick as a whistle. See The Breadworks, Inc., in Sources (page 331) for more information.

BAKING STONES are like large, flat tiles that sit on the rack in your oven during baking. They gather heat that helps produce crisp crusts. I prefer using a single large stone because I can bake multiple loaves and rolls at once on it. These stones are not cheap. While smaller tiles are less expensive, they are not nearly as effective as a large stone, since they don't conduct the heat as well. If you use commercial or professional stones, you can clean them in a self-cleaning oven.

For the best results, baking stones must be hot all the way through. Preheat the stone in the oven at least 30 minutes before you bake so that your loaves will cook evenly throughout.

LAVA ROCKS: Baking stones produce nice crusts, but to achieve an even crispier crust, you can use lava rocks and some water to create steam in the oven. I recommend lava rocks—the kind you use with a grill—over others because they are safer and less likely to explode under high heat. Use other rocks only if you know how well they withstand extreme temperatures. Before you preheat the oven, place a small shallow pan on the bottom shelf and fill it with rocks. When you put the bread in the oven to bake, pour ½ cup boiling water over the rocks and close the door quickly to preserve the steam—it's like giving your bread a sauna. The water will evaporate after the first few minutes of baking and will help your crust to expand and become extra crisp.

BREAD MACHINES are appliances that mix, knead, raise, and bake a loaf of bread with the push of a button. You put the ingredients in the bread pan, turn on the machine, and walk away to return a few hours later to the pleasant aroma of freshly baked bread. Some machines are equipped with timers, so you can set them to begin the process at a time convenient for you. See page 28 for directions to make perfect bread using your machine.

Dutch Ovens. These deep pots with heavy lids can be used on top of the stove or in the oven for cooking or baking. I use them for poaching bagels, frying, and for special loaves that require steam as they bake. Once, on a camping trip in Michigan, I buried a Dutch oven under the coals of our campfire to bake bread. As the bread was baking, a small tornado swept past the area, forcing us to take cover. By the time the winds had calmed, we were able to enjoy the finished product!

Food Processors are familiar to many cooks for cutting, shredding, chopping, and mixing food. They make a variety of kitchen tasks quick and easy. Buy the most powerful processor you can afford—you will not be sorry. A good processor can effortlessly and efficiently mix and knead bread dough as well as a mixer or bread machine. See page 27 for directions to make perfect bread using your food processor.

Graters. If you remove the zest from a citrus fruit with a standard grater or zester, you might scrape too deep and pick up the bitter white pith. Since many of the breads in this book call for zest, I recommend using a Microplane grater. What makes this grater different is its razor-sharp teeth—it makes removing zest from citrus fruits a quick and easy job. Microplane graters come in all sizes and are available in kitchen stores and through catalogs.

Heavy-Duty Mixer. For those who don't have the time or inclination to knead dough by hand, these tough strong-motored machines are fantastic. When you master the technique of using a mixer, your bread will come out exactly as if you had made it by hand. See page 26 for directions to make perfect bread using your mixer. I love getting my hands on the dough whenever I have time; however, I hate the mixing-and-stirring part before the dough is kneadable, so I always start my dough in the mixer. If I have the time, I turn the dough out on the work surface and knead by hand, and if I don't, I let the mixer finish the task for me.

Instant-Read Thermometer. Although many people have a good feel for the temperature of liquids that go into a recipe, an instant-read thermometer never lies. It lets you know the exact temperature of the liquid in your recipe so you get the most out of your yeast. Using an instant-read thermometer is also a foolproof way to tell if your bread is done baking: Stick it into the center of the bread, and when it registers 190°F, it's done.

KITCHEN TIMER. A timer is an absolute necessity when making bread or doing most any task in the kitchen. I use a battery-operated triple timer so that I can keep track of many things at once. If you prepare recipes that require timing for longer than an hour, you will need a timer that can be set for over an hour—mine can be set for up to ten hours.

LARGE CERAMIC BOWL with a 4- to 6-quart capacity. Ceramic bowls hold heat longer than metal or plastic bowls and give a wonderful "incubating" warmth to rising dough. If your kitchen is cool or you need to speed up the rising process slightly, heat the bowl first by filling it with lukewarm water and letting it sit for about 5 minutes; then pour out the water, dry the bowl, and add the dough. I prefer deeper bowls with straighter sides, which allow less air to reach the surface of the dough as it rises.

LARGE WIRE RACK. A wire rack is one of the most essential items for the serious bread baker. You should have at least one, if not two! As soon as bread comes out of the oven, it should be removed from its pan and placed on a rack. Racks allow air to circulate freely around the cooling loaves and keep the bread from sweating and becoming soggy. I like racks with the wires in grids instead of rows; they keep cookies and small baked goods from sliding through onto the work surface.

MEASURING CUPS—both liquid and dry. Liquid cups have a pouring lip and are most often clear for easier measuring. The flat rim of a dry measuring cup allows you to swipe across the ingredient for a level and uniform measurement.

MEASURING SPOONS. I use long-handled spoons with long, narrow bowls. This kind fits through the small mouth of a spice jar easier than the round-bowled spoon.

PANS AND BAKING SHEETS. I use heavyweight, dull to dark baking sheets and pans for bread. Shiny pans and air-cushioned baking sheets and pans reflect the heat rays of the oven and prevent breads from browning properly. Lightweight pans do not conduct heat well and prevent bread from baking evenly. The professional half-sheet pans that I use are 13 by 18 inches with a 1-inch rim and handle all of my baking needs. Several specialty pans are also available:

Bundt pans have a tube in the center, which promotes even baking. They are fluted or designed to give the bread a pretty shape. Any tube pan may be substituted for this pan.

Gugelhopf/kugelhopf pans are tube pans with designed sides. You can substitute a 10-inch Bundt pan.

Springform pans are usually round, though I have seen some square and heart-shaped pans. These pans have removable bottoms; their sides are often expandable and close with a spring or snap device. Springform pans are invaluable when making filled or shaped breads that might be awkward to turn out of a pan. Simply remove the sides of the pan and slip the bread from the base onto a cooling rack.

PASTRY BLENDERS are made of a series of blades or wire loops shaped into a U and attached to a handle. They are used to cut fat into flour. I prefer blenders with blades because they cut through the fat better than wire blenders.

PASTRY BRUSHES are handy for brushing butter, eggs, and other glazes on breads. When I want to remove excess flour from dough during the rolling process, I use them as little brooms. I have a ½-inch brush for small items like thin pretzels or breadsticks and a 2-inch brush for really big loaves. Practically speaking, a 1-inch brush will probably take care of all your needs.

PLASTIC DOUGH SCRAPER AND/OR METAL BENCH SCRAPER. I have both kinds of scrapers, and each serves a different purpose. I use the plastic scraper to clean bowls and to scrape the film that develops on my work surface when I knead dough. The plastic scraper won't gouge a work surface as a metal one might. I use a metal scraper—very carefully—to divide dough. The stiff blade makes cutting the dough easier.

PROFESSIONAL PARCHMENT PAPER. I do most of my baking on parchment paper. It's easy to clean up and gives my breads a softer bottom crust. It also keeps breads made with sugar from caramelizing on the bottom as they do on greased baking sheets. Professional parchment paper can be used in ovens heated up to 425°F. Less expensive brands of parchment become brittle and shatter if they are placed in ovens over 375°F and cannot be reused. I use one sheet of professional parchment several times unless I've baked something particularly messy. Parchment paper is also handy for moving risen dough onto a baking stone. Shape the dough on parchment, then slip both the paper and dough onto your preheated stone.

Rolling Pin. I use 16- to 18-inch, heavyweight, solid cylinder rolling pins. They are called pasta pins and don't have handles. By rolling the pin with my hands in the center of the cylinder rather than at the ends, I keep the thickness of my dough more uniform. I season and clean my hardwood rolling pin with vegetable oil so it won't stick to my dough. Never clean a wooden pin with soapy water. Use oil to clean the pin, and if you need a little abrasion, use salt. Washing a pin in water will dry it out and make it more likely to stick to dough.

Scoops. Scoops are great for measuring dough accurately. I have them in all sizes for making cookies, doughnuts, pancakes—and measuring dough. For greater ease, I use a mechanical scoop; it has a spring-loaded handle that activates a piece of metal that sweeps the dough or batter from the scoop. I recommend buying the more expensive, higher-quality scoop, which stands up to bread dough better than the cheaper ones.

Serrated Knives. Serrated knives make slicing your finished loaves an easy task. Invest in a high-quality 8- to 10-inch serrated blade to prevent tearing and squishing the loaf when you slice it. I use a 3-inch serrated knife, which works better than a razor, to slit the tops of my loaves before baking. It cuts so precisely I can make curved designs on tops of loaves.

Tightly Woven Towels or Plastic Wrap are great for covering dough as it rises; both keep the air away from the bread. I prefer towels, since they can be reused. With the amount of baking I do, I can't afford to throw away that amount of plastic wrap! Tightly woven towels, such as linen or flour sacks, work best. Terrycloth and loosely woven towels allow too much air to reach the dough.

WHISKS

Balloon whisks are large whisks that are ideal for whipping egg whites or heavy cream. When I whip by hand, a balloon whisk gives me total control over the final texture of the aerated ingredient. If egg whites are at room temperature or the cream is very cold, whisking by hand doesn't take much longer than using an electric mixer.

8-inch whisk. I use professional whisks that will last a long time and are sealed so that liquid can't get into the handle. The whisks are long and thin so they fit into a measuring cup as well as the corner of a saucepan. I use an 8-inch whisk to dissolve yeast—yeast dissolves instantly when whisked but sticks to other utensils. I also use it to beat an egg for glaze and mix confectioners' sugar with liquid for a smooth icing.

Heavy-duty roux whisk. My favorite whisk in the kitchen is my heavy-duty roux whisk. This whisk is 12 to 14 inches long, and the wires are flat and strong. Women usually prefer the 12-inch whisk, while men prefer the 14-inch. The roux whisk beats dough efficiently because the wires are flat with no place to trap the dough on the inside. The whisk's handle is thick and easy to hold.

I get a lot of mileage out my roux whisk. I use it to stir batters, fold egg whites into other mixtures, to transfer breads such as doughnuts, pretzels, or bagels into pans containing water or oil, and for general stirring whether in bowls or saucepans. It works the same as a slotted spoon. Oh, yes, and the whisk works great for roux!

3

How to Make Bread

The Four Basic Rules of Bread Baking

I tell my students that there are four things you need to master in order to make perfect bread: how to properly activate the yeast, correctly knead the dough, add just the right amount of flour, and make certain the bread is done baking before removing it from the oven. If you purchase an instant-read thermometer, you immediately take care of the first and last steps. You're already halfway there!

RULE #1: PROPERLY ACTIVATE THE YEAST

Thermometers are a must-have for bread bakers. They give you specific information that your senses alone might not provide. If the liquid for your bread is too cool, then your yeast will not properly activate. If the liquid is too hot, you can severely damage or kill the yeast and your dough will not rise. An instant-read thermometer accurately measures the temperature of the liquid so there is no guesswork. Each type of yeast—active dry, fresh or compressed, and rapid- or quick-rise—has its own method for activating.

ACTIVATING ACTIVE DRY YEAST

There are three basic ways to activate active dry yeast. I prefer the second method below simply out of habit—it's how I was taught. However, each method produces the same results in the finished loaf. Experiment to find which method suits you.

1. **Proofing method of activating yeast:** Before yeast came in packages with expiration dates, bakers had to "prove" that the yeast was good before using it. This old-fashioned method is still popular today. Many people still proof their yeast because they feel it gives the bread more flavor. It is my experience that flavor develops as the dough rises—the longer it rises, the deeper the flavor. Since proofing takes only 5 minutes, I doubt that it really enhances the flavor of the bread, but I do proof yeast when I am concerned about its freshness or when I will be using a food processor. Because the ingredients are combined more quickly in a processor, proofing the yeast first allows it to mix with the other ingredients better.

    To proof the yeast, put the warm water from your recipe in a bowl or measuring cup. The yeast will double in size, so use a container large enough to hold three to four times the amount of water you are using. Add ½ teaspoon of sweetener, such as sugar, honey, or syrup, for every scant tablespoon or package of yeast. Whisk the ingredients until the yeast dissolves, then let it sit uncovered. If the yeast is good, it will double in about 5 minutes.

2. **Standard method of activating yeast:** Now that yeast comes marked with a freshness date, proofing is not essential. I like this method for its ease and simplicity. Soften the yeast by sprinkling it over warm water that is between 105° and 115°F (see page 22 for information about instant-read thermometers). If the water is cooler than 105°F, the yeast may not activate properly. If it is over 115°F, you can severely damage or kill the yeast and your bread will not rise. As soon as each granule of yeast has been moistened, you are done. You do not need to stir the yeast. If you are a creature of habit and feel that stirring is necessary to dissolve the yeast, use a whisk, because the yeast will stick to a spatula, spoon, or fork. If all of the granules are moist, the yeast will dissolve as other ingredients are added and mixed.

3. **Rapid or quick method of activating yeast:** This is the method preferred by most yeast manufacturers. Mix the undissolved yeast with roughly two-thirds of the dry ingredients called for in the recipe. Whisk to combine. Heat the liquid(s) to 120° to 130°F. Pour the liquid ingredients into the dry and mix together thoroughly. Continue the recipe by gradually adding the remaining dry ingredients. The flour and other dry ingredients insulate the yeast from the higher temperature of the liquid so that no damage is done to the yeast.

ACTIVATING COMPRESSED OR FRESH YEAST
To activate fresh yeast, crumble it over water that has been heated to between 80° and 90°F and let it sit for 10 minutes until soft and creamy. Stir until smooth.

ACTIVATING FAST-RISING OR QUICK-RISING YEAST
With rare exceptions, this type of yeast is activated by the rapid or quick method of activating described above. When using rapid- or quick-rising yeast, it is important to cut the rising time in half for each rising period.

RULE #2: CORRECTLY KNEAD THE DOUGH

Whether you use your hands, a heavy-duty mixer, food processor, or bread machine, it is essential to knead the dough correctly. If the dough isn't kneaded well, the bread will not rise to its fullest potential, the texture will be uneven, and you'll probably have more crumbs on the cutting board than in the loaf.

Mix your ingredients in a large bowl according to your recipe's directions, but add only about one-third of the flour. Beat vigorously to start the gluten development—gluten is the meshwork that forms when flour and liquid are mixed and agitated. This process will make your kneading a little easier. At the end of the beating time, gradually add flour ¼ cup at a time. When the dough begins to draw to the middle of the bowl when you add flour—but spreads back out and sticks to the sides of the bowl after you beat it a few seconds—you have a kneadable dough. Turn it out onto a floured work surface to begin kneading.

Kneading forms tiny blisters throughout the dough that fill with gas formed by the yeast. The gas is what makes the dough rise. When you make white bread, you can actually see the blisters just under the skin of the dough. They look like small blisters that might form on your hand or arm if you were splattered by hot grease.

HOW TO KNEAD DOUGH:

1. With your fingertips, pull the far edge of the dough toward you and fold it in half.

2. Roll the dough from the tips of your fingers to the heel of your hands, pushing the dough away from you. This action should roll the dough over, not squish it down on the work surface.

3. With your fingertips, flip the far edge of the dough over toward you.

4. Repeat steps 2 and 3 until the dough becomes long, then give the dough a quarter turn. Starting with step 1, repeat the steps until the dough becomes smooth and elastic.

It is important to develop a steady rhythm when kneading. Not only is it therapeutic but it also helps keep the dough from sticking to the work surface. Each person will develop his or her own rhythm. Some people use a four count: fold-1, push-2, pull-3, turn-4; while others use an eight count. I prefer a light waltz: fold-1, push-2, pull-3, push-4, pull-5, turn-6.

It takes a proficient kneader at least 8 to 10 minutes to knead dough properly by hand. So many of my students tell me they have mastered kneading and can do it in 3 to 4 minutes. You can get the right amount of flour into the dough in that short time, but the dough needs the extra kneading time to allow the gluten meshwork to develop fully.

RULE #3: ADD THE RIGHT AMOUNT OF FLOUR

Too much flour produces doorstops and hockey pucks. Most people add flour to the work surface when kneading just because there isn't any there. This is one of the biggest mistakes bakers make. Add flour only if the dough is sticking, and then just the lightest covering of flour possible. If the dough gets sticky as you knead it, pat the sticky spots with flour but don't overdo it. The secret to keeping your dough from sticking lies in learning to knead with a good rhythm by pushing out and away from you and not down toward the work surface—and in being judicious when adding flour.

In many bread cookbooks you will find a wide range in the amount of flour called for in each recipe—3 to 4 cups, for example. This is because different kinds of flour absorb liquids at different rates. A variety of factors affect a flour's rate of absorption: the age of the flour, how it has been stored, and the weather or humidity level. In the humid southeast you will need a lot more flour than in the arid southwest.

Different measuring techniques are another reason authors call for a range of amounts. For example, I "fluffle" flour into a measuring cup. This is very simple to do but difficult to explain. By gently scooping upward with my cup, I loosen and break up the flour so that it is not packed. I level it by swiping off the excess flour with a dough scraper or knife blade. "Fluffling" yields about 4 ounces flour in a 1-cup measure. You might simply be a "scoop-and-swipe" person, with no scraping; this process that yields about 5 ounces because more flour is packed in the cup. That's a big difference between cooks. I recommend learning to make bread by feel rather than by what the recipe says. If you can develop your ability to "read" dough and understand when to add flour and when not to, you'll be better able to control the quality of your finished loaves.

My goal is to develop what I call "slack" dough. When I've finished the kneading process, my dough should be smooth but still slightly sticky if I squeeze it. To keep dough slack, knead it a lot but add as little flour as possible. Adding too much flour makes your loaves dry and heavy. The dough shouldn't be too stiff, because it needs to continue absorbing liquid during the rising time. Stiff dough will become hard after it has risen, but slack dough remains pliable and easy to shape.

As you learn to add flour by feel, you will need to "test" the dough to make sure you have added the right amount. To test the dough, form it into a football shape—you may have to use your imagination here. With the dough lying on the work surface, use your hands to pat the edges into a diamond or an oval with pointed ends. Lift the "football" about a foot from the work surface and drop it on one pointed end. If the dough doesn't settle at all—that is, you have a tall lump before you—you definitely have too much flour in your dough. If your football relaxes into a flat, thick pancake, you should add a bit more flour. If the top surface remains slightly domed as it settles, you have enough flour in your dough no matter how sticky it is. Another way to visualize the test is to imagine you are making a freestanding loaf of bread—one without a pan. If you form the dough into a ball and place it on a baking sheet, would the dough keep its shape or would it flatten out? If it would keep its shape, you don't need any more flour.

If you don't pass the football test, don't worry. Your bread will still be good. It will be better next time when you don't add too much flour. Each loaf is an opportunity to improve your bread-baking skills.

Before we get to Rule #4, we will cover mixing—using a heavy-duty mixer, food processor, or bread machine—and rising, shaping, and baking.

MIXING INGREDIENTS

Using a heavy-duty mixer. My method of preparing bread in mixers that use a paddle and dough hook usually differs from the manufacturer's directions. My method, however, produces light, lovely bread, and it prevents the dough from crawling up the dough hook into the mixer head.

Start with the paddle attachment, not the dough hook. In the mixing bowl, soften the yeast in the liquid. Add all the moist ingredients from your recipe to the yeast, then all the dry ingredients except the flour. Add about one-third to one-half of the flour from the recipe and beat for 2 minutes on the medium setting.

Reduce the speed to the lowest setting and add the remaining flour ¼ cup at a time. The dough is ready to knead when it begins to ball up on the paddle but spreads back out to the sides of the bowl after a few seconds of mixing.

Now you can turn out the dough onto a work surface to knead it by hand, or you can remove the paddle and change to the dough hook to let the mixer do the kneading. Scrape the sides of the bowl. Turn the mixer to low, and add flour, about 1 tablespoon at a time, until the dough balls up on the hook but spreads back out to the sides of the bowl after a few seconds–just the way it did on the paddle.

Increase the speed to medium and let the mixer knead the dough for 4 to 5 minutes. Usually at the end of the 5-minute kneading period, the dough begins to clean the sides of the bowl. If it does not, gradually add flour 1 tablespoon at a time until it does. When the sides of the bowl are clean, put the dough into an oiled bowl to rise.

Using a food processor. Almost any bread recipe can be converted for use with a food processor. Before you begin, make sure your food processor will accommodate the amount of flour the recipe calls for. If not, you will need to cut the recipe in half.

Since the steps in a recipe happen faster when using a food processor, I proof my yeast before adding it to the processor. Put the warm water (between 105° and 115°F) into a large cup. The mixture will double, so use a container large enough to accommodate the expansion. Dissolve the yeast in the water along with ½ teaspoon sugar for each scant tablespoon or ¼-ounce package of active dry yeast. Let the mixture sit uncovered at room temperature for 5 minutes or until bubbly.

I recommend using the plastic dough blade when using the food processor, or the new metal dough blade that was introduced in 2000 by Cuisinart. Both create less friction and reduce the chance of overheating the dough. Put all but ½ cup of the flour from your recipe into the food processor bowl, then add all the remaining dry ingredients. If you are using solid shortening or butter, add it with the dry ingredients. If you use oil, add it with the liquid ingredients. Eggs are considered a liquid ingredient. Pulse the food processor six or seven times to combine the mixture.

Add the proofed yeast to the dry ingredients and pulse six or seven times to combine. Heat the liquid ingredients to 90° to 100°F, but no warmer, since the processor will create some heat in the mixing and kneading process. With the food processor running, add the liquid as fast as the dry ingredients will accept it. If you hear a sputtering sound from the flour mixture in the processor, pour the liquid slower or the dough will go up under the blade—not only messy to clean but also stressful on the processor's motor. As soon as you have added all the liquid, turn the processor off immediately.

To adjust the liquid-to-flour ratio, pulse the machine seven or eight times to see if the dough balls up on top of the blade. Watch where the side and bottom of the food processor meet. If there are dry crumbly bits there, add water 1 tablespoon at a time and pulse until the dough forms a ball. If the dough is too wet and sticky to pull together, add flour 1 tablespoon at a time and pulse until the dough forms a ball. Pulsing does not create as much friction or heat as running the machine.

When the dough forms a ball, turn the processor on and let it knead. If using the plastic or new metal blade, knead for 60 seconds. If using the metal chopping blade, knead for 45 seconds in the processor, then knead by hand on a work surface for 3 to 4 minutes. Put the dough into an oiled bowl to rise.

Using a bread machine. The recipes in this book can be made in a 1½- or 2-pound bread machine. Put all of the liquid ingredients from your recipe into the pan of the bread machine. Next add the dry ingredients except the flour and yeast on top of the liquid ingredients. Cover the ingredients in the pan with all but ½ cup of the flour. Make an indentation in the top of the flour. Put the yeast in the indentation. The yeast goes in last to keep it separated from the liquids until the mixing starts.

If you are using the sponge method by mixing the yeast, water, and certain ingredients specified in your recipe into a runny batter, mix the sponge and put it into the pan first. Add all the other ingredients on top of the sponge and add the flour last. You do not need to proceed with the recipe at this point but can set the bread machine's timer to start at a later time. The sponge will rise under the flour but not mix with it. When the machine begins its mixing and kneading cycle, it will combine the flour with the sponge and reactivate it if it has relaxed.

Once the machine turns on and all of the ingredients are mixed, open the top of the bread machine to check the liquid-to-flour ratio. If there are dry crumbly bits of dough in the bottom of the pan, add water, 1 tablespoon at a time, and let it mix for a minute. If needed, add more water, but give it time to work itself into the dough before adding more. If the dough is too wet and sticky to come together into a soft ball, add 1 tablespoon of flour, and let it mix for a minute. If needed, add more flour, 1 tablespoon at a time, giving it time to work itself into the dough before adding more.

Some bread machines have a cycle that beeps to let you know when you should add fruits and/or nuts. If your machine does not have this cycle, add the fruits and/or nuts with the yeast.

Bread machines are designed to mix, knead, rise, punch, rise, and bake your dough. Some people object to the size of the loaves produced in a bread machine or do not like the hole in the bottom of the loaf created by the blade. If you would like more control over the shape of the finished loaf, you can remove the dough from the machine and shape it however you like it. Just let the machine do the mixing, kneading, and first rise.

RISING

I have been told many clever ways to make bread rise better. One little old lady carefully wrapped her dough and bowl in an army blanket and placed it on top of a heating pad. Some have suggested putting the dough in an oven with a pot of boiling water next to it, putting the dough in an oven with the light turned on, or placing it in the microwave at 30 percent power for 2 minutes before letting it rise. Some people even buy expensive "rising" boxes. None of this is necessary!

For your dough to rise all you need is a bowl, preferably ceramic, about 1 tablespoon oil, and a tightly woven towel. I prefer deeper bowls with straighter, less rounded sides. These allow less air to reach the surface of the dough as it rises. The oil serves several functions: It keeps the air away from the dough, expands as the dough rises, and keeps the dough from sticking to the bowl. Solid fats such as butter and shortening are not as versatile. Pour the oil into the bowl and use the dough to smear it around a bit.

Cover the dough with the towel and put the bowl in a draft-free place. I use tightly woven towels like old-fashioned tea towels or flour sacks because they help block the air from the dough. Terrycloth towels allow too much air to flow through and can dry out the dough.

You can use plastic wrap to cover the rising dough, but if the dough is warm enough to create steam, condensation may form on the underside of the plastic. If the drops of moisture touch the dough, they will create gooey places in the finished loaf. Plastic wrap is also expensive to use, especially when you bake as much as I do. Throwing a towel into the weekly wash is much more cost efficient.

In about an hour, your dough will double in size. If your dough doubles in less than one hour, either your rising place is too warm or you have added too much yeast. Dough needs the full rising time to develop the gluten's strength. Only if I am in a hurry will I use a warmed ceramic bowl for my rising dough. I heat the bowl by placing warm, not hot, water in it for about 5 minutes before drying it and putting in the oil and dough. It acts as an incubator, retaining the cozy temperature needed during the rising period.

You really don't have to keep the dough warm if you've properly activated the yeast. It will grow regardless of the temperature. Many European recipes activate the yeast in warm water, then add cold water as the remaining liquid, or they let the dough rise in a cool room. The long, slow rise gives the dough plenty of time for the flavors to fully develop. Under normal circumstances I just let my dough rise at room temperature, which is about 65°F in the winter and 70°F in the summer.

Has My Dough Risen Properly? There are two methods for testing if your dough has doubled in size. The old-fashioned method entails pressing two fingertips about ½ to 1 inch into the dough. If the dents stay, the dough is doubled. The only problem with this method is that the dents also stay if the dough has risen too much.

The measure method is more practical and accurate. After you have kneaded your dough, place it in a measuring cup. You may have to measure it in pieces, but try to get as accurate a total as you can. Then, with your dough still out of the bowl, fill the bowl with twice as much water as you have dough. The water line is your doubled-in-size line. Some people mark this line with fingernail polish or indelible ink so they can remember where the double mark is.

SHAPING THE DOUGH

I do two things at this point that differ from what many other bakers do. I don't punch the dough down if I'm going to roll it into a shape, and I turn it from the rising bowl to a lightly oiled work surface. If you punch the dough down, it makes the gluten in the dough become elastic again. It's difficult to roll the dough when it's like this. If you have trouble rolling the dough, cover it with a towel on the work surface, let it rest for 5 minutes, then try again. If you don't punch the dough down, you can roll it easily in any shape you wish.

I use a lightly oiled work surface rather than a lightly floured surface because the dough doesn't accept flour evenly after it has risen. A lightly oiled surface allows the dough to slide easily when I roll it out or shape it. The dough will absorb the oil with no effect on the finished bread.

Shape your dough as the recipe directs. Once you have shaped the dough, cover it again with a tightly woven towel, and allow it to rise until it is *almost* doubled in size, about 45 minutes. If it rises too long before going into the oven, it will collapse like a baked soufflé. If it has risen too long, you can turn it out, reshape it, and let it rise once more. Don't be surprised when your dough continues to rise for a bit after it goes into the oven. Bakers call this brief rising "oven spring."

Slashing the top of a freestanding loaf or baguette before baking it allows the dough to rise under controlled circumstances. If you don't give the gases and moisture a place to escape, they will make their own. You may have seen loaves that look as if they have a "blowout" on the side. They were not slashed.

BAKING THE DOUGH

Before you bake your bread, make sure the oven is fully preheated. This takes about 10 minutes. Your breads will not bake properly if the oven hasn't reached the correct temperature. I recommend placing the oven racks in a position that will allow the center of whatever you are baking to sit as close to the center of the oven as possible. The rack will be lower for loaves, higher for rolls. This rule applies as well for any baked goods—cookies, cakes, and so on. There should be at least 1 inch of air space around all sides of your pans for air to flow evenly. If you use a baking stone, preheat your stone in the oven for a minimum of 30 minutes before you bake.

RULE #4: MAKE CERTAIN THE BREAD IS DONE

Check the center of your bread with an instant-read thermometer. When it reads 190°F, your bread is ready to come out of the oven.

When I bake for my family, I just stick the thermometer in the top of the bread, which leaves a small hole. If you are giving your loaf as a gift, you can lift the loaf out of the pan and stick the thermometer in the bottom; don't do it from the end or every slice will have a hole in it. Don't worry about your yeast bread falling like a cake. Once the crust has risen and set, the bread will hold its shape.

The old-fashioned way to determine if bread was done was to thump the loaf on the bottom to see if it sounded hollow. But what does "hollow" sound like? Bread made with eggs has a different "hollow" thump than whole-grain breads or breads made with water. The only fail-safe and consistently accurate method of testing the loaves is to use an instant-read thermometer. Every bread baker should have one.

As soon as the bread is done, remove it from the pan or baking sheet and put it on a rack to cool. This prevents the bread from sweating, which makes the crust soggy.

4

Tips and Techniques

Some of the tips and techniques I will share with you in this chapter are covered in other sections of this book, but I think they are important enough to mention again.

Cooling Bread

As soon as bread comes out of the oven, remove it from the pan and put it on a cooling rack. This prevents the bread from sweating, which makes the crust soggy. Let bread cool completely before wrapping it. The average loaf of bread takes about 5 hours to cool all the way through. If you wrap the bread in plastic before it has totally cooled, it will steam in the enclosed wrap and become soggy. This soggy bread will become solid as an ice cube if frozen, and when you thaw the bread, the inside will be a mushy disaster.

Storage

Once bread has cooled completely, you can wrap it for storage. Anything that goes into your freezer needs to have a thickness of at least 2 mil of protection. You cannot see nutrients leave food, but they do if the bread isn't properly wrapped. Plastic wrap and foil used together is the equivalent of 2 mil. Freezer zip-style bags—which are what I use—offer over 2 mil protection.

I reuse freezer bags up to five times, wiping them out with a paper towel after each use. When they begin to get flimsy and tired looking, I throw them out. Bread crust becomes soft when wrapped in plastic, but for sandwich loaves that's okay with me. Never use plastic bags from the produce section of your supermarket for bread storage. These bags have minuscule holes in them that let fruits and vegetables breathe but dry out baked goods.

The new jumbo-size bags are wonderful for freezing large loaves such as challah and baguettes. Be sure to squeeze the air out of the bag before zipping it closed. Excess air makes bread go stale, allows the formation of ice crystals that can make your bread soggy, and invites mold. To remove most of the air from a zip-style bag after putting the bread in, put a straw in one end of the zip top and close the bag to the straw. Suck the air out of the bag, quickly remove the straw with your teeth, and pinch the top of the bag closed to seal it. You are your very own vacuum sealer!

If you plan to eat them soon, some sourdough and heavy peasant-type breads can be stored for a short time in a breadbox without being wrapped. However, if you live in a humid climate, your bread will mold more quickly.

Refrigeration also causes bread to go stale quickly. I think it's better to slice it, freeze it, then take it out and defrost it a slice or two at a time. It takes only 5 to 10 minutes for a slice to thaw, or you can pop it in the toaster immediately.

Slowing Down the Bread-Making Process

There are a number of ways to slow down the rising process so that bread fits your schedule. Bread is extremely forgiving as long as you activate the yeast at the correct temperature and knead the dough correctly.

- If you have too much dough to go into an oven at one time, it is best to cover one pan with a tightly woven towel and place it in the refrigerator to slow down the rising while the other loaf is baking. Remove it from the refrigerator about 5 minutes before the first pan is finished baking. Then put the dough in the oven and bake as directed in the recipe.

- Another solution is to shape half the dough and put the remaining half back into the bowl for a second rise. Shape the second dough 30 to 45 minutes after the first so that it will be ready to go into the oven when the first one comes out.

- After the dough has risen the first time, you can punch all the air out of it and let it rise again. To punch the dough down, put your fist into the dough and press to the bottom of the rising bowl in two or three places, then fold the outside edges of the dough to the center of the bowl, pushing down each time to remove the excess air. Flip the dough over and cover it again with the towel. In fact, you can actually punch the dough down, let rise, punch it down, and so on up to five times total before the dough starts to get tired. Each successive time the dough is punched down, it will rise just a little faster; for example, it will take an hour to double in size the first time, about 55 minutes the second time, 50 minutes the third, as so on. Each successive rising gives more time for the flavors to develop and produces a more finely textured bread.

- You can activate the yeast with warm water, then add the remaining liquid called for in the recipe very cold—even ice-water cold—instead of warm. This increases the rising time from 1 hour to 4 or 5 hours.

- You can put the kneaded dough into a bowl, cover it with plastic wrap and a towel (both layers of protection are necessary), then place it in the refrigerator for 2 to 24 hours. About 3 hours before baking, remove the dough from the refrigerator and let it sit at room temperature for an hour. Shape it and let it rise 2 more hours before baking.

- You can knead the dough, then let it rest covered with a towel on the work surface for about 20 minutes. This resting time allows the gluten to relax, which makes dough easier to shape. Shape the dough and brush it lightly with oil; I use canola oil, since it has no flavor. Cover the dough with plastic wrap, then a towel, and put it in the refrigerator for 2 to 24 hours. Fifteen minutes before baking, remove the shaped dough from the refrigerator and allow it to sit at room temperature. Bake according to recipe directions. If the bread is large, it may require an additional 5 minutes of cooking.

Speeding Up the Bread-Making Process

I've discovered that you can make good bread quickly, but you can make better bread slowly. It is much easier to slow dough down than to speed it up, but here are a couple of things you can do.

- The most obvious way to speed up the process is to use quick-rise or rapid-rise yeast. You can convert any recipe for use with this type of yeast, but you must use the quick- or rapid-rise method of preparing the dough. See page 23 for more information.

- Letting dough rise in a fairly warm place can speed up the time, but if you speed it up too much, the dough won't develop the strength and flavor needed to make good bread. When I teach classes and need to complete three or four different bread recipes from start to finish in a 3-hour class, I use warmed bowls. Ceramic bowls are best since they retain heat, but you can use metal. Place plastic wrap over the top of the warm bowl containing the dough. The dough will double in about 40 minutes.

Miscellaneous Tips

Here are a few other tips that you might find interesting:

- Don't wash bread pans with soap unless absolutely necessary. Soap encourages bread dough to stick to the pans, even if they've been well greased. Let pans build up a natural patina and become dull or dirty looking. Dull or dark pans absorb heat and produce a dark, crisp crust. If something needs to be scrubbed off the pans, use a mixture of equal parts salt and oil to scrub, then rinse with hot water and dry.

- Remember, heat is the enemy when making bread. Anything hot can damage or kill the yeast, and your bread will not rise. People will carefully measure the temperature of the liquids when activating the yeast, but then forget and do something like toast sesame seeds and dump them hot into the recipe. Be conscious of the temperature of all ingredients when preparing a bread recipe.

- Almost any loaf recipe can be shaped into rolls, and almost any roll recipe can be shaped into loaves.

- Breads containing eggs tend to brown more quickly than other breads. Watch your bread the last 10 minutes of baking. You may need to cover the bread with foil to keep it from getting too dark. When covering bread with foil, always make sure the shiny side of the foil is facing up. The shiny surface reflects the heat rays and lets the bread cook on the inside but not brown further. If the dull side is facing up, the foil will draw in the heat rays and brown the bread more.

- Whenever you braid loaves, start in the middle. If you braid from one end to the other, the loaf invariably gets thinner as you braid. Start in the center and braid to one end, then turn the loaf and braid from the center to the other end. The loaf will be plump in the center and tapered to the ends, giving a balanced shape.

- When using a bread machine, if your loaves seem to fall during the baking process, try using less yeast. The natural tendency is to add more yeast when the loaves fall or are not as tall as desired. What actually happens is that the dough rises too much, then when the heat comes on, the loaf collapses. This also happens if you let the dough rise too long before baking it in a conventional oven.

- Use stale bread to make croutons, bread crumbs, bread puddings, or French toast. Never throw away bread if you can help it.

5

Africa

Matzo

Matzo (also matzot, matzoh, or matza) is served for the Jewish festival of Passover, which celebrates the flight of the Israelites from Egypt. During Passover, leavened food—any food that is raised by yeast or chemical leavening agents, like baking powder or baking soda—or any food that comes in contact with leavened food, is not eaten. When Moses led the Jews out of Egypt, they left in such a hurry there was no time for their daily bread to rise, and they made flat, unleavened bread instead. The only breadlike food allowed is matzo, a flat wheat bread similar to a cracker or the "bread of affliction or sorrow" used by the Jews during their flight.

Matzo is a major part of the ceremonial Seder dinner, the highlight of Passover. The food prepared for Seder is very symbolic. A roasted shank bone represents the paschal lamb, a roasted egg symbolizes the mourning for the destruction of the Temple in Jerusalem, and bitter herbs serve as a reminder of the bitter suffering under slavery. A mixture of chopped apples, nuts, cinnamon, and wine called *charoses* represents the mortar used by the slaves to build the Egyptian monuments, and parsley, celery, or lettuce symbolizes the meager diet in Egypt. The parsley is dipped in salty water as a reminder of tears shed in hardship.

There are five obligations performed by Jews during Seder. The first is eating matzo, the second is drinking wine, the third is eating bitter herbs, the fourth is reading the Haggadah (the story of the flight of the Jews), and the fifth is reciting the psalms of praise.

IF YOU ADHERE STRICTLY to Jewish dietary law, matzo made for Passover must be prepared in front of a rabbi and must be mixed, kneaded, and in the oven within 18 minutes so there is no time for natural yeasts to ferment. This is nearly impossible to do alone but makes for great fun working with a friend. Taking longer than 18 minutes won't adversely affect the taste or texture of your matzo, but it should not be served at a Seder.

MAKES 12 FLATBREADS

1½ cups warm spring or well water (water without chemicals), or bottled water, about 110°F

3 to 3½ cups finely ground whole-wheat flour

Preheat oven Thirty to forty minutes before baking, place a baking stone on a rack in the lower third of the oven. Preheat the oven to 475°F.

By hand Place the water in a large bowl. Add 2 cups of the flour and mix well. Add the remaining flour ¼ cup at a time, beating well after each addition. When the dough begins to pull away from the side of the bowl, turn it out onto a well-floured work surface and knead until smooth, adding flour only as necessary. Continue to knead until the dough becomes very pliable, about 2 minutes of quick, vigorous kneading.

Shape Divide the dough into 12 equal pieces. Work with 4 pieces of dough at a time. Roll each piece into an 8- or 9-inch circle. The dough is very soft, so that it can be rolled thinly. You might find it easier to roll the dough on lightly floured parchment paper in order to get it from the work surface to the baking stone without reshaping the dough.

Pierce the dough all over, making the holes about ¼ inch apart (I use an Afro comb for this task). Stretch the dough slightly to open the holes. Immediately place on the stone in the oven. Work with the next 4 pieces of dough while the first 4 are baking. Repeat with the remaining matzo.

Bake and cool Bake the 4 matzo for 2 to 3 minutes, just until the edges begin to color. Repeat with the remaining matzo. Remove from the oven and place on a rack to cool and dry.

NOTE: Matzo should be stored in an airtight container. Do not freeze.

Zalabya

Although Egypt's population is mostly Muslim, a large number of Egyptians are Christians belonging to the Coptic Orthodox Church. In preparation for Christmas, Christian Egyptians fast from November 25 until January 6. During this time they do not eat meat, dairy, or poultry.

Prior to Christmas, Christian Egyptians also decorate their homes and churches with small mangers, and trees filled with numerous lights. The churches are decorated with special lamps and candles during this season.

At midnight on the eve of January 6, Christians go to church to celebrate the birth of Christ—Egyptian Christians rely on the Julian calendar rather than the Gregorian calendar, used by Roman Catholics and most Protestants. After this glorious ceremony the bells of all Christian churches in Egypt ring in celebration. Following the service, families go home to break their fast. Christmas Day is observed on January 7, when children receive new clothes and gifts.

It is an Egyptian Christian custom that the rich give candles to the poor. These candles are said to represent the candles Joseph used to protect Mary on the night of Jesus' birth. They also prepare and give *bouri* (fried mullet) and Zalabya (special fried bread similar to a fritter or doughnut) to the less fortunate.

VIGOROUS BEATING is what makes these small fried breads extremely light and crisp. Using a whisk or the whisk attachment on a mixer adds the needed air to the batter. The food processor and bread machine don't incorporate enough air, so I don't recommend them for this recipe. The combination of orange flower water and rose water add a subtle but rich flavor to the syrup.

MAKES 48 FRITTERS

FOR THE SYRUP

3 cups granulated sugar

1 cup honey

1 cup water

2 tablespoons lemon juice

1 tablespoon orange flower water

1 tablespoon rose water

FOR THE DOUGH

1 scant tablespoon or 1 (¼ ounce) package active dry yeast

¼ cup warm water (about 110°F)

3 cups water

2 teaspoons granulated sugar

1 teaspoon salt

3 cups unbleached all-purpose flour

FOR FRYING

Vegetable oil

Prepare syrup Combine the sugar, honey, water, and lemon juice in a large heavy pot and bring to a boil. Reduce the heat and cook for 20 minutes until the mixture coats a metal spoon. Remove from the heat and stir in the orange flower and rose waters. Set aside to cool.

Prepare dough In a large bowl, sprinkle the yeast in the warm water to soften. Heat the 3 cups water to 110°F and add it to the yeast along with the sugar, salt, and all the flour. (This will be a heavy batter.) Whisk vigorously for 2 minutes either by hand or by mixer. A spoon or spatula can be used, but the goal is to get as much air into the mixture as possible.

First rise Cover with plastic wrap and let rise until light, about one hour.

Beat dough #1 Uncover the dough and whisk vigorously for 4 minutes. Recover and let rise for 30 minutes.

Beat dough #2 Uncover the dough and whisk vigorously for 4 minutes. Recover and let rise for 30 minutes.

Heat oil Heat about 2 inches oil in a large Dutch oven or other deep pan to 375°F. For safety's sake there should be at least 2 inches of space between the oil and the top of the pan.

Fry Carefully drop a heaping teaspoon or small scoop of dough into the hot oil; do not stir down the dough. Dipping the spoon in the oil before scooping up the dough ensures a quick release. Do not crowd the fritters. As soon as the fritters rise to the top of the oil and are lightly browned, turn them over. Usually 2 minutes on each side will cook them all the way through and brown them. Adjust your heat accordingly.

Final preparation Remove the fritters from the hot oil and drain on layers of paper towels. Dip in syrup while hot and drain on a rack.

NOTE: Fritters are best eaten fresh and slightly warm or at room temperature. They do not freeze well.

Abadir

Every year at the end of the summer after the crops are harvested and before the rainy season begins, the Ait Hdiddou tribe in Morocco hosts an immensely popular festival called the Moussem. Part religious observance, family reunion, craft show, and swap meet, the Moussem brings members from all the nomadic Berber tribes of the Atlas Mountains to the Imilchil Valley in Morocco for three days of praying, singing, dancing, and feasting. The event attracts more than twenty-five thousand people, who come with their flocks, horses, donkeys, and camels. Quite a celebration!

The Moussem is held near two lakes, Isli (meaning bridegroom) and Tislite (meaning bride). Legend claims that the lakes were formed when two young people were forbidden to marry by their respective families and tribal leaders. They were so heartbroken that they cried until the two lakes formed. Then they drowned in their own tears. Now each year the Moussem is held to pay homage to the two young lovers and to respect the freedom of children to marry whomever they choose.

Weddings that occurred during the previous year are celebrated at this time. However, the main purpose of the gathering is to give young men and women a chance to meet prospective mates from different tribes. All of the events are chaperoned. Once a young man finds someone who strikes his fancy, he must act quickly or she might be spoken for by another while he is thinking about it. Many engagements are arranged on sight, and the weddings are quickly performed soon after. A mass wedding is held at the end of the Moussem.

Once a young man selects the girl of his choice, his family visits the girl's family and offers a sheep and Abadir, one of the traditional breads of the Ait Hdiddou tribe. If the match is acceptable to both families, much food is prepared and served by the girl's family to bless the union.

ABADIR, THE BREAD that is presented to the prospective bride's family, is made by the men of the tribe and involves a complex cooking process. A large stone is heated in a huge fire, the ashes are swept off, and the bread is placed directly on top of the stone. The exposed side of the bread is covered with burning *armoise* branches, an aromatic plant of the region. The ashes add a unique flavor to the bread, a flavor that is impossible to replicate in the home kitchen. The bread is baked for one hour, then turned over. Another layer of burning branches is placed on top of the loaf, and it is cooked for another hour. To follow the tradition of adding flavor this way, I have substituted fresh rosemary sprigs. The original recipe for this huge, round unleavened loaf called for 55 pounds flour, 10½ quarts water, and just under an ounce of salt. It served forty people and was 2 inches thick and over 3 feet across. I've adapted the recipe for home kitchens.

The recipe testers preferred more salt than is added to the traditional recipe, which explains the range of salt in the recipe. A mixer is a lifesaver when making this bread, since it should be kneaded for 15 minutes. Because there is no yeast in this bread, the loaf is heavy, but not as heavy as one might think. Keep this dough as light as possible and make sure it is still sticky when you set it aside to rest. If you use fresh whole-wheat flour, the loaf will have a delightfully nutty taste.

MAKES 1 LARGE LOAF

1½ cups hot water (about 150°F)

½ to 1½ teaspoons salt

4½ to 5 cups whole-wheat flour

3 (4-inch) sprigs fresh rosemary

Preheat baking stone If using a baking stone, preheat the oven to 400°F for 45 minutes prior to baking.

Prepare dough Put the water and salt in a large bowl. Stir in the flour a little at a time until it begins to pull away from the side of the bowl. Turn the mixture out onto a well-floured work surface and knead for 15 minutes until very smooth and elastic. If using a heavy-duty mixer, knead the dough for 10 minutes on medium speed.

Rest Leave the dough on the work surface and invert the mixing bowl over the dough to cover it. Let rest for 30 minutes.

Preheat oven If using a baking stone, place the stone on the lower shelf of the oven. About 30 minutes before baking, preheat the oven to 400°F. If not using a stone, preheat the oven about 10 minutes before baking.

Shape Knead the dough into a round ball, then flatten to about 2 inches thick. Carefully lift the loaf and place it in the oven directly on the hot baking stone, or place the dough on a parchment-lined or well-greased baking sheet and place in the lower third of the oven.

Bake and cool Place the rosemary sprigs on top of the loaf and bake for 1 hour 10 minutes. The loaf should be very hard and lightly browned. An instant-read thermometer will not work with this recipe. Turn off the oven and let the loaf cool in the closed oven, about 2 hours. Discard the rosemary. Remove the bread from the oven or baking sheet and allow it to mellow for 2 hours before serving.

To serve Slice thinly and serve with stew or cheese.

NOTE: This bread does not freeze well.

Sephardi Bread

The Jews of Spain and Portugal were the original Sephardim. Their descendants settled in Western Europe and in countries bordering the Mediterranean, North Africa, and the Middle East. The Sephardim observe customs that are different from those of the Ashkenazim, or Middle European, Jews. One of the most important differences is that they do not bake challah, the special Sabbath bread. Instead, the Spanish and Moroccans make plain leavened breads, while the North African and Middle Eastern Jews favor flatbreads.

As do Jews around the world, Sephardic Jews celebrate Yom Kippur, the holiday that follows eight days after Rosh Hashanah. Yom Kippur is the Day of Atonement, the Day of Divine Judgment, and the day of the "affliction of the souls" when individuals are cleansed of their sins. On this day each Jew is expected to pray for forgiveness for sins between man and God and correct any wrongful deeds against his fellow men. At sunset on the day before Yom Kippur, a full day of fasting begins.

After the fast of Yom Kippur, many Sephardim stuff their bread with a spicy mixture of nuts and spices to revive themselves and to symbolically bridge the old year and the new.

THE AUTHENTIC RECIPE for this bread calls for whole almonds in the stuffing. My testers and I did not like them whole, so I substituted slivered almonds and liked it much better. This bread is at its best when baked on a stone. If you use a stone, place the shaped dough on a piece of parchment paper to help transfer the stuffed loaf from the rising surface to the oven in one piece.

MAKES 1 LARGE LOAF

FOR THE DOUGH

1 tablespoon or 1 (¼-ounce) package active dry yeast

¾ cup warm water (about 110°F)

3 tablespoons olive oil

1 teaspoon salt

2¾ to 3¼ cups semolina flour

FOR THE FILLING

2 tablespoons olive oil

2 teaspoons freshly ground coriander seeds

½ teaspoon turmeric

1 cup whole blanched almonds

FOR THE GLAZE

1 large egg

1 tablespoon cold water

Toasted sesame seeds, optional

By hand In a large bowl, sprinkle the yeast in the water to soften. Add the olive oil, salt, and 1 cup of the flour to the yeast. Beat vigorously for 2 minutes. Add the remaining flour ¼ cup at a time until the dough begins to pull away from the side of the bowl. Turn the dough out onto a floured work surface. Knead, adding flour a little at a time, until the dough is stiff and elastic.

By mixer In the mixer bowl, sprinkle the yeast in the water to soften. Add the olive oil, salt, and 1 cup of the flour to the yeast. Using the mixer paddle, beat on medium-low speed for 2 minutes. Add the remaining flour ¼ cup at a time until the dough begins to pull away from the side of the bowl. Change to the dough hook. Continue to add flour 1 tablespoon at a time until the dough is stiff and cleans the bowl. Knead 4 to 5 minutes on medium-low.

By food processor In a measuring cup or small bowl, sprinkle the yeast in the water to soften. Add the olive oil to the yeast. In the bowl of the food processor fitted with the dough blade, combine the salt and 2¾ cups of the flour with 4 or 5 pulses. With the food processor running, add the liquid ingredients as fast as the dry ingredients will accept them. If you hear a sputtering sound, pour the liquid slower. As soon as all the liquid is added, turn the processor off. Check the liquid-to-flour ratio (see page 28). Pulse until the dough forms a ball, then process for exactly 60 seconds.

By bread machine For the dough, put the water and olive oil into the bread pan. Add the salt and 2¾ cups flour, then sprinkle with the yeast. Select the Dough cycle and press Start. While the dough is mixing, check the liquid-to-flour ratio (see page 29). The machine stops after the kneading cycle. You may let the dough rise in the bread machine or a bowl.

First rise Put the dough in an oiled bowl and turn to coat the entire ball of dough with oil. Cover with a tightly woven towel and let rise until doubled, about 1 hour.

Prepare filling Heat the olive oil in a large skillet over medium heat. Add the coriander and turmeric and cook for 1 minute. Add the almonds and cook for 5 minutes until the almonds begin to brown slightly (they'll cook more while baking). Remove from the heat and cool.

Prepare glaze Beat the egg with the cold water. Set aside.

Shape Turn the dough out onto a lightly oiled work surface and divide it in half. Roll each piece of dough into a 14-inch circle. If using a baking stone, place one circle on a piece of parchment paper or on a paddle that has been sprinkled heavily with semolina flour (you need enough semolina to allow the dough to slide easily). If not using a stone, place the dough on a parchment-lined or well-greased pizza pan or stretch the dough to fit a large baking sheet. Spread the almond mixture over the circle, leaving a ½-inch border at the edge. Brush the edge lightly with the egg glaze. Place the other circle over the nut-covered circle. Press the circles together. With the side of your thumb and forefinger, pinch the top to the bottom to seal the filling inside and create a scalloped edge.

Second rise Cover with a tightly woven towel and let rise for 30 minutes.

Preheat oven If using a baking stone, place the stone on the lower shelf of the oven. About 30 minutes before baking, preheat the oven to 425°F. If not using a stone, preheat the oven about 10 minutes before baking.

Final preparation Brush the top of the loaf with the egg glaze. With a fork or skewer, punch holes about every 2 inches in the top to prevent air bubbles from forming under the crust. Sprinkle the top of the loaf liberally with sesame seeds.

Bake and cool If using a baking stone, slide the bread onto the hot stone. If not using a stone, put the pan in the oven. Bake for 20 minutes until the bread is golden brown. A thermometer does not work for thin, filled breads. You need to go by the color of the loaf. Immediately remove the bread from the oven and place it on a rack to cool. Serve warm.

NOTE: This bread is best served fresh. It does not freeze well because the almonds become rubbery.

6

The
Americas

Oppone

Native Americans were deeply spiritual. In many southeastern tribes each meal was preceded by a prayer. Before they ate they shared a little of what they had with the spirit world by tossing a small piece of food into the wind. They considered all food a precious gift. Corn bread was an important part of many celebrations, but perhaps the most common celebration bread was Oppone. Oppone gained widespread favor with European settlers who adopted the breads and renamed them "pones."

STONE-GROUND CORNMEAL produces a much more flavorful bread than the enriched degerminated cornmeal found on most grocery store shelves. Check to see if there is a local mill in your area; if not, try one of the mail-order sources on page 331. Though this is a very quick bread to make, the cornmeal mixture must sit for an hour before frying.

MAKES 12 PONES

FOR THE BREAD

2 cups yellow cornmeal

1 teaspoon salt

1½ cups boiling water

FOR THE PAN

Lard or vegetable shortening

FOR SERVING

Syrup

Prepare bread Combine the cornmeal and salt. Gradually stir in the water until the mixture is smooth. Cover and let sit for one hour.

Heat oil About 10 minutes before frying, heat about ½ inch of melted lard in a deep skillet to 375°F, until the fat sputters and spits when a drop of water is thrown into it.

Fry and drain Indian women would take a handful of the cornmeal and drop it into the hot lard. I use a scoop or very large spoon, something that will measure about ¼ cup. Drop the cornmeal mixture carefully into the hot fat. Fry until golden and crisp, about 3 minutes; turn over and fry the other side until golden. Remove the bread from the hot lard and drain on paper towels. Serve hot, dipped into or drizzled with warm syrup.

NOTE: This bread is best eaten fresh and hot.

Kneeldown Bread

Navajo tribes consider it an honor to prepare food. For traditional celebrations women would grind corn for many hours, using four grinding stones of varying degrees of coarseness. The men would sing grinding songs, creating a mesmerizing rhythm to keep them from growing tired. When corn was scarce, breads were made from ground acorns, cattail roots, nuts, and seeds.

Bread was always served for important occasions, such as when a bride was chosen for a son. When the time was right for the boy to receive a mate, his mother would go searching for the perfect bride. She had to make certain the girl was strong, had a good nature, and was a hard worker. Once the right girl was chosen, bread would be prepared by the boy's family and taken to the girl's parents to ask for her. As soon as the girl "became a woman"—marked by her first menstruation—there would be a four-day celebration. On the last night of this puberty ceremony, Kneeldown Bread was baked in the ground.

IN THE OLD DAYS this puddinglike bread was prepared by women who knelt over a metate—a grinding stone. Then the bread was baked in a hole in the ground where again the women knelt over the bread, hence the name Kneeldown Bread. I've written instructions to make this bread by the old Indian method and by more modern methods. The bread is much better, not to mention a lot of fun to prepare, when baked the traditional way because of the flavor imparted by the ashes.

MAKES 8

8 ears fresh corn

2 tablespoons lard or vegetable shortening

½ to 1 teaspoon salt (to taste)

½ cup water

By the old method Build a fire using about 20 wrist-thick pieces of wood measuring about 14 inches long.

Cut the kernels from the corn cobs with a sharp knife. Scrape the back side of the blade (not the cutting edge) of the knife over the corn cobs to release the remaining corn. Grind the corn on a metate to a fine paste. Combine the corn paste with the lard, salt, and water. Divide the mixture into 8 equal portions and wrap each portion in corn husks to make a small packet. You will need 4 or 5 layers of husks to completely seal the mixture.

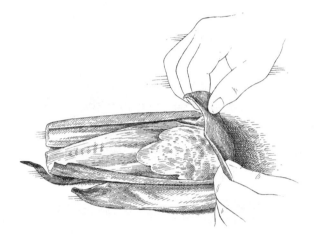

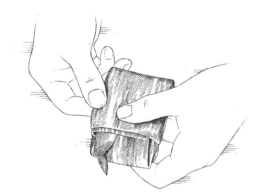

Dig a hole in the ground about 10 inches deep and 16 inches square. Place about ½ inch of ashes from the fire in the bottom of the hole. Place the packets in a single layer on the ashes. Cover the packets with the corn silk and remaining husks. If the packets aren't completely covered, add fresh leaves. Cover the leaves with about 2 inches of slightly moist dirt, then pile the fire over the dirt. Bake for one hour.

By modern methods Preheat the oven to 375°F. Cut the kernels from the corn cobs with a sharp knife. Scrape the back side of the blade (not the cutting edge) of the knife over the corn cobs to release the remaining corn. Put the corn, lard, salt, and water in a food processor or blender and process to form a fine paste. Divide the mixture into 8 equal portions and wrap each portion in corn husks to make a small packet. You will need 4 or 5 layers of husks to completely seal the mixture.

Line a baking sheet with 5 layers of wet paper towels. Arrange the packets on the towels and cover with 5 more layers of wet paper towels. Cover the baking sheet with foil, sealing in the towels and packets completely. Bake for one hour until firm.

To serve Remove the bread from the husks and eat at once.

Navajo Blue Bread

*T*he Navajo people do not observe birthdays, but they have a wonderful tradition celebrating a baby's first laugh. Whoever makes the baby laugh first furnishes a basket of food. This person holds the baby and the basket that holds Navajo Blue Bread, cookies, and other foods to share with all who come. Visitors can choose what they want from the basket to take with them. It is believed that by sharing the food, the baby will be kind and generous.

BEFORE BAKING POWDER and baking soda, Native Americans made culinary ash by burning specific kinds of trees or bushes, such as juniper, soaking the ashes in water, straining the mixture, and using the liquid in the recipe. The optional addition of eggs in this recipe is definitely not traditional but does make the bread tastier.

MAKES 10 TO 12

1 cup boiling water

2 tablespoons juniper ashes or 2 teaspoons baking powder

2 cups finely ground blue cornmeal

½ to 1 teaspoon salt (to taste)

2 large eggs, optional

If using juniper ashes Combine the water and ashes and let the mixture sit 5 minutes. Strain the water into a bowl. Add the remaining ingredients and stir to combine.

If using baking powder Combine the baking powder, cornmeal, and salt in a bowl. Add the eggs if using and stir. Add the water and stir to combine.

Preheat skillet Lightly grease a skillet and place over medium-low heat.

Shape and cook Roll about 3 tablespoons of dough into a ball and flatten to about ½ inch thick. Place in the heated skillet and cook about 10 minutes on each side. Serve fresh and warm.

Hartford Election Cake

Many early American settlers left their own countries to seek the freedom that America offered. One of the enduring symbols of American freedom is Election Day. Although the tradition of celebrating Election Day has dwindled over the last few decades, it was a time of great celebration and festivity throughout the eighteenth and nineteenth centuries.

For example, in Connecticut back in the 1800s Election Day was an important social and political event for the residents of Hartford. People from the outskirts came to town to escape the isolation of rural farm living, visit with friends, and revel in the celebration of freedom, while local women worked hard to show up their neighbors by producing the best cakes and food.

Politicians would frequently hire the best bakers to bake cakes to share with those who voted a straight-party ticket. Carnival-like vendors sold cakes in the streets. Although the idea of Election Cakes began in Great Britain, it caught on in Connecticut and other New England states. As the pioneers moved westward, the tradition of the Election Cake followed and became popular across the nation. With the advent of modern communications, this tradition has slowly dwindled.

TRADITIONALLY CALLED A CAKE, this recipe is prepared by the basic method for a sponge-type batter bread. The original recipes of the 1600s produced loaves weighing a whopping 5 to 20 pounds to serve large groups of people. As with many English-style breads, this recipe is lightly spiced, sweet, rich, and filled with fruit that has been steeped in spirits. Since this dough is prepared by the batter method, it is sticky and does not work well in a food processor or bread machine. Note that the finished bread needs a minimum of two days after baking to mellow. Be patient . . . it gets better with age.

MAKES 2 LOAVES

FOR THE SPONGE

1 scant tablespoon or 1 (¼-ounce) package active dry yeast

¼ cup warm water (about 110°F)

¼ cup warm milk (about 110°F)

½ cup brown sugar, firmly packed

1 cup unbleached all-purpose flour

FOR THE FRUIT

1½ cups golden raisins

¼ cup brandy

FOR THE DOUGH

¾ cup (1½ sticks) unsalted butter, softened

½ cup granulated sugar

2 large eggs, beaten

¼ cup milk

3 cups unbleached all-purpose flour

½ teaspoon salt

½ teaspoon ground mace

1 teaspoon ground nutmeg

1 teaspoon ground cinnamon

FOR THE LOAVES

Brandy, optional

Prepare sponge In a large bowl, sprinkle the yeast in the water to soften. Add the milk, sugar, and flour. Beat vigorously for 2 minutes. The mixture will be thick.

First rise Cover with plastic wrap and let rise at room temperature for 2 to 24 hours. The longer the sponge sits, the more strength and flavor it will impart. The sponge often rises and then falls. That's fine. It will rise again once you add the remaining ingredients.

Prepare fruit Combine the raisins and brandy. Cover and let sit 8 to 12 hours at room temperature, shaking or stirring occasionally.

Prepare dough Either by hand or mixer with a paddle attachment, cream the butter and sugar until light, about 5 minutes. Add the eggs and milk and beat for 3 minutes more. Add the sponge (no need to stir it down) ¼ cup at a time, beating well after each addition. Add the raisin mixture. Whisk the flour, salt, mace, nutmeg, and cinnamon together. Add the flour mixture to the creamed mixture ¼ cup at a time, beating well after each addition.

Shape Divide the mixture in half and place each half in a well-greased 8½ by 4½ -inch loaf pan.

Second rise Cover with a tightly woven towel and let rise for one hour. The dough will not rise very much until it is in the oven.

Preheat oven About 10 minutes before baking, preheat the oven to 375°F.

Bake and cool Bake for 50 minutes until the internal temperature of the bread reaches 190°F. Immediately remove the bread from the pans and place on a rack to cool. If desired brush the tops of the loaves with brandy.

Ripen loaves When the loaves are cooled, brush the tops and sides of the loaves with brandy (optional) once more, wrap in plastic wrap, and let sit at room temperature for 2 days before eating.

NOTE: This bread/cake freezes nicely for up to 6 months after ripening. It is best served at room temperature.

President Abraham Lincoln issued the Emancipation Proclamation on January 1, 1863, freeing more than 250,000 slaves after the War Between the States (many Southerners to this day don't call it the Civil War because they find nothing civil about it).

It took more than a year and a half for the news to travel around the country. Some speculate that the information was withheld by white slave owners so that another crop could be harvested, while others think the original bearer of the news was killed—also by the slave owners.

In Texas the news arrived on June 19, 1865. Each year on this date, the anniversary of the emancipation is celebrated with picnics, music, and storytelling. The tradition of celebrating Juneteenth is still observed across the South. The holiday is called Juneteenth because the official date falls in June somewhere between the 13th and 19th each year.

Soul food, African American cooking prepared with traditional African techniques but made with American ingredients, is a tradition at Juneteenth celebrations. The selections might include fried chicken, fried catfish, gumbo-thickened okra (seeds for okra were brought from Africa), potato salads, and green beans. Collard, beet, or turnip greens are cooked in the traditional manner for several hours with a little pork and often spiced with hot sauce. Meats such as ham hocks, chitterlings or chitlins (pork intestines), and maw (stomach lining) are prepared, as well as biscuits, spoon bread, hush puppies, and all kinds of pies, cobblers, and cakes.

The food of the slaves was usually food that wasn't considered good enough to serve to the white folks, or that was overabundant; the slaves were allowed to take what wasn't used by their masters. Ingenious slave women concocted some of the best food in the world. The foods served for Juneteenth are part of our American heritage and are truly soul satisfying.

Spoon Bread is similar to a soufflé but not as light or fragile. It is brought directly to the table from the oven in the baking dish and is spooned onto plates. It is usually served with meat and gravy but is also extremely good drizzled with melted butter and cane syrup or light molasses (that is, if you are a Southerner—Yankees seem to like maple syrup poured on everything!). Spoon Bread is eaten with a fork.

SERVES 6

FOR THE DISH

Butter or vegetable shortening

Cornmeal

FOR THE BREAD

1 cup white cornmeal, preferably stone ground

1 teaspoon baking powder

1 teaspoon salt

2 tablespoons melted bacon fat or vegetable oil

3 large eggs, separated

3 cups milk

Preheat oven About 10 minutes before baking, preheat the oven to 400°F.

Prepare dish Liberally grease a 1½-quart soufflé dish or tall casserole with butter or shortening. Lightly sprinkle the bottom and sides of the dish with cornmeal.

Prepare bread In a large bowl, whisk together the cornmeal, baking powder, and salt until well combined. Whisk the bacon fat with the egg yolks and milk until combined. Add the liquid ingredients to the dry ingredients and stir just until blended.

Beat the egg whites until stiff peaks form—almost to the dry stage. (If they are not stiff enough, the cornmeal will sink to the bottom of the dish.) Stir ½ cup of the cornmeal mixture into the egg whites, then gently fold the egg whites into the batter, taking care not to deflate the mixture. Pour into the prepared dish.

Bake Place the dish in the middle of the hot oven and bake for 45 minutes until lightly browned. When it is done, a knife inserted into the center will come out clean. Best served warm.

VARIATION: Add 2 cups shredded cheese—Cheddar, Monterey Jack, or any pepper cheese—to the dry ingredients before adding the liquid ingredients.

NOTE: This bread does not freeze well and is best eaten fresh.

Montreal Bagels

Yom Kippur, the Day of Atonement, is the holiest of Jewish holidays. Two holiday candles are blessed and lit to signal the beginning of the celebration. Strict fasting and a day of prayer are observed, starting at sunset the day before Yom Kippur. Jews who hold to strict religious laws not only prohibit eating and drinking on Yom Kippur but also refuse to bathe, use creams and oils, wear leather shoes, and have sexual relations.

The holiday is spent attending services that begin in the morning and go throughout the day. One of the services, the Musaf, is the longest of the year and contains two parts—one that recounts temple service and one that describes the ten Jewish wise men who were tortured to death by the Romans.

The blowing of the shofar, a ram's horn, follows the afternoon service. Families and close friends go home and break the fast with a meal beginning with coffee and a small sweet, like an apple slice dipped in honey, followed by a bit of salty food such as herring. The meal that follows traditionally includes lox and bagels.

An important tradition that by no means overshadows Yom Kippur takes place in Montreal and New York City with the bragging of bagel aficionados. Canadians consider the Montreal bagel to be *the* ultimate bagel. The recipe for the Montreal bagel was handed down to the current owner of the Fairmount Bagel Bakery, Irwin Shlafman, by his grandfather Isidore, who came to Montreal in 1918 from the Ukraine. His bagels are sweeter than New York bagels and contain eggs, oil, and malt (not all American bagels use malt) but no salt. Just before baking, they are poached in honey-sweetened water, which gives them extra shine and a chewy texture.

The Canadian popular press boasts that Montreal is the center of the bagel world and suggests New Yorkers need to learn how to make a proper bagel. One writer even stated that what he "saw in New York was not a pretty sight . . . No hole! No class . . . bagels looked like king-sized doughnuts with rigor mortis . . . more like a life preserver than a bagel." Duck! The bagels may start flying at any moment.

MONTREAL BAGELS are saltless; however, I prefer a little salt in mine. Try it both ways to see what you like. These bagels are thinner than New York bagels, less bready, have a bigger hole, and are heavily seeded. To get the special smoky flavor of a Montreal Bagel, bake them in a wood-fired oven.

MAKES 18 BAGELS

FOR THE DOUGH

> 1 scant tablespoon or 1 (¼-ounce) package active dry yeast
>
> 1 cup warm water (about 110°F)
>
> 1 large egg, beaten
>
> ¼ cup honey
>
> 2 tablespoons vegetable or canola oil
>
> 1 tablespoon malt syrup or 2 teaspoons malt powder
>
> 1 teaspoon salt, optional
>
> 4 to 4½ cups unbleached all-purpose flour

FOR POACHING

> 4 quarts boiling water
>
> 3 tablespoons honey

FOR THE TOPPING

> 1 cup sesame and/or poppy seeds

By hand In a large bowl, sprinkle the yeast in the water to soften. Add the egg, honey, oil, malt, salt if using, and 2 cups of the flour. Beat vigorously for 2 minutes. Gradually add the remaining flour ¼ cup at a time until the dough begins to pull away from the side of the bowl. Turn the dough out onto a floured work surface. Knead, adding flour a little at a time, until the dough is smooth and elastic.

By mixer In the mixer bowl, sprinkle the yeast in the water to soften. Add the egg, honey, oil, malt, salt if using, and 2 cups of the flour. Using the mixer paddle, beat on medium-low speed for 2 minutes. Gradually add the remaining flour ¼ cup at a time until the dough begins to pull away from the side of the bowl. Change to the dough hook. Continue to add flour 1 tablespoon at a time until the dough just begins to clean the bowl. Knead 4 to 5 minutes on medium-low.

By food processor In a large measuring cup or bowl, sprinkle the yeast in the water to soften. Combine the yeast with the egg, honey, oil, and malt. In the bowl of the food processor fitted with the dough blade, mix the salt if using and 4 cups flour with 4 or 5 pulses. With the food processor running, add the liquid ingredients as fast as the dry ingredients will accept them. If you hear a sputtering sound, pour the liquid slower. As soon as all the liquid is added, turn the processor off. Check the liquid-to-flour ratio (see page 28). Pulse until the dough forms a ball, then process exactly 60 seconds.

By bread machine Put the water, egg, honey, oil, and malt into the bread pan.

Add the salt if using and 4 cups flour, then sprinkle with the yeast. Select the Dough cycle and press Start. While the dough is mixing, check the liquid-to-flour ratio (see page 29). The machine stops after the kneading cycle. You may let the dough rise in the bread machine or a bowl.

First rise Put the dough in an oiled bowl and turn to coat the entire ball of dough with oil. Cover with a tightly woven towel and let rise until doubled, about 1 hour.

Shape Turn the dough out onto a lightly oiled work surface and divide into 18 equal pieces. Roll each piece into a 10-inch rope. Bring the ends together, overlapping them by about 1 inch. With your fingertips on the inside of the bagel, gently roll the two ends back and forth until the ends have joined and the joined section is the same size as the rest of the bagel.

Second rise Cover with a tightly woven towel on the work surface and let rest for 20 minutes.

Preheat oven About 10 minutes before baking, preheat the oven to 375°F.

Final preparation Combine the boiling water with the honey in a large, deep pan, over high heat.

Poach Gently lower 2 or 3 bagels at a time (do not crowd) into the boiling water, poach about 1 minute, turn the bagels over, and poach for 2 minutes. Remove with a slotted spoon or spatula and drain for a few seconds on a cloth towel to absorb most of the water. Dip the slightly damp bagels into the seeds to coat them thickly and place on parchment-lined or well-greased baking sheets.

Bake and cool Bake for 20 minutes until lightly browned. Using a thermometer doesn't work well with bagels, since they are so flat. Immediately remove the bagels from the baking sheets and place on a rack to cool.

NOTE: Bagels freeze nicely for up to 6 months. To serve, first thaw the bagels, then reheat on a baking sheet in a 375°F oven for 7 to 10 minutes.

Inca Festival Bread

In June (around the time of the southern hemisphere's winter solstice), Inti Raimi, the Festival of the Sun, is celebrated in Cuzco, Peru. The modern celebration is a reconstruction or reenactment of the solemn festivals celebrated by the Incas. It is a time for the Indians to worship the sun as their Incan brothers and sisters once did.

The families and clans that attend from neighboring nations compete with displays of wealth, beauty, and family pride. All persons in a clan's entourage (from the head of the clan to the servants) dress in the finest costumes, covered in gold and silver with huge wreaths and headdresses. Great paintings of the deeds they have accomplished during the year in the service of the sun are presented for show.

To prepare for Inti Raimi, the men fast for three days prior to their journey, eating only a little uncooked white corn *(chúcam)*, herbs, and water to give them the strength to travel. They do not light fires, nor do they sleep with their women, until the festival is over.

The night prior to the festival, the participants acting as Inca priests take charge of gathering sacrificial animals and other food and drink to offer as a sacrifice to the sun. These offerings have to feed all the Inca nations that come to Inti Raimi. The women spend the night grinding large quantities of cornmeal in large, flat stone vessels to make Inca Festival Bread—a corn bread containing cheese, chiles, and roasted red pimientos. Today the bread is shaped into a round loaf and baked in an oven. Years ago it was spread into a circle about the size of an apple on either a hot stone or a griddle to cook it.

The morning of the festival, everyone gathers to wait for the sun to rise. They take off their shoes and face the east. As soon as the sun becomes visible, they squat down, raise their arms and hands upward to the sun, and kiss the air. The celebration continues for nine days. Each day there is an abundance of food and drink, along with many festivities.

THE INCAS USE white cornmeal for this bread, though yellow can be substituted. Stone-ground or water-ground cornmeal will be much more flavorful than the degerminated meal offered on the shelves of most supermarkets. See page 331 for mail-order sources. The Incas also scrape fresh white corn from the cobs and cook it with a little heavy cream or milk until creamy. I substitute cream-style corn as a convenience. They also make a hard farmer's-type cheese to use in this bread. Since it is unavailable, I have substituted a mild Cheddar cheese.

MAKES 1 LARGE LOAF

FOR THE BREAD

4 ounces whole, sweet roasted red pimientos (or substitute roasted red peppers)

¾ cup milk

2 large eggs

¼ cup (½ stick) unsalted butter, melted

1 (8-ounce) can cream-style corn

½ cup coarsely chopped chiles, fresh or canned

1 to 1¼ cups white cornmeal

1 teaspoon baking soda

1 teaspoon salt

2 cups diced (¼ inch) mild Cheddar cheese, about 8 ounces

FOR THE PAN

1 tablespoon unsalted butter

FOR THE TOPPING

½ cup coarsely shredded Cheddar cheese, about 2 ounces

Preheat oven Preheat the oven to 400°F. Place a 10- to 12-inch round pan in the oven.

Prepare peppers Divide the pimientos in half. Coarsely chop half the pimientos and set them aside. Cut the other half into long, thin strips for the top of the bread and set aside.

Make bread In a large bowl, whisk the milk and eggs together. Add the butter, corn, chiles, and chopped pimientos and stir well. Whisk 1 cup cornmeal, the baking soda, and salt together. Add to the milk mixture along with the diced cheese and mix thoroughly. The mixture should be thick and mushy and "plop" off a spoon rather than drizzle off. If the mixture is too thin, add more cornmeal 1 tablespoon at a time until a good consistency is reached.

Final preparation Remove the hot pan from the oven and add the butter. Let sit until the butter melts. Swirl the butter around to coat the bottom and sides of the pan. Add the bread mixture. Sprinkle the shredded cheese over the top and arrange the pimiento strips on top of the cheese in a decorative manner.

Bake Place the pan in the middle of the oven and bake for 45 minutes. Using an instant-read thermometer is not a good test to see if this bread is done. If you stick a knife into the center of the bread and it comes out clean, the bread is done.

Cool Remove the bread from the oven and let sit for 15 minutes in the pan. To serve, remove from the pan and cut into wedges.

NOTE: This bread does not freeze well. It can be stored in the refrigerator for up to 2 days but is best served warm. To reheat, wrap the bread in foil and bake in a 375°F oven for 10 minutes. Open the foil and let warm 2 minutes uncovered.

Bread of the Dead
PAN DE MUERTOS

*D*ía de los Muertos, or the Day of the Dead, Mexico's festive annual celebration of life—and death—takes place on November 2. The modern celebration, now an official Catholic holiday, owes its roots to the Aztecs, who devoted two full months of the year to honor the dead and assist departed souls to their final destination. During and after the Spanish conquest, the culture of the Aztecs became infused with the beliefs of the Catholic Church. Consequently, the Day of the Dead coincides with All Souls' Day, the day after All Saints' Day.

The Day of the Dead is a time of smiles, not tears. During the day, children dress in ghost and goblin costumes and parade gaily through the streets of towns and villages. Many special candies and foods are prepared for the day, such as skulls and skeletons made from marzipan, chocolate, or sugar. Bakers make sweet breads in the shape of bones, humans, flowers, and animals.

Along with formal religious ceremonies (three requiem masses), people attend more personal rituals with their families. In honor of the dead, families create brightly decorated shrines both in their homes and at cemeteries. The shrines or altars are covered with pictures, favorite items of the deceased, flowers, candies, mescal or tequila, and food, especially loaves of decorated bread.

The breads are placed on shrines and altars as offerings for the deceased and are given to visitors arriving for the celebration. Bread is sold in large quantities on the streets of towns and villages and shared with family and friends. So great is the demand for the Bread of the Dead that big-city bakers call on small-town master bakers to meet the demand. Bread of the Dead is shaped into a wide variety of death-related shapes and figures but is most commonly decorated with dough in the shape of human bones.

THE ORANGE FLOWER WATER used in this recipe is available in many large supermarkets and specialty food stores. It gives a subtle orange flavor. One teaspoon of finely grated orange zest can be substituted, but the bread will have a bolder taste.

MAKES 1 LARGE LOAF

FOR THE DOUGH

1 scant tablespoon or 1 (¼-ounce) package active dry yeast

¼ cup warm water (about 110°F)

½ cup milk

3 large eggs, beaten

¼ cup (½ stick) unsalted butter, softened

2 teaspoons orange flower water

1 teaspoon salt

1 teaspoon anise seeds

¼ cup granulated sugar

4 to 4½ cups unbleached all-purpose flour

FOR THE TOPPING

1 large egg

1 tablespoon granulated sugar

By hand In a large bowl, sprinkle the yeast in the water to soften. Heat the milk to 110°F and add it to the yeast along with the eggs, butter, orange flower water, salt, anise seeds, sugar, and 2 cups of the flour. Beat vigorously for 2 minutes. Gradually add the remaining flour ¼ cup at a time until the dough begins to pull away from the side of the bowl. Turn the dough out onto a floured work surface. Knead, adding flour a little at a time, until the dough is smooth and elastic.

By mixer In the mixer bowl, sprinkle the yeast in the water to soften. Heat the milk to 110°F and add it to the yeast along with the eggs, butter, orange flower water, salt, anise seeds, sugar, and 2 cups of the flour. Using the mixer paddle, beat on medium-low speed for 2 minutes. Gradually add the remaining flour ¼ cup at a time until the dough begins to pull away from the side of the bowl. Change to the dough hook. Continue to add flour 1 tablespoon at a time until the dough just begins to clean the bowl. Knead 4 to 5 minutes on medium-low.

By food processor In a large measuring cup or bowl, sprinkle the yeast in the water to soften. Heat the milk to 100°F and add it to the yeast along with the eggs, butter, and orange flower water. In a bowl, combine the salt, anise seeds, sugar, and 4 cups flour. Put the dry ingredients in the bowl of the food processor fitted with the dough blade. Add the liquid ingredients and pulse 9 or 10 times until the ingredients begin to come together in a ball. Check the liquid-to-flour ratio (see page 28). Once the dough begins to come together, process exactly 60 seconds.

By bread machine Put the water, milk, eggs, butter, and orange flower water in the bread pan. Add the salt, anise seeds, sugar, and 4 cups flour to the bread pan, then sprinkle with the yeast. Select the Dough cycle and press Start. While the dough is mixing, check the liquid-to-flour ratio (see page 29). The machine stops after the kneading cycle. You may let the dough rise in the bread machine or a bowl.

First rise Put the dough in an oiled bowl and turn to coat the entire ball of dough with oil. Cover with a tightly woven towel and let rise until doubled, about one hour.

Shape Turn the dough out onto a lightly oiled work surface. Remove a tennis-ball-sized portion of dough and set aside. Shape the larger piece of dough into a smooth ball and place on a parchment-lined or well-seasoned baking sheet. Flatten the dough into a 1-inch-thick disk. Divide the remaining dough in half and roll each piece into an 8-inch rope. Lay the ropes on top of the loaf parallel to each other about 3 inches apart. With scissors or a knife, cut into the end of each rope about ¾ inch and spread the ends apart slightly to resemble bones.

Second rise Cover with a tightly woven towel and let rise for 45 minutes.

Preheat oven About 10 minutes before baking, preheat the oven to 375°F.

Prepare topping Beat the egg and sugar until the sugar dissolves, then brush the mixture on the top and sides of the bread.

Bake and cool Bake for 30 minutes until the internal temperature of the bread reaches 190°F. Immediately remove the bread from the baking sheet and place on a rack to cool.

NOTE: This bread freezes nicely for up to 6 months. To serve, first thaw the bread, then reheat on a baking sheet or directly on the oven rack in a 375°F oven for 7 to 10 minutes.

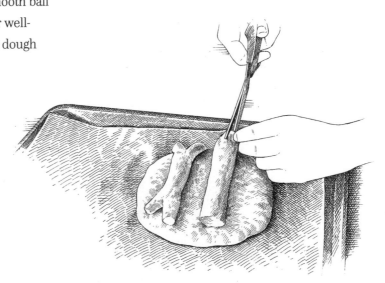

7

The British Isles

Hot Cross Buns ◆ Chelsea Buns

Perhaps no cry used to be more familiar to a Londoner than the ditty:

Hot Cross Buns! Hot Cross Buns!
One a penny,
Two a penny,
Hot Cross Buns!
If you have no daughters,
Pray give them to your sons!
One a penny,
Two a penny,
Hot Cross Buns!

However, this from Poor Robin in his Almanack for 1733:

Good Friday comes this month, the old woman runs
With one- or two-a-penny hot cross buns,
Whose virtue is, if you believe what's said
They'll not grow mouldy like the common bread.

As with many breads and customs, Hot Cross Buns most likely originated with pagan celebrations honoring the goddess Eastore. The church tried to stop the making of these sacramental cakes, but they were too popular, so the church made them a Christian symbol by blessing them and decorating them with a cross. Some say the cross on top of the bun represents the four quarters of the moon or Christ's cross; others say the bun is slashed to let the devil fly out.

Many superstitions are associated with the buns. People believed that buns baked on Good Friday would never mold. Some immigrants still say that the housewife who bakes on Good Friday and the five Fridays afterward is truly blessed, but the housewife who washes her clothes on those days is cursed. According to legend, when Christ was on his way to Golgotha, he stopped to rest at the home of a woman who was washing clothes and she turned him away. Christ then knocked at the door of a woman who was baking and asked for bread and water. The woman gave him a loaf of fresh bread and a cup of water.

Buns were also nailed to the ceilings of homes and bakeries to protect them from fire; and crumbled in water, they were used to treat a number of ailments of both man and beast. The buns also protected corn from mice, sailors from shipwrecks, and clothes from moths.

Hot Cross Buns are baked all over the British Isles. Many historians believe that the original buns were made by the fourteenth-century monk Father Rocliff of Saint Albans. He gave every person who came to the abbey for their usual dole of soup a spiced bun to accompany it. His secret recipe was considered the best in the world, but, unfortunately, it died with him.

Two bun houses competed to produce the best buns in London. In 1792 there was almost a riot when 50,000 patrons rushed the Old Original Royal Bun House on the morning of Good Friday to purchase Hot Cross Buns. The following year the proprietress issued an early notice to her patrons that on Good Friday they could order Chelsea Buns as usual, but no Hot Cross Buns. Even the king went without his buns that year! The next year orderly lines were formed, and the bun house has sold thousands of Hot Cross Buns without incident since.

Following are the recipes for Hot Cross Buns and the famous Chelsea Buns from the same bun house. As one Brit explained, we celebrate every day that we have such a marvelous treat as the Chelsea Bun! I guess this makes it a true celebration bread.

Hot Cross Buns

THE DOUGH for these spiced buns is slightly firmer than most so that the slits forming the cross remain when the buns are baked. Many bakers used candied peel or strips of pastry to emphasize the cross, but I prefer filling the slit with a light icing after baking.

MAKES 24 BUNS

FOR THE DOUGH

1 scant tablespoon or 1 (¼-ounce) package active dry yeast

¼ cup warm water (about 110°F)

¾ cup milk

½ cup (1 stick) unsalted butter, softened

½ cup light brown sugar, packed

2 large eggs, beaten

1 teaspoon salt

1 teaspoon ground cinnamon

¼ teaspoon ground ginger

¼ teaspoon ground nutmeg

¼ teaspoon ground pepper

4½ to 5½ cups unbleached all-purpose flour

1 cup currants

1 tablespoon finely grated lemon zest

FOR THE TOPPING

2 tablespoons milk

2 tablespoons granulated sugar

FOR THE ICING

1 cup confectioners' sugar

1 tablespoon lemon juice

2 to 3 tablespoons heavy cream

By hand In a large bowl, sprinkle the yeast in the water to soften. Heat the milk to 110°F and add it to the yeast along with the butter, brown sugar, and eggs. Whisk the salt, cinnamon, ginger, nutmeg, pepper, and 2 cups of the flour together and add it to the yeast mixture. Beat vigorously for 2 minutes. Add the currants and lemon zest and stir to combine. Gradually add the remaining flour ¼ cup at a time until the dough begins to pull away from the side of the bowl. Turn the dough out onto a floured work surface. Knead, adding flour a little at a time, until the dough is smooth and elastic.

By mixer In the mixer bowl, sprinkle the yeast in the water to soften. Heat the milk to 110°F and add it to the yeast along with the butter, brown sugar, and eggs. Whisk the salt, cinnamon, ginger, nutmeg, pepper, and 2 cups of the flour together and add it to the yeast mixture. Using the paddle, beat on medium-low speed for 2 minutes. Add the currants and lemon zest and stir to combine. Gradually add the remaining flour ¼ cup at a time until the dough begins to pull away from the side of the bowl. Change to the dough hook. Continue to add flour 1 tablespoon at a time until the dough just begins to clean the bowl. Knead 4 to 5 minutes on medium-low.

By food processor In a large measuring cup or bowl, sprinkle the yeast in the water to soften. Heat the milk to 100°F and add it to the yeast along with the butter and eggs. In the bowl of the food processor fitted with the dough blade, combine the brown sugar, salt, cinnamon, ginger, nutmeg, pepper, 4 cups flour, currants, and lemon zest with 4 or 5 pulses. With the food processor running, add the liquid ingredients as fast as the dry ingredients will accept them. If you hear a sputtering sound, pour the liquid slower. As soon as all the liquid is added, turn the processor off. Check the liquid-to-flour ratio (see page 28). Pulse until the dough forms a ball, then process exactly 60 seconds.

By bread machine Put the water, milk, butter, and eggs in the bread pan. Add the brown sugar, salt, cinnamon, ginger, nutmeg, pepper, lemon zest, and 4 cups flour. Sprinkle with the yeast. Select the Dough cycle and press Start. If your machine has an Add Fruit cycle, add the currants when prompted; if not, add them with the yeast. While the dough is mixing, check the liquid-to-flour ratio (see page 29). The machine stops after the kneading cycle. You may let the dough rise in the bread machine or a bowl.

First rise Put the dough in an oiled bowl and turn to coat the entire ball of dough with oil. Cover with a tightly woven towel and let rise until doubled, about one hour.

Shape Turn the dough out onto a lightly oiled work surface and divide into 24 equal pieces. Shape each piece into a ball and arrange in 2 well-greased 9 by 12-inch baking pans.

Second rise Cover with tightly woven towels and let rise for 45 minutes.

Preheat oven About 10 minutes before baking, preheat the oven to 375°F (350°F if your pans are glass).

Final preparation Just before baking, cut a cross about ¼ inch deep in the top of each bun with a sharp serrated knife or razor. For the topping, combine the milk and granulated sugar and brush over the top of each bun.

Bake and cool Bake for 20 minutes until the internal temperature of the buns reaches 190°F. Remove the buns from the oven and let cool in the pans for about 10 minutes.

Finish In a measuring cup with a pouring lip, mix the confectioners' sugar with the lemon juice and enough heavy cream to reach the consistency of honey. Drizzle the icing into the slits to form a cross on top of each bun.

NOTE: These buns freeze nicely for up to 6 months and can easily be reheated after thawing. Wrap the buns in foil and bake in a preheated 375°F oven for 7 to 10 minutes until heated through.

Chelsea Buns

CHELSEA BUNS are rolled and cut like cinnamon rolls. To keep their shape, cut them with a long strand of unwaxed dental floss. Wrap the floss around both of your index fingers and lightly score the top of the cylinder with the floss so you'll know where to cut. Slip the floss under the roll where you scored it, bring up the ends of the floss, cross them, and pull straight out to the sides (see page 81).

MAKES 24 BUNS

FOR THE DOUGH

1 scant tablespoon or 1 (¼-ounce) package active dry yeast

¼ cup warm water (about 110°F)

¾ cup milk

2 large eggs, beaten

½ cup (1 stick) unsalted butter, softened

2 tablespoons granulated sugar

1 teaspoon salt

4 to 5 cups unbleached all-purpose flour

FOR THE FILLING

½ cup light brown sugar, packed

½ cup (1 stick) unsalted butter, softened

1 cup currants

1 cup finely chopped golden raisins

FOR THE TOPPING

2 tablespoons milk

3 tablespoons granulated sugar

By hand In a large bowl, sprinkle the yeast in the water to soften. Heat the milk to 110°F and add it to the yeast along with the eggs, butter, sugar, salt, and 2 cups of the flour. Beat vigorously for 2 minutes. Gradually add the remaining flour ¼ cup at a time until the dough begins to pull away from the side of the bowl. Turn the dough out onto a floured work surface. Knead, adding flour a little at a time, until the dough is smooth and elastic.

By mixer In the mixer bowl, sprinkle the yeast in the water to soften. Heat the milk to 110°F and add it to the yeast along with the eggs, butter, sugar, salt, and 2 cups of the flour. Using the mixer paddle, beat the mixture on medium-low speed for 2 minutes. Gradually add the remaining flour ¼ cup at a time until the dough begins to pull away from the side of the bowl. Change to the dough hook. Continue to add flour 1 tablespoon at a time until the dough just begins to clean the bowl. Knead 4 to 5 minutes on medium-low.

By food processor In a large measuring cup or bowl, sprinkle the yeast in the water to soften. Heat the milk to 100°F and add it to the yeast along with the eggs and butter. In the bowl of the food processor fitted with the dough blade, combine the sugar, salt, and 4 cups flour. Pulse 4 or 5 times to combine. With the food processor running, add the liquid ingredients as fast as the dry ingredients will accept them. If you hear a sputtering sound, pour the liquid slower. As soon as all the liquid is added, turn the processor off. Check the liquid-to-flour ratio (see page 28). Pulse until the dough forms a ball, then process exactly 60 seconds.

By bread machine Put the water, milk, eggs, and butter in the bread pan. Add the sugar, salt, and 4 cups flour to the bread pan, then sprinkle with the yeast. Select the Dough cycle and press Start. While the dough is mixing, check the liquid-to-flour ratio (see page 29). The machine stops after the kneading cycle. You may let the dough rise in the bread machine or a bowl.

First rise Put the dough in an oiled bowl and turn to coat the entire ball of dough with oil. Cover with a tightly woven towel and let rise until doubled, about one hour.

Prepare filling In a small bowl, cream the brown sugar and butter. Add the currants and raisins and stir to combine.

Shape Turn the dough out onto a lightly oiled work surface and divide it in half. Roll each half into a 12 by 18-inch rectangle. Thinly spread half the filling on each rectangle, leaving a ½-inch border along one 18-inch side (leaving an open border assures the dough will adhere to itself). Roll each rectangle into an 18-inch cylinder and pinch the seams to seal. Cut each cylinder into 12 equal slices and place about 1 inch apart on parchment-lined or well-greased baking sheets.

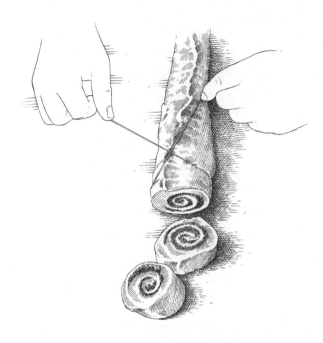

Second rise Cover with tightly woven towels and let rise for 45 minutes.

Preheat oven About 10 minutes before baking, preheat the oven to 375°F.

Final preparation For the topping, brush the top of the buns with the milk, then sprinkle with the granulated sugar.

Bake and cool Bake for 20 minutes until the internal temperature of the buns reaches 190°F. Immediately remove the buns from the baking sheets and place on a rack to cool.

NOTE: These buns freeze nicely for up to 6 months and can easily be reheated after thawing. Wrap the buns in foil and bake in a preheated 375°F oven for 7 to 10 minutes until heated through.

Shrovetide Pancakes

The Great Pancake Race began on Shrove Tuesday in Olney, England, in 1445. Over the years the popularity of this event has fluctuated, but after World War II, it gained status each year.

Shrove Tuesday, also referred to as Fat Tuesday, is the day before Ash Wednesday, which is the beginning of the Christian Lenten season. This is a day of festivity—one last fling before the six-week fast of Lent begins. Shrove Tuesday in Great Britain has always been a day of frivolity, pranks, and mischief. Throughout the ages it has also been a day of excessive eating, since many dread the long fast. Pancakes have been a favorite for Shrove Tuesday because they are ideal for using up the fat and eggs in the household that might go bad in the following weeks, when they are forbidden.

Before the Reformation, the church bell (called a shriving bell) tolled on Shrove Tuesday to call people to church. They came to confess their sins to the parish priest so they could be shriven—forgiven—of their sins. The Great Pancake Race began when a harassed housewife who was late preparing her family's pancakes became flustered when she heard the church bell ring. In her excitement, she ran from her home still holding the hot frying pan with that last pancake, wearing her apron over her skirt and her kerchief still wrapped around her head. The women of the village thought this was great sport and each year raced from their homes to the church when the bells tolled. It was soon organized into an annual event.

Today this centuries-old tradition begins when the church warden, or verger, rings a large bronze "Pancake Bell" at 11:55 A.M. on Shrove Tuesday. The entrants are all women over the age of eighteen who must have lived in the town of Olney for at least three months prior to the race; they don't have to be married. The entrants must wear the traditional skirt, apron, and kerchief and carry a pancake in a frying pan.

At the start of the race, the warden yells, "Toss your pancakes! Are you ready?," and gives the signal for the race to begin. The women toss their pancake, then run from the marketplace to the finish line, 415 yards away on Church Lane, where they must toss their pancake one more time. The winner is greeted with the Kiss of Peace by the verger, and the vicar offers the blessing, "The peace of the Lord be always with you." When the race is over, the runners, officials, townsfolk, and visitors all go to the parish church for the shriving service. Competitors place their frying pans around the font and occupy reserved seats for the service.

In 1949 the Jaycees in Liberal, Kansas, were planning a pancake breakfast to raise money for equipment for the local hospital when *Time* magazine ran a story about the Shrove Tuesday race in Olney, England. R. J. Leete, president of the Liberal Jaycees, wrote to the Reverend Ronald Collins, vicar of Olney and supervisor of the Olney race, issuing a challenge for a Pancake Race with the housewives of Liberal. Vicar Collins quickly accepted the challenge, and the first race took place February 21, 1950. The two races have taken place every year since. The running times of the winners are compared in a telephone call and the winner is declared.

PANCAKES FOR SHROVE TUESDAY can be thick or thin, large or small, whole grain, or just about anything you want them to be. The main thing is that they should be rich, with lots of butter and eggs! The pancake most associated with this special day is sprinkled liberally with confectioners' sugar and drizzled with fresh lemon juice. Being a southern-born syrup lover, I thought this was a strange combination until I gave it a try and found it to be absolutely delightful.

MAKES ABOUT TWENTY-FOUR
4-INCH PANCAKES

2½ cups unbleached all-purpose flour

½ teaspoon salt

1 teaspoon baking soda

½ teaspoon cream of tartar

1 tablespoon granulated sugar

4 large eggs

2 to 2½ cups buttermilk

½ cup (1 stick) unsalted butter, melted

Confectioners' sugar

Lemon wedges

Prepare batter In a large bowl, whisk the flour, salt, baking soda, cream of tartar, and granulated sugar together. Whisk together the eggs, buttermilk, and butter. Combine the dry ingredients with the wet ingredients. The batter should be the consistency of heavy cream.

Preheat pan About 5 minutes before cooking, preheat a lightly greased heavy skillet or griddle over medium-high heat to 375°F or until water sprinkled on the hot pan dances across the surface.

Cook Pour about 3 tablespoons batter in the skillet to make a 4-inch circle. Cook until delicately browned on one side, about one minute; turn and cook on the other side.

To serve For an English-style treat, serve sprinkled with confectioners' sugar, with lemon wedges to squeeze over the tops of the pancakes.

NOTE: Pancakes freeze nicely for up to 6 months and can easily be reheated after thawing. Wrap the pancakes in foil and bake in a 375°F oven for 10 minutes.

Simnel Cake

Simnel Cake (the English call many of their sweet breads cakes) is made for the British holiday Mothering Sunday, which is celebrated on the Sunday before Lent. Originally Mothering Sunday was a tribute to the mother church but eventually evolved into a day to honor one's mother.

The holiday waned in popularity during the eighteenth century. American soldiers stationed in England after World War II captivated the English with their tradition of honoring their mothers on Mother's Day in May, so the English began honoring mothers again on Mothering Sunday.

In pre-Christian times, Simnel Cake was decorated with twelve balls of marzipan, which represented the twelve signs of the zodiac. English desserts tend to be quite sweet; this rich bread is no exception.

HOMEMADE ALMOND PASTE is not difficult to make if you have a food processor. Three 7-ounce cans of commercial almond paste softened slightly with about 2 tablespoons orange juice can be substituted, but there is a vast difference in flavor and texture. This dough is not kneaded and has a heavy batter consistency. I don't recommend preparing it in a food processor or bread machine.

MAKES 1 LARGE LOAF

FOR THE ALMOND PASTE

4 cups (1 pound) blanched almonds

4 cups (1 pound) confectioners' sugar

2 egg yolks, optional

½ teaspoon almond extract

2 to 4 tablespoons orange juice

FOR THE DOUGH

1 scant tablespoon or 1 (¼-ounce) package active dry yeast

¼ cup warm water (about 110°F)

½ cup (1 stick) unsalted butter, softened

½ cup light brown sugar, packed

6 large eggs, beaten

¼ teaspoon freshly grated nutmeg

½ teaspoon ground cinnamon

1 teaspoon salt

4 cups unbleached all-purpose flour

2 cups currants

½ cup finely chopped candied orange peel (see Notes)

DECORATIONS FOR TOP

Almond paste flowers, whole blanched almonds, candied cherries (either halves or whole), thin slices of candied citron, lemon or orange slices

Prepare almond paste In a food processor fitted with the metal blade, process the almonds until the oil from the nuts begins to bring the mixture together like a chunky peanut butter. Add the confectioners' sugar, yolks, and almond extract. Pulse until most of the sugar is absorbed. Add 2 tablespoons juice and pulse to combine. Remove the top of the processor and remove a pinch of the mixture. If you can roll this mixture into a ball that keeps its shape, then you have added enough liquid. If the mixture is too crumbly, continue to add juice 1 teaspoon at a time until the mixture can keep its shape. This amount can vary a great deal if you are not using the egg yolks. Cover the mixture tightly and set aside.

By hand In a large bowl, sprinkle the yeast in the water to soften. Add the butter, brown sugar, eggs, nutmeg, cinnamon, salt, and 2 cups of the flour. Beat vigorously for 2 minutes. Add the currants and orange peel, then gradually add the remaining flour ¼ cup at a time until completely incorporated.

By mixer In the mixer bowl, sprinkle the yeast in the water to soften. Add the butter, brown sugar, eggs, nutmeg, cinnamon, salt, and 2 cups of the flour. Using the mixer paddle, beat on medium-low speed for 2 minutes. Add the currants and orange peel, then gradually add the remaining flour ¼ cup at a time until completely incorporated.

First rise Cover with a tightly woven towel and let rise until doubled, about one hour.

Shape Divide the almond paste in half. Roll each half between 2 pieces of waxed or parchment paper into a 10-inch circle. Set aside.

Beat the dough to completely deflate it. Put half the dough in a well-greased 10-inch-round, 3-inch-tall pan. With buttered fingers, pat the dough to an even thickness. Place one of the rounds of almond paste over the dough and put the remaining dough over the paste. With buttered fingers, pat the dough to make it completely flat.

Second rise Cover with a tightly woven towel and let rise for 45 minutes.

Preheat oven About 10 minutes before baking, preheat the oven to 375°F.

Bake and cool Bake for 25 minutes. Place the final layer of almond paste on the top and bake 10 minutes more until the internal temperature of the bread reaches 190°F. Allow the bread to cool 10 minutes, then remove it from the pan.

Decorate When the bread is cool, decorate the top with almond paste flowers, almonds, candied cherries, thin slices of candied citron, and/or lemon or orange slices.

NOTES: If you prefer to make your own candied peel, see page 326.

I don't like the texture of this bread or the almond paste after it is frozen. It is much better served fresh at room temperature or just slightly warm.

English Soul Cakes

The ancient Celtic people who inhabited England, Wales, Scotland, Ireland, and Brittany (northwestern France) celebrated New Year's Day on what would be November 1 on our calendar. The Celtic festival marked the end of the "season of the sun" and the beginning of the "season of darkness and cold." On that night Samhain, the Lord of Death and Prince of Darkness, took the Sun God prisoner. As the earth passed into the "death" of winter, the spirits of the dead entered the world of the living.

These spirits of death were imprisoned in the bodies of people or animals during the next year until they moved into the afterlife. On this night ghosts, goblins, demons, witches, and other evil spirits roamed the countryside. It was believed that they would leave you alone if you dressed and acted like them.

The villagers extinguished hearth fires in their houses, and people paraded through their cold homes, making as much noise as possible to make their homes as undesirable as possible to the evil spirits.

The Druids, Celtic priests, lit huge bonfires on hilltops in sacred oak forests to honor the Sun God and frighten away the lost souls. They offered gifts and sacrificed crops and animals to Samhain. As the sun passed to the season of darkness, each family took a hot ember from the bonfire to start new fires in their homes, which would now be free of evil spirits.

The Roman Catholic Church, in its efforts to do away with pagan celebrations, changed All Saints' Day from May to November 1 to honor all of its saints. Years later the Church set All Souls' Day on November 2 to honor the dead and allowed bonfires, parades, and dressing up as saints, angels, and devils.

Eventually all these customs mixed together and became known as All Hallow Even, then All Hallows' Eve, then Hallowe'en, and finally Halloween. The custom of dressing as black cats, evil spirits, ghosts, skeletons, and such prevailed, and the sacrifices changed to the giving of small cakes known as Soul Cakes. These cakes were given in return for prayers for departed souls. Children would go from home to home chanting:

Soul! Soul! For a souling cake.
I pray you, good missus, a souling cake!
Apple, or pear, or plum, or cherry
Anything good to make us merry.

THESE BUNS are placed close together on the baking sheet or pan so that they rise together, which creates soft-sided buns. The buns look as if they were made with whole-wheat flour, but they're not. The brown color comes from the addition of cinnamon to the dough.

MAKES 24 LARGE BUNS

FOR THE DOUGH

1 scant tablespoon or 1 (¼-ounce) package active dry yeast

¼ cup warm water (about 110°F)

1 cup milk

2 tablespoons unsalted butter, softened

2 tablespoons granulated sugar

2 teaspoons ground cinnamon

1 teaspoon salt

4 to 5 cups unbleached all-purpose flour

FOR THE GLAZE

1 large egg

1 tablespoon cold water

Additional granulated sugar, optional

By hand In a large bowl, sprinkle the yeast in the water to soften. Heat the milk to 110°F and add it to the yeast along with the butter, sugar, cinnamon, salt, and 2 cups of the flour. Beat vigorously for 2 minutes. Gradually add the remaining flour ¼ cup at a time until the dough begins to pull away from the side of the bowl. Turn the dough out onto a floured work surface. Knead, adding flour a little at a time, until the dough is smooth and elastic.

By mixer In the mixer bowl, sprinkle the yeast in the water to soften. Heat the milk to 110°F and add it to the yeast along with the butter, sugar, cinnamon, salt, and 2 cups of the flour. Using the mixer paddle, beat on medium-low speed for 2 minutes. Gradually add the remaining flour ¼ cup at a time until the dough begins to pull away from the side of the bowl. Change to the dough hook. Continue to add flour 1 tablespoon at a time until the dough just begins to clean the bowl. Knead 4 to 5 minutes on medium-low.

By food processor In a cup or small bowl, sprinkle the yeast in the water to soften. Heat the milk to 100°F and add it to the yeast. In the bowl of the food processor fitted with the dough blade, combine the butter, sugar, cinnamon, salt, and 4 cups flour. Pulse 4 or 5 times to combine. With the food processor running, add the liquid ingredients as fast as the dry ingredients will accept them. If you hear a sputtering sound, pour the liquid slower. As soon as all the liquid is added, turn the processor off. Check the liquid-to-flour ratio (see page 28). Pulse until the dough forms a ball, then process for exactly 60 seconds.

By bread machine Put the water, milk, and butter in the bread pan. Add the sugar, cinnamon, salt, and 4 cups flour, then sprinkle with the yeast. Select the Dough cycle and press Start. While the dough is mixing, check the liquid to flour ratio (see page 29). The machine stops after the kneading cycle. You may let the dough rise in the bread machine or a bowl.

First rise Put the dough in an oiled bowl and turn to coat the entire ball of dough with oil. Cover with a tightly woven towel and let rise until doubled, about one hour.

Shape Turn the dough out onto a lightly oiled work surface and divide into 24 equal pieces. Shape each piece into a ball and place on a parchment-lined or well-greased baking sheet about ½ inch apart. The buns can also be placed in 2 well-greased 9 by 13-inch baking pans.

Second rise Cover with a tightly woven towel and let rise for 45 minutes.

Preheat oven About 10 minutes before baking, preheat the oven to 375°F.

Final preparation Whisk the egg and cold water together to form a glaze and lightly brush it over the tops of the buns. Sprinkle the buns with granulated sugar if using.

Bake and cool Bake for 20 minutes until the internal temperature of the buns reaches 190°F. Immediately remove the buns from the baking sheet and place them on a rack to cool.

NOTE: These buns freeze nicely for up to 6 months and can easily be reheated. Wrap the thawed buns in foil and reheat in a 375°F oven for 7 to 10 minutes.

Wiggs

Wiggs, wygges, wigges, whigs, or wigs are small, lightly spiced, wedge-shaped breads served in Great Britain during Lent. Christians observe Lent as the annual season of fasting and penitence in preparation for Easter. It begins on Ash Wednesday and lasts forty weekdays—not weekends—ending with Easter.

Wiggs came to Great Britain around the fourteenth century from Holland. In Dutch the word *wigge* means wedge-shaped cake. Breads were often named by their shape, so very few old recipes described how to shape the dough.

Wiggs were extremely popular in the eighteenth century. Recipes varied from the extremely rich, with lots of cream, butter, and eggs, to the very plain, containing only caraway seeds, a very popular flavoring for English cakes, buns, and biscuits during the eighteenth and nineteenth centuries.

Wiggs were usually eaten plain or lightly buttered to accompany a pint of ale, but they were also served for breakfast with a "cuppa"—English for a cup of tea. For a light lunch, Wiggs were often lightly toasted with Leicester or Cheddar cheese and placed in a bowl of red wine or ale.

For some reason Wiggs lost their popularity. In and around the town of Bath they are still served in some restaurants and pubs, but otherwise they seem to have all but disappeared from modern cookbooks and tables.

THIS BREAD is shaped into dough rounds that are flattened slightly. Then the rounds are cut into wedges like scones but not separated so they rise together. When they have baked, break them apart where they were cut.

MAKES 24 BUNS

FOR THE SPONGE

1 scant tablespoon or 1 (¼-ounce) package active dry yeast

2 tablespoons warm water (about 110°F)

1 cup warm light cream or half-and-half (about 110°F)

1 teaspoon granulated sugar

1 cup unbleached all-purpose flour

FOR THE DOUGH

½ cup granulated sugar

½ cup (1 stick) unsalted butter, melted

1 large egg, beaten

3 tablespoons finely chopped candied ginger

1 teaspoon caraway seeds

1 teaspoon salt

½ teaspoon ground nutmeg

½ teaspoon ground mace

¼ teaspoon ground cloves

3 to 4 cups unbleached all-purpose flour

FOR THE TOP

3 tablespoons caraway seeds

Prepare sponge In a large bowl, sprinkle the yeast in the water to soften. Stir in the cream, sugar, and 1 cup flour. Cover with plastic wrap and let sit for 30 minutes.

By hand Combine the sponge, sugar, butter, egg, ginger, caraway, salt, nutmeg, mace, cloves, and 1 cup of the flour. Beat vigorously for 2 minutes. Gradually add the remaining flour ¼ cup at a time until the dough begins to pull away from the side of the bowl. Turn the dough out onto a floured work surface. Knead, adding flour a little at a time, until the dough is smooth and elastic.

By mixer In the mixer bowl, combine the sponge, sugar, butter, egg, ginger, caraway, salt, nutmeg, mace, cloves, and 1 cup of the flour. Using the mixer paddle, beat on medium-low speed for 2 minutes. Gradually add the remaining flour ¼ cup at a time until the dough begins to pull away from the side of the bowl. Change to the dough hook. Continue to add flour 1 tablespoon at a time until the dough just begins to clean the bowl. Knead 4 to 5 minutes on medium-low.

By food processor Add the egg to the sponge. In the bowl of the food processor fitted with the dough blade, combine the sugar, ginger, caraway, salt, nutmeg, mace, cloves, and 3 cups flour. Pulse 4 or 5 times to combine. Add the butter and pulse 4 or 5 times more to combine. With the food processor running, add the sponge as fast as the dry ingredients will accept it. If you hear a sputtering sound, pour the sponge slower. As soon as all the sponge is added, turn the processor off. Check the liquid-to-flour ratio (see page 28). Pulse until the dough forms a ball, then process exactly 60 seconds.

By bread machine Put the sponge, butter, and egg in the bread pan. Add the sugar, ginger, caraway, salt, nutmeg, mace, cloves, and 3 cups flour. Select the Dough cycle and press Start. While the dough is mixing, check the liquid-to-flour ratio (see page 29). The machine stops after the kneading cycle. You may let the dough rise in the bread machine or a bowl.

First rise Put the dough in an oiled bowl and turn to coat the entire ball of dough with oil. Cover with a tightly woven towel and let rise until doubled, about one hour.

Shape Turn the dough out onto a lightly oiled work surface and divide into 3 equal pieces. Shape each piece into a ball and place about 3 inches apart on parchment-lined or well-greased baking sheets. Sprinkle the tops of the loaves with caraway seeds. Press the seeds into the loaves while flattening the loaves to about 1½ inches thick.

Second rise Cover with a tightly woven towel and let rise for 30 minutes.

Final preparation Cut each dough round into 8 wedges, leaving the wedges in place; you need to cut all the way through to the pan. I find a rectangular dough blade/scraper or bench knife perfect for this task.

Third rise Recover the loaves and let rise 20 minutes.

Preheat oven About 10 minutes before baking, preheat the oven to 400°F.

Bake and cool Bake for 20 minutes until the internal temperature of the bread reaches 190°F. Immediately remove the bread from the baking sheet and place on a rack to cool. Break into wedges to serve.

NOTE: This bread freezes nicely for up to 6 months. To serve, wrap the thawed bread in foil and reheat in a 375°F oven for 10 to 12 minutes.

Irish Soda Bread

For old Irish weddings, the festivities began at the home of the bride in the early morning. Large weddings brought many problems—mostly the logistics of housing and feeding the large number of guests. To accommodate everyone, the house, garden, and many of the farm buildings were pressed into service for the wedding feast, and everyone hoped for good weather.

Tables—usually doors taken off their hinges—were laid in the barn and often the farmyard. They were loaded with corned beef, legs of mutton, salt pork, bacon, turkeys, geese, chickens, potatoes and other vegetables from the garden, and enriched soda breads, all offered with copious quantities of alcoholic beverages. The food was simple and often inferior in status to the drink.

Outside of family members, the piper and the priest were the most important guests and were treated with equal importance. While the priest only sanctified the ceremony, the piper ensured lively entertainment until daybreak. Two hats were passed to take up collections, since both of their contributions were considered indispensable.

Guests feasted until it was time for the young couple to take their wedding vows, which could be pronounced at the local chapel or the home where the couple would live. Though the groom was present at the feast at the bride's home, they traveled separately until they were married.

After the wedding the party would continue at the groom's home. The religious ceremony was not the most important part of the wedding; it simply divided the two periods of festivity. The feasting, drinking, and merriment at the groom's home lasted until daybreak the following morning.

The custom of breaking bread over the bride's head has different meanings in different parts of Ireland. In most instances, bread was broken over the bride as she entered her new home and became the woman of the house. To emphasize this change of status, her new mother-in-law would greet her at the door, hand her the fire tongs, and invite her to adjust the fire in the hearth. She was also given the churn dash as a sign that she had control of the butter-making and the kitchen.

In other locales the bread was broken over the bride as she sat at the table after the wedding feast or stood among the guests, to signify her change from maiden to wife. Another custom was that guests broke the bread into crumbs and threw bits at the bride to wish that she would not want or go hungry. Young unmarried girls gathered these crumbs to place under their pillows to prompt dreams of their future husbands. The next time you plan to break bread over the head of an Irish bride, Irish Soda Bread should do the trick.

SODA BREAD is made daily in most Irish homes, because it goes stale quickly. It is an insult and a sign of careless hospitality to offer your guest anything but that day's bread. Everyday soda bread can be made with white or whole-wheat flour and does not contain caraway seeds, sugar, orange zest, or fruit. References to sweet cake, raisin bread, currant cake, and treacle cake must be interpreted as fancy versions of the basic soda bread. The bread should be mixed gently, like a good biscuit, to prevent it from becoming tough. My husband, Keith, and I were most fortunate to be shown the proper method of preparing Irish Soda Bread by Tim Allen in the kitchens of the Ballymaloe Cookery School in County Cork, Ireland.

Tim and his wife, Darina, who founded the school, share their love of food with several hundred people each year in one of the most beautiful culinary schools in the world.

MAKES 1 LARGE ROUND LOAF

2 cups unbleached all-purpose flour

½ teaspoon baking powder

½ teaspoon baking soda

½ teaspoon salt

2 teaspoons caraway seeds

2 tablespoons granulated sugar

1 tablespoon finely grated orange zest

4 tablespoons (½ stick) cold unsalted butter

½ cup currants or raisins

1 cup buttermilk

Preheat oven Preheat the oven to 375°F degrees.

Prepare dough Whisk together the flour, baking powder, baking soda, salt, caraway, sugar, and orange zest until well combined. With a pastry blender or 2 knives, cut the butter into the dry ingredients until it is about the size of little peas. Add the currants to the dry mixture and toss until combined. Add the buttermilk all at once and mix just until moistened. Turn out onto a floured board and knead gently 8 or 9 times.

Shape Place the dough in the center of a parchment-lined or well-seasoned baking sheet and pat into an 8-inch circle about 3 inches thick. Dust the loaf with flour. With a sharp serrated knife, cut a cross on the top of the loaf about ½ inch deep.

Bake and cool Bake for 35 minutes until the internal temperature of the bread reaches 190°F. Immediately remove the bread from the baking sheet and cool on a rack to prevent the crust from becoming soggy.

Scottish Black Bun

New Year's Eve is called Hogmanay in Scotland. Though Christmas is celebrated rather somberly, there are always rowdy parties to welcome the New Year. On Hogmanay, large barrels of tar are set on fire to "burn out the old year," and "Auld Lang Syne," the song written by Scottish poet Robert Burns in the early 1700s, is always sung at midnight.

Traditionally two foods are eaten for Hogmanay—haggis, a pudding from sheep's stomach that is stuffed with oatmeal and sheep's innards, which is drenched in Scotch whisky; and Black Bun, a heavily fruited bread loaded with spices, butter, eggs, and whisky.

The recipe for Black Bun varies by region. In some parts it is shaped like a sandwich loaf; in others, the fruited bread is wrapped in a plain layer of the same dough. Black Bun originally belonged to Twelfth Night celebrations, but it became a New Year's Eve bread when religious reformers banned Christmas as a festival.

THIS RECIPE for Black Bun calls for wrapping the bread in a plain version of the same dough. This bread needs two to three weeks from the time it is baked to mellow and develop the flavors.

MAKES 1 LARGE LOAF

FOR THE DOUGH

1 scant tablespoon or 1 (¼-ounce) package active dry yeast

¼ cup warm water (about 110°F)

¾ cup milk

¼ cup (½ stick) unsalted butter, softened

2 large eggs, beaten

2 large egg whites

¼ cup granulated sugar

1 teaspoon salt

4 to 5 cups unbleached all-purpose flour

FOR THE FILLING

1 cup coarsely chopped almonds

1 cup currants

1 cup golden raisins

¼ cup candied orange peel (see Notes)

¼ cup candied lemon peel (see Notes)

2 tablespoons finely chopped candied ginger

¼ cup Scotch whisky or brandy

1 teaspoon cinnamon

FOR THE GLAZE

2 egg yolks

1 tablespoon cold water

By hand In a large bowl, sprinkle the yeast in the water to soften. Heat the milk to 110°F and add it to the yeast along with the butter, eggs, egg whites, sugar, salt, and 2 cups of the flour. Beat vigorously for 2 minutes. Gradually add the remaining flour ¼ cup at a time until the dough begins to pull away from the side of the bowl. Turn the dough out onto a floured work surface. Knead, adding flour a little at a time, until the dough is smooth and elastic.

By mixer In the mixer bowl, sprinkle the yeast in the water to soften. Heat the milk to 110°F and add it to the yeast along with the butter, eggs, egg whites, sugar, salt, and 2 cups of the flour. Using the mixer paddle, beat on medium-low speed for 2 minutes. Gradually add the remaining flour ¼ cup at a time until the dough begins to pull away from the side of the bowl. Change to the dough hook. Continue to add flour 1 tablespoon at a time until the dough just begins to clean the bowl. Knead 4 to 5 minutes on medium-low.

By food processor In a large measuring cup or bowl, sprinkle the yeast in the water to soften. Heat the milk to 100°F and add it to the yeast along with the eggs and egg whites. In the bowl of the food processor fitted with the dough blade, combine the butter, sugar, salt, and 4 cups flour. Pulse 4 or 5 times to combine. With the food processor running, add the liquid ingredients as fast as the dry ingredients will accept them. If you hear a sputtering sound, pour the liquid slower. As soon as all the liquid is added, turn the processor off. Check the liquid-to-flour ratio (see page 28). Pulse until the dough forms a ball, then process exactly 60 seconds.

By bread machine Put the water, milk, butter, eggs, and egg whites in the bread pan. Add the sugar, salt, and 4 cups flour to the bread pan, then sprinkle with the yeast. Select the Dough cycle and press Start. While the dough is mixing, check the liquid-to-flour ratio (see page 29). The machine stops after the kneading cycle. You may let the dough rise in the bread machine or a bowl.

First rise Put the dough in an oiled bowl and turn to coat the entire ball of dough with oil. Cover with a tightly woven towel and let rise until doubled, about one hour.

Prepare filling Combine the almonds, currants, raisins, orange peel, lemon peel, candied ginger, Scotch, and cinnamon. Let the mixture sit while the dough rises, stirring often.

Shape Turn the dough out onto a lightly oiled work surface and cut off about one-third of the dough. Set aside this piece and cover with a towel. Knead the fruit mixture into the remaining dough. This is a messy process, but do not add more flour. Use a dough scraper or spatula to help scrape the dough from the work surface. This task is easily done in a heavy-duty mixer. When the fruit is incorporated in the dough, shape the dough into a ball and cover with a towel.

Take the reserved dough and remove one-third of it. Cover this piece with a towel. On a lightly oiled work surface, roll the larger portion of dough into a 15-inch round. Carefully ease the rolled dough into a well-greased 9-inch springform pan, letting the excess dough extend over the sides of the pan. Flatten the fruited dough into a 9-inch round and place it in the dough-lined pan. Lay the excess dough over the top of the loaf and pleat to make it fit.

On a lightly oiled work surface, roll the remaining piece of dough into a 10-inch round and center it on top of the dough in the pan. Carefully slide the excess dough between the side of the pan and the loaf. (See top illustration, next page.)

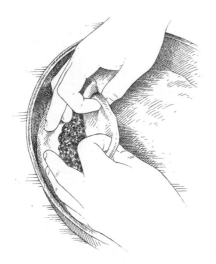

Final preparation Prick the loaf with a skewer or toothpick about 1 inch apart and one inch deep all over the top. The dough must be compressed to control the rising. Use something flat like a 10-inch cake pan, an ovenproof plate, or a baking sheet (grease the bottom of the pan, or place a greased piece of parchment paper between the dough and the pan). Put something heavy and ovenproof on top of the pan—a brick, cast-iron frying pan, 4-cup Pyrex measure filled with water—to weight it.

Bake and cool Bake for 1½ hours. Remove the weight from the loaf and the outer ring from the springform pan. For the glaze beat the egg yolks with the cold water and brush over the top and sides of the bread. Return the bread to the oven and bake for 5 to 10 minutes until the internal temperature of the loaf reaches 190°F. Immediately remove the bread from the pan and place it on a rack to cool. When completely cooled, wrap with plastic or foil and let mellow for 2 to 3 weeks before serving.

Second rise Cover with a tightly woven towel and let rest for 30 minutes. The dough should not double in size.

Preheat oven About 10 minutes before baking, preheat the oven to 375°F.

NOTES: If you prefer to make your own candied peel, see page 326.

This bread freezes nicely for up to 6 months and is best served at room temperature. This very dense bread does not reheat well.

Barmbrack

The origin of the word *February* comes from Febrarius, the Roman feast of purification. The name is apt, since the festival falls at the beginning of Lent. The first feast in the month of February is that of Saint Bridget, who is also known as Mary of the Gael. Saint Bridget is known for her work with Saint Patrick in converting the pagans of Ireland to Christianity. She founded the first nunnery in Ireland.

On Bridget's feast day, a bread called Barmbrack, or Barinbreac, was served. *Barm* is the old word for yeast—a by-product of making beer—and *brack* means speckled, referring to the addition of raisins and currants. Eventually Saint Bridget's Day faded in popularity, and the custom of eating Barmbrack moved to another popular holiday, All Hallows' Eve or Halloween.

Over time changes were made to the traditional recipe. Small items were added to the loaf before baking to foretell the future. The person who found a small piece of rag in the bread was destined to be poor. A pea or bean meant you were doomed to be an old maid or bachelor. You would rule the house if you found a small stick, and you'd marry within a year if you found a ring.

ONE OF THE UNIQUE QUALITIES of this Celtic bread is that the raisins and currants are macerated in strong hot tea before being added to the dough. This step imparts a slight bitterness to the fruit that is counterbalanced by the addition of sugar and a subtle mixture of spices. This Welsh version of Barmbrack calls for a mixture of raisins and currants. The Irish typically use only currants in the recipe, and the Scots and English use mainly raisins.

MAKES I LARGE LOAF

1 cup raisins

1 cup golden raisins

¾ cup currants

1 cup extremely hot strong tea

2 large eggs, beaten

1 scant tablespoon or 1 (¼-ounce) package active dry yeast

¼ cup warm water (about 110°F)

½ cup (1 stick) unsalted butter, softened

¾ cup light brown sugar, packed

1 teaspoon salt

¼ cup finely chopped candied lemon peel (See Notes)

½ teaspoon ground cinnamon

¼ teaspoon ground nutmeg

¼ teaspoon ground allspice

4 to 5 cups unbleached all-purpose flour

Optional additions: 1-inch square of cloth, dried pea, dried bean, toothpick, and a ring, individually wrapped in foil

Milk to brush on loaf

Prepare fruit Combine both types of raisins and the currants. Pour hot tea over the raisin mixture, cover, and cool to about 110°F. Drain the raisin mixture, reserving the liquid.

Put the beaten eggs into a measuring cup and add enough of the reserved liquid to measure 1 cup; add water if needed. Stir to combine.

By hand In a large bowl, sprinkle the yeast in the water to soften. Add the egg mixture, butter, sugar, salt, and lemon peel to the yeast. Whisk the cinnamon, nutmeg, allspice, and 2 cups of the flour together, then add to the yeast mixture. Beat vigorously for 2 minutes. Add the raisin mixture, then gradually add the remaining flour ¼ cup at a time until the dough begins to pull away from the side of the bowl. Turn the dough out onto a floured work surface. Knead, adding flour a little at a time, until the dough is smooth and elastic.

By mixer In the mixer bowl, sprinkle the yeast in the water to soften. Add the egg mixture, butter, sugar, salt, and lemon peel to the yeast. Whisk the cinnamon, nutmeg, allspice, and 2 cups of the flour together, then add to the yeast mixture. Using the mixer paddle, beat on medium-low speed for 2 minutes. Add the raisin mixture, then gradually add the remaining flour ¼ cup at a time until the dough begins to pull away from the side of the bowl. Change to the dough hook. Continue to add flour 1 tablespoon at a time until the dough just begins to clean the bowl. Knead 4 to 5 minutes on medium-low.

By food processor In a cup or small bowl, sprinkle the yeast into the water to soften. Add the egg mixture to the yeast and stir to combine. In the bowl of the food processor fitted with the dough blade, combine the sugar, salt, lemon peel, cinnamon, nutmeg, allspice, and 4 cups flour. Pulse 4 or 5 times to combine. Add the butter and pulse 4 or 5 more times. With the food processor running, add the egg mixture as fast as the dry ingredients will accept it. If you hear a sputtering sound, pour the liquid slower. As soon as all the liquid is added, turn the processor off. Check the liquid-to-flour ratio (see page 28). Pulse until the dough forms a ball, then process exactly 60 seconds. Turn the dough out onto a work surface and knead in the raisin mixture.

By bread machine Put the egg mixture, water, and butter in the bread pan. Add the sugar, salt, lemon peel, cinnamon, nutmeg, allspice, and 4 cups flour to the bread pan, then sprinkle with the yeast. If your machine has an Add Fruit cycle, add the raisin mixture when prompted; if not, add it with the egg mixture. Select the Dough cycle and press Start. While the dough is mixing, check the liquid-to-flour ratio (see page 29). The machine stops after the kneading cycle. You may let the dough rise in the bread machine or a bowl.

First rise Put the dough in an oiled bowl and turn to coat the entire ball of dough with oil. Cover with a tightly woven towel and let rise until doubled, 1 to 1½ hours.

Shape Turn the dough out onto a lightly oiled work surface and shape into a ball. Press the 5 foil-wrapped packets into the bottom of the ball, evenly spaced, so they are not visible. Turn the loaf over and place on a parchment-lined or well-greased baking sheet. Flatten the center of the loaf to about 3 inches thick.

Second rise Cover with a tightly woven towel and let rise for 45 minutes.

Preheat oven About 10 minutes before baking, preheat the oven to 375°F.

Final preparation Brush the loaf with milk.

Bake and cool Bake for 30 minutes until the internal temperature of the bread reaches 190°F. Immediately remove the bread from the baking sheet and place on a rack to cool.

NOTES: If you prefer to make your own candied peel, see page 326.

This bread freezes nicely for up to 6 months. To serve, first thaw the bread, then reheat on a baking sheet or directly on the oven rack in a 375°F oven for 7 to 10 minutes.

8

Eastern Europe

Challah

Braided breads are not of Jewish origin, though most challahs for Shabbat, the Jewish Sabbath, are braided. Braided challahs came into popularity sometime during the fifteenth century in Ashkenazic (Central and Eastern European Jewish) communities. There are many customs and traditions surrounding this wonderful bread.

Customarily the "head" or "rosh" of the dough (a small piece of dough about the size of an olive) is separated from the mass after all the ingredients are mixed. This tradition of "taking challah" or "separating challah" is mentioned in the Bible, Numbers 15, and was originally a portion of dough offered to the temple priests. Today a small piece of dough is thrown into the oven and burnt, and the following blessing recited: "Blessed are You, Lord God, King of the Universe, who has sanctified us with His commandments and commanded us to separate challah." Some people save all of the challah offerings gathered throughout the year and burn them just before Passover when they remove all leavened bread from their homes.

The word *challah*—pronounced with a soft *h* as in *ha-la*—means dough and refers specifically to the bread remaining after the small piece was separated from it. (Dough has to be separated only if the bread is made from wheat, barley, maize, spelt, or oats.) Challah is usually eaten on Shabbat and other Jewish festivals, except the eight days of Passover. The custom of sprinkling challah with poppy or sesame seeds symbolizes God's offering manna in the desert. Manna did not fall on the Sabbath, but a double portion fell the day before so there would be plenty for Shabbat.

In the homes of Orthodox Jewish families, two loaves of challah are placed on an embroidered tablecloth. A cloth is placed over the loaves until after the wine is blessed. Knives on the table are covered; knives are not used to cut the challah on Shabbat. Cutting the challah with a knife—a weapon of war—is considered sacrilege.

A blessing is said over the bread, then the challah is broken and passed to each person at the table. One does not hand bread directly to another person but places a piece of bread on a plate, to symbolize that it is not from man that we receive our bread but from the hand of God. The old custom still prevails that bread should be salted just before eating to symbolize the Temple sacrifices and the sweat of sacrifice.

This traditional braided bread, eaten on Jewish Shabbat and holidays, is made from a sponge. For the sponge a few of the ingredients are mixed together without salt, which would inhibit the growth of the yeast, and allowed to rise. The sponge is the consistency of a batter. After the sponge rises, the remaining ingredients are added and the process is finished like regular dough. By creating a sponge and letting it rise, the flavors have more time to develop, and the texture is changed into a smooth, velvety crumb unlike dough made by the regular methods of just mixing, kneading, and baking. It's amazing what that one small sponge can do!

MAKES 2 LARGE BRAIDS

FOR THE SPONGE

1 scant tablespoon or 1 (¼-ounce) package active dry yeast

1 cup warm water (about 110°F)

1 tablespoon granulated sugar

1 cup unbleached all-purpose flour

FOR THE DOUGH

3 to 4 cups unbleached all-purpose flour

3 tablespoons granulated sugar

1 teaspoon salt

2 large eggs

¼ cup vegetable or canola oil

FOR THE TOPPING

1 large egg, beaten

1 tablespoon cold water

Poppy or sesame seeds, optional

Prepare sponge In a large bowl, sprinkle the yeast in the water to soften. Add the sugar and flour and beat until the mixture is smooth. Cover with plastic wrap and let sit for 1 to 12 hours at room temperature. The longer the sponge sits, the more the flavor develops.

By hand Add 2 cups of the flour, the sugar, salt, eggs, and oil to the sponge. Beat vigorously for 2 minutes. Gradually add the remaining flour ¼ cup at a time until the dough begins to pull away from the side of the bowl. Turn the dough out onto a floured work surface. Knead, adding flour a little at a time, until the dough is smooth and elastic.

By mixer In the mixer bowl using the paddle, add 2 cups of the flour, the sugar, salt, eggs, and oil to the sponge. Beat on medium-low speed for 2 minutes. Gradually add the remaining flour ¼ cup at a time until the dough begins to pull away from the side of the bowl. Change to the dough hook. Continue to add flour 1 tablespoon at a time until the dough just begins to clean the bowl. Knead 4 to 5 minutes on medium-low.

By food processor Add the eggs and oil to the sponge and stir to combine. In the bowl of the food processor fitted with the dough blade, add 3 cups flour, the sugar, and salt. Pulse 4 or 5 times to combine. With the food processor running, add the sponge mixture as fast as the dry ingredients will accept it. If you hear a sputtering sound, pour the liquid slower. As soon as all the sponge is added, turn the processor off. Check the liquid-to-flour ratio (see page 28). Pulse until the dough forms a ball, then process exactly 60 seconds.

By bread machine Add the salt, eggs, and oil to the sponge and stir to combine. Pour the mixture into the bread pan and add 3 cups flour and the sugar. Select the Dough cycle and press Start. While the dough is mixing, check the liquid-to-flour ratio (see page 29). The machine stops after the kneading cycle. You may let the dough rise in the bread machine or a bowl.

First rise Put the dough in an oiled bowl and turn to coat the entire ball of dough with oil. Cover with a tightly woven towel and let rise until doubled, about one hour.

Shape Turn the dough out onto a lightly oiled work surface and divide in half. Divide each half into thirds (6 pieces of dough in all). Shape each piece of dough into a 20-inch-long rope. Working with 3 ropes at a time, lay the ropes side by side. Starting in the center of the ropes, place the right rope over the middle rope (note that the right rope has now become the middle rope), then place the left rope over the middle, the right over the middle, left over the middle, and so on. Continue this process until the ropes are too short to braid. Pinch the ends together and tuck them under.

To braid the other end of the loaf, place the middle rope over the right rope, then the rope that is now in the middle over the left, middle over the right, middle over the left, and so on, until the ends are too short to braid. Pinch the ends together and tuck them under. Carefully lift and place the braid on one side of a large parchment-lined or well-greased baking sheet. Repeat with the remaining ropes and place on the other side of the baking sheet.

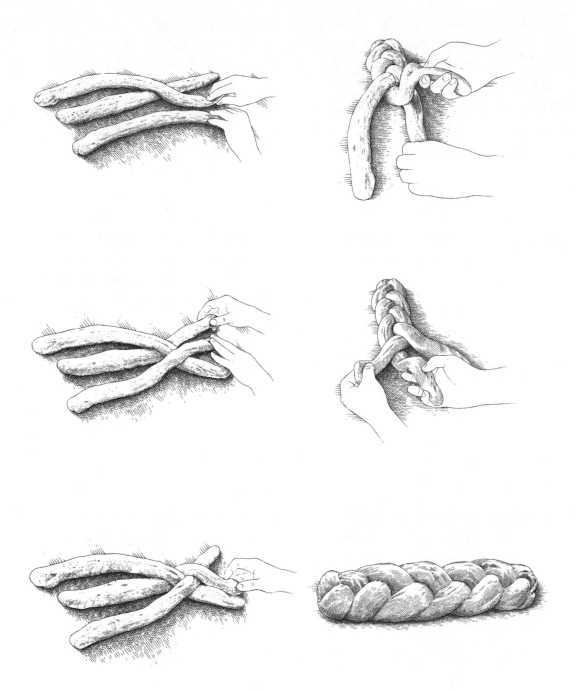

Second rise Cover with a tightly woven towel and let rise for 45 minutes.

Preheat oven About 10 minutes before baking, preheat the oven to 375°F.

Final preparation Combine the beaten egg with the cold water and brush on the braids. Let sit 5 minutes and brush the braids again. Sprinkle with poppy or sesame seeds if using.

Bake and cool Bake for 25 minutes until the internal temperature of the bread reaches 190°F. Immediately remove the bread from the baking sheet and place on a rack to cool.

NOTE: This bread freezes nicely for up to 6 months. To serve, first thaw the bread, then reheat on a baking sheet or directly on the oven rack in a preheated 375°F oven for 7 to 10 minutes.

New Year's Challah or Faigele

Uring Rosh Hashanah, the beginning of the Jewish New Year, it is customary to eat sweet foods to symbolize the "sweetness and good fortune" of the coming year. The Rosh Hashanah meal, for example, begins with challah and apple slices dipped in honey. Festive meals are served the evening that marks the beginning of Rosh Hashanah and through the next day.

Challah and other foods are both symbolic and nourishing. The challah contains saffron and raisins for long life and is formed into a ring, representing life without end and continuous health and happiness. Sesame or anise seeds might be served for plenty and fruitfulness, dried fruits for a sweet year, carrots for a good year, olives for beauty and peace, and pomegranates because they are said to have the same number of seeds as there are Jewish laws.

The crown-shaped challah that originated in Lithuania and the Ukraine around the eighteenth century symbolized the King of Kings. The Hungarian Faigele incorporated an actual bird or bird head on the top of the loaf to represent one's sins flying away (*faigele* means "birds"). It was also thought that the bird flies straight to God with prayers for salvation.

IF YOU USE WARM EGGS in this recipe, you will get extra volume or height. Crack the eggs into a small glass bowl, place the glass bowl in a slightly larger bowl that contains warm, not hot, water, and let sit for 5 minutes before using in the recipe.

MAKES 2 COILED LOAVES

FOR THE SPONGE

1 scant tablespoon or 1 (¼-ounce) package active dry yeast

¼ cup warm water (about 110°F)

4 large eggs, warmed

¼ cup vegetable or canola oil

¼ cup honey

2 cups unbleached all-purpose flour

FOR THE DOUGH

¼ cup boiling water

¼ teaspoon or large pinch saffron

1 cup golden raisins

1 teaspoon salt

2 to 3 cups unbleached all-purpose flour

FOR THE TOPPING

1 large egg, beaten

1 tablespoon cold water

Poppy seeds, optional

Prepare sponge In a large bowl, sprinkle the yeast in the water to soften. Add the eggs, oil, honey, and 2 cups flour and beat until the mixture is smooth. Cover with plastic wrap and let sit for 30 minutes at room temperature.

Prepare raisins Combine the boiling water, saffron, and raisins. Cover and let sit for 15 minutes until cooled to warm.

By hand Combine the sponge, raisin mixture, and salt. Gradually add the flour ¼ cup at a time until the dough begins to pull away from the side of the bowl. Turn the dough out onto a floured work surface. Knead, adding flour a little at a time, until the dough is smooth and elastic.

By mixer In the mixer bowl using the paddle, combine the sponge, raisin mixture, and salt. Gradually add the flour ¼ cup at a time until the dough begins to pull away from the side of the bowl. Change to the dough hook. Continue to add flour 1 tablespoon at a time until the dough just begins to clean the bowl. Knead 4 to 5 minutes on medium-low.

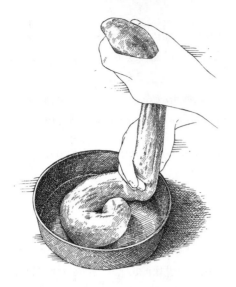

By food processor Add the raisin mixture to the sponge and stir to combine. In the bowl of the food processor fitted with the dough blade, add the salt and 2 cups flour. Pulse 4 or 5 times to combine. With the food processor running, add the liquid mixture as fast as the dry ingredients will accept it. If you hear a sputtering sound, pour the liquid slower. As soon as all the liquid is added, turn the processor off. Check the liquid-to-flour ratio (see page 28). Pulse until the dough forms a ball, then process exactly 60 seconds.

By bread machine Add the sponge and raisin mixture to the bread pan. Add the salt and 2 cups flour. Select the Dough cycle and press Start. While the dough is mixing, check the liquid-to-flour ratio (see page 29). The machine stops after the kneading cycle. You may let the dough rise in the bread machine or a bowl.

First rise Put the dough into an oiled bowl and turn to coat the entire ball of dough with oil. Cover with a tightly woven towel and let rise until doubled, about one hour.

Shape Turn the dough out onto a lightly oiled work surface and divide in half. Shape each half into a 26-inch-long rope with one end twice as thick as the other. Starting with the larger end of one rope in the center of a well-greased 10-inch round pan, coil the rope in the pan. Repeat with the other rope and a second pan.

Second rise Cover with tightly woven towels and let rise for 45 minutes.

Preheat oven About 10 minutes before baking, preheat the oven to 375°F.

Final preparation Combine the beaten egg and cold water and brush on each loaf. Let stand uncovered for 5 minutes, then brush again with the egg mixture. Sprinkle with poppy seeds if using.

Bake and cool Bake for 25 minutes until the internal temperature of the bread reaches 190°F. Immediately remove the bread from the pans and place on a rack to cool.

NOTE: This bread freezes nicely for up to 6 months. To serve, first thaw the bread, then reheat on a baking sheet or directly on the oven rack in a preheated 375°F oven for 7 to 10 minutes.

Potica

Potica is to Slovenia what apple pie is to America. Pronounced *po-tee-cia,* the word is derived from the Slovenian word *povitica,* meaning "something rolled in." The Ukraine, Poland, and Yugoslavia all claim Potica as a favored bread originating in their country. Each region of these countries has a different filling—nuts, honey, poppy seeds, raisins, chocolate, herbs, cottage cheese, or cracklings—though walnut is the most common.

In some of the poorer areas, Potica is baked with three types of dough—one made from white flour, one from rye flour, and one from maize—that give the appearance of a filling. This type of bread is called mottled bread. Making Potica with all white flour is a symbol of wealth, festivity, and well-being.

Potica as we know it today is a relatively new bread—just two hundred years old. Before that time molds for baking were unknown, so the bread was rolled and placed directly in the oven. Once clay and earthenware molds were developed, bakers used them to bake their Potica.

Though Potica is baked for almost every important occasion, it is essential to the celebration of Palm Sunday, when Christians remember Jesus Christ's triumphal entry into Jerusalem and his last days as a man; and Easter, when Christ was crucified, died on the cross, was buried, and arose into heaven.

TRADITIONALLY, FLOUR for Potica was kept in a warm corner near the oven to ensure that the dough didn't "catch cold." If you don't have a space large enough to roll out the dough, cover a table with a sheet and use that. Traditionally Potica is baked in a toroidal, a large, round ceramic mold with a hole in the middle. A tube or Bundt pan is a good alternative.

MAKES 1 LARGE LOAF

FOR THE DOUGH

1 scant tablespoon or 1 (¼-ounce) package active dry yeast

2 tablespoons warm water (about 110°F)

3 large egg yolks

¾ cup milk

1 teaspoon salt

¼ cup granulated sugar

3 to 4 cups unbleached all-purpose flour

½ cup (1 stick) unsalted butter, melted

FOR THE FILLING

4 cups walnuts

2 cups golden raisins

½ cup heavy cream, scalded

¼ cup honey

¼ cup (½ stick) unsalted butter, softened

2 teaspoons ground cinnamon

3 large egg whites, beaten stiff

FOR THE TOPPING

¼ cup (½ stick) unsalted butter, melted
Confectioners' sugar

By hand In a large bowl, sprinkle the yeast in the water to soften. Beat the egg yolks and add to the yeast along with the milk, salt, sugar, and 2 cups of the flour. Beat vigorously for 2 minutes. Add the butter. Gradually add the remaining flour ¼ cup at a time until the dough begins to pull away from the side of the bowl. Turn the dough out onto a floured work surface. Knead, adding flour a little at a time, until the dough is smooth and elastic.

By mixer In the mixer bowl, sprinkle the yeast in the water to soften. Beat the egg yolks and add to the yeast along with the milk salt, sugar, and 2 cups of the flour. Using the mixer paddle, beat on medium-low speed for 2 minutes. Add the butter. Gradually add the remaining flour ¼ cup at a time until the dough begins to pull away from the side of the bowl. Change to the dough hook. Continue to add flour 1 tablespoon at a time until the dough just begins to clean the bowl. Knead 4 to 5 minutes on medium-low.

By food processor In a large measuring cup or bowl, sprinkle the yeast in the water to soften. Beat the egg yolks and add to the yeast along with the milk and butter. In the bowl of the food processor fitted with the dough blade, combine the salt, sugar, and 3 cups flour with 4 or 5 pulses. With the food processor running, add the liquid ingredients as fast as the dry ingredients will accept them. If you hear a sputtering sound, pour the liquid slower. As soon as all the liquid is added, turn the processor off. Check the liquid-to-flour ratio (see page 28). Pulse until the dough forms a ball, then process exactly 60 seconds.

By bread machine Beat the egg yolks and put into the bread pan along with the milk, water and butter. Add the salt, sugar, and 3 cups flour to the bread pan, then sprinkle with the yeast. Select the Dough cycle and press Start. While the dough is mixing, check the liquid-to-flour ratio (see page 29). The machine stops after the kneading cycle. You may let the dough rise in the bread machine or a bowl.

First rise Put the dough in an oiled bowl and turn to coat the entire ball of dough with oil. Cover with a tightly woven towel and let rise until doubled, about one hour.

Prepare filling While the dough is rising, grind or very finely chop the walnuts and raisins together. Add the cream and let sit for 5 minutes. Add honey, butter, and cinnamon and stir well. Gently fold in the beaten egg whites. Cover with plastic wrap and set aside.

Shape Turn the dough out onto a lightly floured surface (see headnote). Roll the dough into an 18 by 30-inch rectangle. If the dough is difficult to roll, you may have to let it rest 2 or 3 times to get it to this size. Spread the filling evenly over the dough, leaving a ½-inch border on one 18-inch side. Start rolling the dough from the 18-inch edge that is covered with filling. After every couple of rolls, pierce the dough at 2-inch intervals with a knitting needle, skewer, or ice pick to help eliminate air pockets. Continue to roll the dough, piercing after each couple of rolls, to the end. Take care while rolling to keep the dough as even as possible. With a sharp serrated knife, trim 1 inch from each end of the cylinder (these are usually placed in a small pan and baked separately for the children). Place in a well-greased 10-inch tube or Bundt pan and carefully join the cut ends. Pierce the loaf at 1-inch intervals going all the way to the bottom of the pan with the same object you used before.

Second rise Cover with a tightly woven towel and let rise for 1½ hours, or cover with plastic wrap and a tightly woven towel and refrigerate for 2 to 24 hours.

Preheat oven About 10 minutes before baking, preheat the oven to 325°F.

Bake and cool Bake for one hour until the internal temperature of the bread reaches 190°F. Immediately invert the bread on a rack and remove the pan.

Just before serving Brush the bread with the butter and sprinkle with confectioners' sugar.

VARIATION: Once the dough has been rolled and the ends trimmed, you can cut the cylinder in half and bake each half in a well-greased 8½ by 4½-inch loaf pan.

NOTE: This bread freezes nicely for up to 6 months. To serve, wrap the thawed bread in foil and reheat in a 375°F oven for 20 minutes.

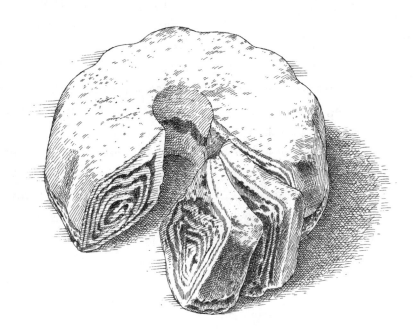

Saint Barbara's Bread

KLETZENBROT

December 4 marks the celebration of Saint Barbara's Day in Bulgaria. Saint Barbara is the patron saint in times of danger; she guards against smallpox and other diseases in children, fire, thunderstorms, and sudden death. Among those who seek her protection are gunners, artillerymen, and miners. There is some doubt as to when she lived (sometime between 235 and 313 C.E.) and where (Rome, Antioch, Tuscany, Nicomedia, or Heliopolis in Egypt). However, there is consensus regarding the general details of her life.

Barbara was the beautiful daughter of Dioscurus. He confined her to a tower to protect her from the outside world; he wanted no man to see her and ask for her hand in marriage. Before leaving on a long trip, Dioscurus commissioned a sumptuous bathhouse to be built just for Barbara and approved the design before he left. While her father was gone, Barbara spent much of her time in contemplation and secretly became a Christian. She had the builders redesign the bathhouse with a third window to symbolize the Holy Trinity.

When Dioscurus returned he was enraged at the changes and even more infuriated when Barbara announced she had converted. He denounced her to the authorities, and the prefect of the province decreed that she should be tortured and beheaded. Barbara refused to forsake her Christianity, and Dioscurus performed the execution himself. On his way home he was struck by lightning and reduced to ashes.

Saint Barbara's Day brings with it several food-related observances. All food is to be cooked by the lady of the house herself, not by any other woman, and no ready-to-cook products are to be used. An old Bulgarian custom on Saint Barbara's Day had housewives going out to the road to give pieces of bread to passersby. Each person who broke a piece off the loaf uttered the blessing, "May God bless you, your family, your cattle, and all." It is also the only time of the year when Kletzenbrot, a traditional fruit bread, is baked.

DUE TO THE ADDITION of fruit, the
dough will be an intriguing dark color.
When the bread is baked the crust is dull,
but when rubbed with soft butter, it shines.
Rubbing the crust with butter also keeps the
crust soft. This bread is best if allowed to sit
a day or two wrapped in plastic to allow the
flavors to mellow.

MAKES 2 BRAIDED LOAVES

FOR THE DOUGH

*1 scant tablespoon or 1 (¼-ounce) package
active dry yeast*

¼ cup warm water (about 110°F)

¾ cup milk

2 large eggs

½ cup (1 stick) unsalted butter, softened

½ teaspoon grated nutmeg

1 teaspoon ground cinnamon

1 cup finely chopped almonds

1 cup finely chopped dried figs

½ cup finely chopped prunes

½ cup finely chopped dates

1 cup raisins

1 teaspoon finely grated lemon zest

1 teaspoon salt

1 cup whole-wheat flour

3 to 4 cups unbleached all-purpose flour

FOR THE TOPPING

Soft butter, optional

By hand In a large bowl, sprinkle the yeast
in the water to soften. Heat the milk to 110°F
and add it to the yeast along with the eggs,
butter, nutmeg, cinnamon, almonds, figs,
prunes, dates, raisins, zest, salt, whole-wheat
flour, and 2 cups of the unbleached flour.
Beat vigorously for 2 minutes. Gradually add
the remaining flour ¼ cup at a time until the
dough begins to pull away from the side of
the bowl. Turn the dough out onto a floured
work surface. Knead, adding flour a little at a
time, until the dough is smooth and elastic.

By mixer In the mixer bowl, sprinkle the
yeast in the water to soften. Heat the milk to
110°F and add it to the yeast along with the
eggs, butter, nutmeg, cinnamon, almonds,
figs, prunes, dates, raisins, zest, salt, whole-
wheat flour, and 2 cups of the unbleached
flour. Using the paddle, beat on medium-low
speed for 2 minutes. Gradually add the
remaining flour ¼ cup at a time until the
dough begins to pull away from the side of
the bowl. Change to the dough hook. Continue to add flour 1 tablespoon at a time until
the dough just begins to clean the bowl.
Knead 4 to 5 minutes on medium-low.

By food processor In a large measuring cup or bowl, sprinkle the yeast in the water to soften. Heat the milk to 100°F and add it to the yeast along with the eggs and butter. In the bowl of the food processor fitted with the dough blade, combine the nutmeg, cinnamon, almonds, zest, whole-wheat flour, and 3 cups unbleached flour with 3 or 4 pulses. With the food processor running, add the liquid ingredients as fast as the dry ingredients will accept them. If you hear a sputtering sound, pour the liquid slower. As soon as all liquid is added, turn the processor off. Check the liquid-to-flour ratio (see page 28). Pulse until the dough forms a ball, then process exactly 60 seconds. Remove the dough from the bowl and knead in the figs, prunes, dates, and raisins.

By bread machine Put the water, milk, eggs, butter, nutmeg, cinnamon, almonds, zest, and salt in the bread pan. Add the whole-wheat flour and 3 cups unbleached flour and sprinkle with the yeast. Select the Dough cycle and press Start. While the dough is mixing, check the liquid-to-flour ratio (see page 29). If your machine has an Add Fruit cycle, add the figs, prunes, dates, and raisins at that time; otherwise add the fruit after you check the liquid-to-flour ratio. The machine stops after the kneading cycle. You may let the dough rise in the bread machine or a bowl.

First rise Put the dough in an oiled bowl and turn to coat the entire ball of dough with oil. Cover with a tightly woven towel and let rise until doubled, about one hour.

Shape Turn the dough out onto a lightly oiled work surface and divide it into 6 equal pieces. Shape each piece into an 18-inch-long rope. Braid 3 of the ropes and tuck the ends under. Place on one side of a parchment-lined or well-greased baking sheet. Repeat with the remaining 3 ropes and place on the other side of the baking sheet.

Second rise Cover with a tightly woven towel and let rise for 45 minutes.

Preheat oven About 10 minutes before baking, preheat the oven to 375°F.

Bake and cool Bake for 25 minutes until the internal temperature of the bread reaches 190°F. Immediately remove the bread from the baking sheet and place on a rack to cool for about 20 minutes.

Finish Rub the crust with soft butter if using.

Vanocka • Hoska

Czech Christmas customs are full of unusual superstitions. Unlike in many other countries, the children, not the parents, decorate the tree, as the mother has too much to do, preparing the large Christmas Eve feast and baking the Vanocka or Hoska for dessert. These two breads are gorgeous, edible works of art.

During the afternoon, the father ties shocks of grain together, dips the shocks in holy water, and sprinkles the water throughout the house, especially in the oven, to protect the home from trouble and fire.

The Christmas table is covered with a pure white cloth, and the legs of the table are wrapped with evergreen garlands. This is done to prevent thieves from stealing the crops in the fields. A bowl of grain, with a smaller bowl of garlic sitting in it, is placed under the table to strengthen and protect the family. These bowls must not be kicked or turned over or it will bring bad luck.

As soon as the first star appears on Christmas Eve the festivities begin. As the family gathers around the table, the father recites the family prayer. A loaf of bread and pot of honey are placed on the table. The bread is sliced, and each slice is spread with honey. A slice is passed to everyone at the table, starting with the oldest and ending with the youngest. Then the meal is served. Even poor families fill the table with food, for it is believed that the more food on the table, the more grain there will be in the fields.

After dinner, traditional Christmas desserts are served—usually strudels and always Vanocka or Hoska. When leaving the table, everyone tries to stand up at the same time, for it is believed that the first to stand will die within a year. The head of the house takes all the leftovers from dinner to the farmyard. The chickens are given peas and poppy seeds to ensure they lay plenty of eggs. The rooster, ganders, and dogs are given lots of garlic to assure they will have keen senses throughout the next year. The livestock are given a slice of the Vanocka so they remain healthy and safe from evil spirits.

Vanocka

Many customs are followed in preparing the dough for Vanocka. The mother must always wear a white apron and kerchief. To produce the perfect Vanocka, she cannot talk while preparing the dough and should jump up and down periodically while the dough rises.

Makes one 6-stranded braid

For the Sponge

1 scant tablespoon or 1 (¼-ounce) package active dry yeast

¼ cup warm water (about 110°F)

¾ cup milk

1 cup unbleached all-purpose flour

For the Creamed Mixture

½ cup (1 stick) unsalted butter, softened

½ cup granulated sugar

2 large eggs, beaten

For the Dough

1 tablespoon finely grated lemon zest

1 teaspoon salt

¾ cup golden raisins

¾ cup coarsely chopped almonds

3 to 4 cups unbleached all-purpose flour

For the Topping

¼ cup (½ stick) unsalted butter, melted

Confectioners' sugar

Prepare sponge In a medium bowl, soften the yeast in the water. Heat the milk to 110°F and add it to the yeast along with the flour. Cover and let rise for 20 minutes.

Cream mixture Beat the butter and sugar together until light, fluffy, and very pale yellow, about 5 minutes. Add the eggs and beat for 2 minutes longer. Set aside.

By hand In a large bowl, combine the sponge, creamed mixture, zest, salt, raisins, almonds, and 2 cups of the flour. Beat vigorously for 2 minutes. Gradually add the remaining flour ¼ cup at a time until the dough begins to pull away from the side of the bowl. Turn the dough out onto a floured work surface. Knead, adding flour a little at a time, until the dough is smooth and elastic.

By mixer In a mixer bowl, combine the sponge, creamed mixture, zest, salt, raisins, almonds, and 2 cups of the flour. Using the mixer paddle, beat on medium-low speed for 2 minutes. Gradually add the remaining flour ¼ cup at a time until the dough begins to pull away from the side of the bowl. Change to the dough hook. Continue to add flour 1 tablespoon at a time until the dough just begins to clean the bowl. Knead 4 to 5 minutes on medium-low.

By food processor To the bowl of the food processor fitted with the dough blade, add 3 cups flour, the sponge, creamed mixture, zest, and salt. Pulse to combine thoroughly. Check the liquid-to-flour ratio (see page 28). Pulse until the dough forms a ball, then process exactly 60 seconds. Turn the dough out onto a work surface and knead in the raisins and almonds.

By bread machine Put the sponge and creamed mixture in the bread pan. Add the salt, zest, and 3 cups flour to the bread pan. If your machine has an Add Fruit cycle, add the raisins and almonds when prompted; if not, add them with the flour. Select the Dough cycle and press Start. While the dough is mixing, check the liquid-to-flour ratio (see page 29). The machine stops after the kneading cycle. You may let the dough rise in the bread machine or a bowl.

First rise Put the dough in an oiled bowl and turn to coat the entire ball of dough with oil. Cover with a tightly woven towel and let rise until doubled, about one hour.

Shape Turn the dough out onto a lightly oiled work surface and divide it into 6 equal pieces. Roll each piece into a 20-inch-long rope. This isn't as difficult as you might expect. There's a rhythm to it.

STEP 1: Lay the ropes vertically on the work surface about ¼ inch apart. Pinch the ends of the ropes together at the top.

Take the rope on the far right and lay it across the other ropes horizontally.

Take the far left rope and lay it horizontally over the remaining 4 ropes. Spread the 4 ropes apart, 2 to the left and 2 to the right to leave more room in the center. Do this each time you have 4 vertical ropes.

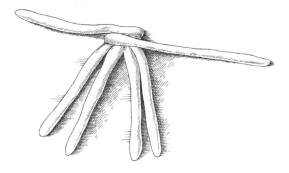

STEP 2: Take the left horizontal rope and lay it in the center between the separated vertical ropes.

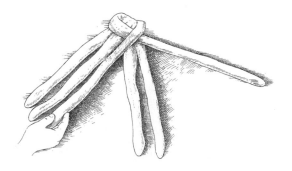

STEP 3: Take the right vertical rope and lay it horizontally over the 4 vertical ropes, then spread the 4 vertical ropes apart.

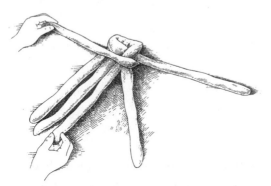

STEP 4: Take the top right horizontal rope and lay it between the separated vertical ropes.

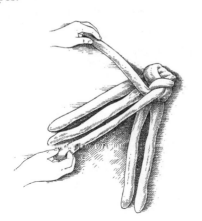

STEP 5: Take the left vertical rope and lay it horizontally over the 4 vertical ropes.

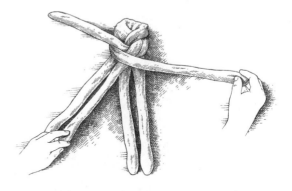

STEP 6: Take the top horizontal rope from the left and lay it between the separated vertical ropes.

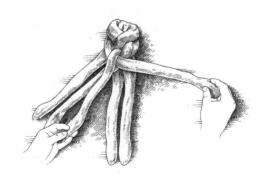

STEP 7: Take the right vertical rope and lay it horizontally over the 4 vertical ropes.

Repeat the braiding process from Step 3 to about 2 inches from the bottom. Bring all the ends to the center and pinch them together. Tuck the pinched ends under the braid. For a neater braid tuck the top ends under the braid. Place the braid on a parchment-lined or well-greased baking sheet.

Second rise Cover with a tightly woven towel and let rise for 45 minutes.

Preheat oven About 10 minutes before baking, preheat the over to 375°F.

Bake and cool Bake for 25 minutes until the internal temperature of the bread reaches 190°F. Immediately remove the bread from the baking sheet and place on a rack to cool.

Finish Brush melted butter over the braid and sprinkle liberally with confectioners' sugar.

NOTE: This bread freezes nicely for up to 6 months. To serve, first thaw the bread, then reheat on a baking sheet or directly on the oven rack in a 375°F oven for 7 to 10 minutes.

Hoska

THE CZECHOSLOVAKIANS consider bread making a true art, and every celebration loaf is formed into some marvelous shape. Hoska is stacked with three layers—a large braid on bottom, then a smaller braid, and then a small twist—to create a visually striking loaf. This loaf is very large, since it is often used as a centerpiece, but you can shape it into two smaller simple braids and bake them for 25 minutes.

MAKES 1 LARGE 3-TIERED LOAF

FOR THE DOUGH

1 scant tablespoon or 1 (¼-ounce) package active dry yeast

¼ cup warm water (about 110°F)

½ cup milk

3 large eggs, beaten

1 tablespoon vanilla extract

1 teaspoon salt

½ cup granulated sugar

4 to 5 cups unbleached all-purpose flour

½ cup (1 stick) unsalted butter, melted

1 cup golden raisins

½ cup finely chopped almonds

FOR THE TOPPING

1 large egg

1 tablespoon cold water

By hand In a large bowl, sprinkle the yeast in the water to soften. Heat the milk to 110°F and add it to the yeast along with the eggs, vanilla, salt, sugar, and 2 cups of the flour. Beat vigorously for 2 minutes. Add the butter, raisins, and almonds, then gradually add the remaining flour ¼ cup at a time until the dough begins to pull away from the side of the bowl. Turn the dough out onto a floured work surface. Knead, adding flour a little at a time, until the dough is smooth and elastic.

By mixer In the mixer bowl, sprinkle the yeast in the water to soften. Heat the milk to 110°F and add it to the yeast along with the eggs, vanilla, salt, sugar, and 2 cups of the flour. Using the mixer paddle, beat on medium-low speed for 2 minutes. Add the butter, raisins, and almonds, then gradually add the remaining flour ¼ cup at a time until the dough begins to pull away from the side of the bowl. Change to the dough hook. Continue to add flour 1 tablespoon at a time until the dough just begins to clean the bowl. Knead 4 to 5 minutes on medium-low.

By food processor In a large measuring cup or bowl, sprinkle the yeast in the water to soften. Heat the milk to 100°F and add it to the yeast along with the eggs, vanilla, and butter. In the bowl of the food processor fitted with the dough blade, combine the sugar, salt, and 4 cups flour with 4 or 5 pulses. With the food processor running, add the liquid ingredients as fast as the dry ingredients will accept them. If you hear a sputtering sound, pour the liquid slower. As soon as all the liquid is added, turn the processor off. Check the liquid-to-flour ratio (see page 28). Pulse until the dough forms a ball, then process exactly 60 seconds. Turn the dough out onto a work surface and knead in the raisins and almonds.

By bread machine Put the water, milk, eggs, vanilla, and butter in the bread pan. Add the sugar, salt, and 4 cups flour to the bread pan, then sprinkle with the yeast. If your machine has an Add Fruit cycle, add the raisins and almonds when prompted; if not, add them with the yeast. Select the Dough cycle and press Start. While the dough is mixing, check the liquid-to-flour ratio (see page 29). The machine stops after the kneading cycle. You may let the dough rise in the bread machine or a bowl.

First rise Put the dough in an oiled bowl and turn to coat the entire ball of dough with oil. Cover with a tightly woven towel and let rise until doubled, about one hour.

Shape Turn the dough out onto a lightly oiled work surface and remove one-fourth of the dough. Shape this into a ball and cover with a towel. Remove a tennis-ball-sized piece of dough (about ½ cup) from the large piece of dough and round it into a ball. Put it under the towel with the other piece of dough.

Divide the large piece of dough into thirds. Shape each third into a rope 20 inches long. Lay the ropes side by side on a parchment-lined or well-greased baking sheet. Turn the baking sheet so the ropes are facing lengthwise away from you. Starting in the center, place the right rope over the middle rope (note that the right rope has now become the middle one), then place the left rope over the middle, the right over the middle, left over the middle, and so on. Continue until the ropes are too short to braid. Pinch the ends together and tuck them under.

To braid the other end of the loaf, turn the baking sheet around so that the unbraided portion is facing you. Place the middle strand over the right strand, then the strand that is now in the middle over the left, middle over the right, middle over the left, etc., until the ends are too short to braid. Pinch the ends together, and tuck them under. With the side of your hand crease the first braid down the center lengthwise to create a trough (this will help keep the top braid in place).

Take the larger piece of reserved dough and divide it into thirds. Shape each third into a rope 22 inches long. Braid as directed but do not tuck the ends under. With the side of your little finger, crease the smaller braid down the center lengthwise to create a trough. Carefully lift the smaller braid and place it down the center of the larger braid. Tuck the ends of the top braid under the larger braid on both ends.

Take the remaining piece of dough and divide it in half. Shape each half into a rope 24 inches long. Starting in the center loosely twist the 2 ropes together, then twist the other end. Place the twist on top of the second braid and secure the ends under the largest braid.

Second rise Cover with a tightly woven towel and let rise for 45 minutes.

Preheat oven About 10 minutes before baking, preheat the oven to 375°F.

Final preparation Whisk the egg with the cold water until frothy. Lightly brush all exposed surfaces of the triple braid with the egg mixture.

Bake and cool Bake for 35 minutes until the internal temperature of the bread reaches 190°F. Immediately remove the bread from the baking sheet and place on a rack to cool.

NOTE: This bread freezes nicely for up to 6 months. To serve, first thaw the bread, then reheat on a baking sheet or directly on the oven rack in a 375°F oven for 7 to 10 minutes.

Hamantashen or Hamantash

Few holidays are happier than the Jewish festival of Purim, the Festival of Lots. Celebrated on the fourteenth day of Adar, which falls in late February or early March, this festival celebrates the deliverance of the Jews in ancient Persia from extermination by Haman, the chief advisor to the king of Persia.

Esther, the queen of Persia, was Jewish and had been raised by her relative Mordechai after her parents died. She had never told the king that she was Jewish. Haman hated Jews and influenced the king to seize the property of the Jews and slaughter them all. The day of the slaughter was determined by casting lots, hence the name Purim from *pur,* or "lot."

Mordecai petitioned Esther to intervene for her people and she agreed to appear before the king. She requested that the Jewish people hold a three-day fast to give her courage. After the fast, Esther entered the king's inner court dressed in her most royal garb. She told the king of Haman's plot and asked that the Jews be spared. The king was furious and ordered Haman to be hanged, ironically on the gallows that his advisor had built to kill Mordecai.

Prior to Purim, there is a day of fasting in memory of the Jews' three-day fast. During the celebration a service is held in which parts of the Book of Esther are read. Each time Haman's name is mentioned in the story, the congregation sets up a good-humored din, often spinning *graggers*—noisemakers. Among the traditional treats served during Purim are Hamantashen, plural for Hamantash, or Haman's pockets.

In America Hamantashen are more like pastries or cookies, but in Eastern Europe (Hungary) they are made with bread dough. This dough isn't recommended for a bread machine, since the other methods of preparation keep small pieces of butter from completely melting and becoming part of the dough.

MAKES 36 INDIVIDUAL OR 2 LARGE

FOR THE BUTTER MIXTURE

¾ cup (1½ sticks) unsalted butter, very cold

2 cups unbleached all-purpose flour

FOR THE SPONGE

1 scant tablespoon or 1 (¼-ounce) package active dry yeast

¼ cup warm water (about 110°F)

¾ cup warm milk (about 110°F)

1 cup unbleached all-purpose flour

FOR THE DOUGH

1 to 2 cups unbleached all-purpose flour

2 large eggs, lightly beaten

1 large egg yolk

½ cup granulated sugar

1 teaspoon salt

FOR THE FILLINGS

Raisin Nut Filling or Poppy Seed Filling or Apricot Filling (recipes follow)

FOR THE TOPPING

1 large egg white

1 tablespoon cold water

Prepare butter mixture Using a pastry blender, 2 knives, or a food processor, cut the butter into the flour until the small pieces of butter are about the size of small peas. Cover with plastic wrap and refrigerate for 30 minutes.

Prepare the sponge In a large bowl, sprinkle the yeast in the water to soften. Add the milk and flour to the yeast and stir to combine. Cover with plastic wrap and let sit for 30 minutes.

By hand Combine the sponge, 1 cup flour, the eggs, egg yolk, sugar, and salt. Beat vigorously for 2 minutes. Add the butter mixture ¼ cup at a time until the dough begins to pull away from the side of the bowl. Turn the dough out onto a floured work surface. Knead, adding the remaining butter mixture, and additional flour only if necessary, until the dough just becomes smooth, about 3 minutes. The dough should be very soft. Excessive kneading will melt the butter.

By mixer In the mixer bowl, combine the sponge, 1 cup flour, the eggs, egg yolk, sugar, and salt. Using the mixer paddle, beat on medium-low speed for 2 minutes. Change to the dough hook and add the butter mixture. Knead on medium-low speed for 2 minutes. Add flour only if necessary. The dough should be very soft. Excessive kneading will melt the butter.

By food processor In the bowl of the food processor fitted with the dough blade, combine the butter mixture, 1 cup flour, the eggs, egg yolk, sugar, and salt with 4 or 5 pulses. With the food processor running, add the sponge as fast as the dry ingredients will accept them. If you hear a sputtering sound, pour the sponge slower. As soon as all the sponge is added, turn the processor off. Check the liquid-to-flour ratio (see page 28). Pulse until the dough forms a ball, then process for 30 seconds only.

First rise Put the dough in an oiled bowl and turn to coat the entire ball of dough with oil. Cover with a tightly woven towel and let rise until doubled, about one hour.

Make filling Prepare the filling while the dough is rising.

Shape *For individual Hamantashen,* turn the dough out onto a lightly oiled work surface and divide into 36 equal pieces. Roll each piece into a ball. Cover with a towel and let

rest for 5 minutes. Roll each ball into a 4-inch circle. Place 2 teaspoons filling in the center of each circle. Picturing the circle as a clock, take the edge at 2 and fold it to the center. Take the edge at 10 and fold it to the center. Then take the edge at 6 and bring it to the center, leaving just a little of the filling peeking through at the center. Pinch the joined edges firmly and place on parchment-lined or well-greased baking sheets.

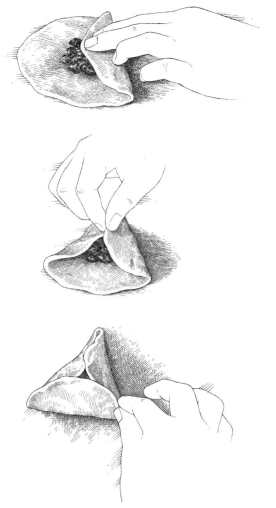

For two large Hamantashen, divide the dough in half. Roll each piece of dough into an 18-inch circle. Spread half the filling over one of the circles, leaving a 2-inch border all around. Shape as directed for Hamantashen and place on a parchment-lined or well-greased baking sheet. Repeat with the second circle.

Second rise Cover with a tightly woven towel and let rise for 45 minutes.

Preheat oven About 10 minutes before baking, preheat the oven to 375°F.

Final preparation Beat the egg white with the cold water until frothy. Brush lightly over each piece of risen dough.

Bake and cool Bake the Hamantashen for 20 minutes or the Hamantash for 30 minutes until golden. Due to the filling, the thermometer test will not work. Immediately remove from the baking sheets and place on a rack to cool.

NOTE: This bread freezes nicely for up to 6 months. To serve, first thaw the bread, then reheat on a baking sheet in a 375°F oven for 7 to 10 minutes.

Raisin Nut Filling

The more finely you chop the raisins and nuts, the better. They should be almost ground. I prefer to use a food processor to achieve the proper consistency.

1 cup very finely chopped walnuts or pecans

½ cup very finely chopped raisins

2 tablespoons honey

1 teaspoon finely grated lemon zest

½ teaspoon ground cinnamon

In a medium bowl, combine the nuts, raisins, honey, zest, and cinnamon.

Poppy Seed Filling

1 teaspoon finely grated lemon zest

½ cup milk

¼ cup granulated sugar

1 tablespoon honey

1 cup poppy seeds

In a medium saucepan over medium heat, combine the lemon zest, milk, sugar, honey, and poppy seeds. When the mixture just begins to bubble slightly, reduce the heat and cook for 10 minutes. Remove from the heat and cool.

Apricot Filling

1½ cups finely chopped dried apricots

¾ cup orange juice

½ cup light brown sugar, packed

1 teaspoon ground cinnamon

½ cup finely chopped walnuts or pecans

In a medium saucepan over medium heat, combine the apricots, orange juice, brown sugar, and cinnamon. When the mixture just begins to bubble slightly, reduce the heat and cook for 10 minutes. Remove from the heat, add the nuts, and cool.

Scalded Bread

In Lithuania, bread is shown great respect. It is always referred to in the feminine gender and is considered holy. Should a piece of bread fall to the floor, it is picked up with great reverence, kissed, and eaten to assure that the home will never be without bread.

Lithuanians believe bread protects them from fire and also helps in extinguishing fires. To defend a new home from evil and trouble, a piece of bread is placed in the foundation as the home is being built. No one would lend anything on bread-baking day for fear the borrower would take away the good taste of the bread. Homemakers are proud of their baking skills and constantly brag that their bread is the best.

Rye bread is eaten at almost every meal and plays an important role in family and holiday rituals. Until a young woman can produce a perfect loaf of bread, she is considered unworthy of marriage. A mother teaches her daughters how to make bread with great ceremony. When a daughter bakes her first loaf, the mother gathers the entire family and their nearest neighbor to taste the bread. The first slice goes to the father, who is master of the house. If the bread is perfect, he kisses his daughter and turns her and her chair toward the door as a sign that the daughter is now ready for marriage.

There are two traditional kinds of rye bread: plain fermented bread and scalded bread. Fermented bread has been around since the earliest times, but scalded bread has been part of the culture only since the start of the twentieth century. Scalded bread is tastier and prepared by a unique technique, so I am including only its recipe here.

THIS RECIPE seems more complicated than it really is, since it takes two to three days to prepare it. There is a lot of rising time but very little work involved. The bread doesn't do well in the food processor or bread machine. This very heavy, dense bread is made with dough saved from a previous batch, which contains leavening. If you don't have dough from a previous batch, make the starter at the end of the recipe. For the traditional loaf, you should use the maple leaves, but you can make an outstanding bread without them. Note that there is no rise in the bowl after the dough is mixed.

MAKES 2 LOAVES

FOR THE FERMENTATION

2½ cups boiling water

2 cups rye flour

2 tablespoons caraway seeds

1 cup dough from previous baking or starter (directions follow)

FOR THE DOUGH

2 teaspoons salt

5½ cups rye flour

FOR THE PAN

Butter or vegetable shortening

Green maple leaves or fresh cabbage leaves

Fermentation Combine the boiling water with the flour and caraway seeds and mix well. Cover and let cool to room temperature. Add the dough or starter and mix well. Cover and let stand in a warm spot for 24 hours.

By hand Add the salt to the fermented mixture and mix well. Gradually add the flour ¼ cup at a time until the dough begins to pull away from the side of the bowl. Turn the dough out onto a floured work surface. This dough is very much like paste and doesn't respond well to regular kneading. Sprinkle the work surface with flour and roll into a log. Fold the ends to the center and roll into a log again. Keep adding flour, rolling, and folding until the dough holds its shape and doesn't sag. Add as little flour as possible. No matter how sticky the dough is, you have plenty of flour if the dough doesn't sag.

By mixer In the mixer bowl, add the salt and 2 cups of the flour to the fermented mixture. Using the mixer paddle, beat on medium-low speed for 2 minutes. Gradually add the remaining flour ¼ cup at a time until all the flour has been added. Remove a fistful of dough and roll it into a ball on a work surface. Add more flour only if the ball sags. No matter how sticky the dough is, you have plenty of flour if the dough doesn't sag.

Prepare pans Grease two 8½ by 4½-inch loaf pans with butter or shortening, then line the sides and bottoms of the pans with maple or cabbage leaves.

Shape Divide the dough in half and shape into loaves. Lightly flour the loaves and put them in the pans. Cover with plastic wrap and tightly woven towel.

Rise Let rise for 2 hours. The dough should come to the top of the pan.

Preheat oven About 10 minutes before baking, preheat the oven to 400°F.

Bake and cool Bake for one hour until the internal temperature of the bread reaches 190°F. Immediately remove the bread from the pans and douse with running water (this should be done quickly, so it won't matter whether the water is hot or cold). Wrap the loaves in a tightly woven towel and place on a rack to cool.

For the starter Combine ¾ cup rye flour, 1 scant tablespoon or 1 (¼-ounce) package active dry yeast, and ½ cup warm sour milk, buttermilk, or water. Cover and let sit for 8 to 12 hours at room temperature. The starter will rise, then fall.

NOTE: This bread freezes nicely for up to 6 months. Serve at room temperature.

Babka

The origin of Babka is disputed. Some food historians believe it arose from the union of early pagan spring rites and the Church's Easter celebrations. Some say it arrived in the sixteenth century with Queen Bona from Italy; others say it is a Ukrainian or western Russian bread. Wherever it came from, Babka made its way to Poland, where it became part of the celebration of Easter.

The celebration of Easter in Poland has changed little through the centuries. It begins at dawn on Palm Sunday. Young girls carry a small decorated spruce tree from house to house in their neighborhood. They knock on their neighbors' windows and sing songs in praise of their little tree. People praise the tree and give the girls gifts of eggs. These eggs, called *pisanky,* are painted in beautiful, intricate patterns through a process similar to batik.

On Saturday the dining table is covered with a pure white cloth to signify the cloth in which Jesus was wrapped when he was interred in the sepulcher. On it is placed a lamb carved from butter or sugar and holding a cross, plus a small bowl of grated horseradish to signify the bitterness and disappointment in life. (The practice of serving horseradish may have been borrowed in the fourteenth century from Polish Jews.) In the afternoon the mother of the household and a child, usually the oldest son, take a basket of food filled with eggs, ham, sausages, pastries, and Babka to the church to be blessed by the priest.

Babka is the diminutive form of *baba,* a colloquialism for "grandmother" or "old woman." Because Babka is traditionally made in fluted molds, people claimed it resembled a woman's full skirt. Some recipes for this rich bread call for 24 egg yolks and ¾ pound butter to 6 cups flour, baked in molds 16 inches tall. Babka is an extremely delicate bread, and much care is given to its preparation. Many bakers believe the dough should be placed on an eiderdown to rise. Men—or anyone who tends to walk heavily—are banned from the kitchen, and no one can speak above a whisper while the dough rises.

OLD POLISH WOMEN think that the dough for Babka should be beaten thoroughly to impart as much air as possible before the butter is added. This is difficult to accomplish in the food processor or bread machine, so I've followed the standard procedure for mixing the bread. The Babka won't be as authentic, but it will certainly be good. True Babka is baked in a tall, fluted mold made of copper. Since I've been unable to find the proper mold, I use a decorative Bundt pan instead. As a substitute, you can also use tall juice cans, the ones that hold about 64 ounces.

MAKES 1 LARGE LOAF

FOR THE DOUGH

1 scant tablespoon or 1 (¼-ounce) package active dry yeast

¼ cup warm water (about 110°F)

½ cup milk

4 large egg yolks, beaten

1 teaspoon salt

1 tablespoon finely grated orange zest

½ cup granulated sugar

3 to 4 cups unbleached all-purpose flour

½ cup (1 stick) unsalted butter, softened

½ cup slivered almonds

1 cup golden raisins

FOR THE PAN

Softened butter or vegetable shortening

¼ cup unflavored bread crumbs

By hand In a large bowl, sprinkle the yeast into the water to soften. Heat the milk to 110°F and add it to the yeast along with the yolks, salt, zest, sugar, and 2 cups of the flour. Beat vigorously for 5 minutes. Add the butter and beat until well incorporated. Gradually add the remaining flour ¼ cup at a time until the dough begins to pull away from the side of the bowl. Add the almonds and raisins and stir to combine. Turn the dough out onto a floured work surface. Knead, adding flour a little at a time, until the dough is smooth and elastic.

By mixer In the mixer bowl, sprinkle the yeast into the water to soften. Heat the milk to 110°F and add it to the yeast along with the yolks, salt, zest, sugar, and 2 cups of the flour. Using the mixer paddle, beat on medium-low speed for 5 minutes. Add the butter and beat until well incorporated. Gradually add the remaining flour ¼ cup at a time until the dough begins to pull away from the side of the bowl. Change to the dough hook and add the almonds and raisins. Continue to add flour 1 tablespoon at a time until the dough just begins to clean the bowl. Knead 4 to 5 minutes on medium-low.

By food processor In a large measuring cup or bowl, sprinkle the yeast in the water to soften. Heat the milk to 100°F and add it to the yeast with the yolks. In the bowl of the food processor fitted with the dough blade, combine the butter, salt, zest, sugar, and 3 cups flour with 4 or 5 pulses. With the food processor running, add the liquid ingredients as fast as the dry ingredients will accept them. If you hear a sputtering sound, pour the liquid slower. As soon as all the liquid is added, turn the processor off. Check the liquid-to-flour ratio (see page 28). Pulse until the dough forms a ball, then process exactly 60 seconds. Remove from the work bowl and knead in the almonds and raisins.

By bread machine Put the water, milk, yolks, and butter into the bread pan. Add the salt, zest, sugar, and 3 cups flour to the bread pan, then sprinkle with the yeast. If your machine has an Add Fruit cycle, add the almonds and raisins when prompted; if not, add them with the yeast. Select the Dough cycle and press Start. While the dough is mixing, check the liquid-to-flour ratio (see page 29). The machine stops after the kneading cycle. You may let the dough rise in the bread machine or a bowl.

First rise Put the dough in an oiled bowl and turn to coat the entire ball of dough with oil. Cover with a tightly woven towel and let rise until doubled, about 2 hours.

Shape Heavily grease a 10-inch Bundt or tube pan with butter or vegetable shortening and sprinkle evenly with bread crumbs. Set aside. Turn the dough out onto a lightly oiled work surface and shape into a ball. Put your fingers through the center of the ball to make a doughnut shape. Slip the hole over the center of the Bundt pan and press the dough evenly in the pan.

Second rise Cover with a tightly woven towel and let rise for 45 minutes.

Preheat oven About 10 minutes before baking, preheat the oven to 375°F.

Bake and cool Bake for 35 minutes until the internal temperature of the bread reaches 190°F. Immediately invert the bread on a rack to cool.

NOTE: This bread freezes nicely for up to 6 months. To serve, wrap the thawed bread in foil and bake in a 375°F oven for 15 minutes.

Paczki

Many religions around the world celebrate a fasting period prior to significant religious holidays. Roman Catholics of Poland observe Paczki Days, when everyone consumes Paczki, jelly-filled fried buns, before the Lenten fast begins. It is the last day of gaiety during Karnawal, or Carnival, the period between Christmas and Lent. Paczki Day marks the last moments of excess before the austerity of Lent and takes place on Fat Thursday, the Thursday before Ash Wednesday (in the United States, Fat Tuesday replaces Fat Thursday).

THIS RECIPE does not produce light Paczki when made in the food processor or bread machine. Paczki is usually made with a strong potato-based spirit or alcohol, which is difficult to find in America. Rum is a good substitute. The Poles fry their Paczki in a combination of lard and vegetable shortening. Traditionally, Paczki are filled with prune butter, jam, or preserves; contemporary Paczki are filled with custard or curd. Because these are better fresh, the recipe can be divided in half if you are making them for just a few people.

MAKES ABOUT 36

For the Sponge

1 scant tablespoon or 1 (¼-ounce) package active dry yeast

2 tablespoons warm water (about 110°F)

10 large egg yolks

½ cup granulated sugar

1 cup warm heavy cream (about 110°F)

1 cup unbleached all-purpose flour

For the Dough

1 teaspoon salt

¼ cup rum or Polish potato spirits

3 to 3½ cups unbleached all-purpose flour

½ cup (1 stick) unsalted butter, melted

Fat for frying

Prune Filling (recipe follows), jam, preserves, or lemon curd

Confectioners' or granulated sugar for topping

Prepare sponge In a cup, sprinkle the yeast in the water to soften. Beat the yolks with the sugar until very light in color, about 5 minutes (this is best done in a mixer). Slowly add the cream to the yolk mixture and continue to beat for 2 minutes more. Add the yeast and flour and beat until well combined. Cover with plastic wrap and let rise 30 minutes.

By hand In a large bowl, combine the sponge, salt, rum, and 1 cup of the flour. Beat vigorously for 2 minutes. Add the butter, then gradually add the remaining flour ¼ cup at a time until the dough begins to pull away from the side of the bowl. Turn the dough out onto a floured work surface. Knead, adding flour a little at a time, until the dough is smooth and elastic.

By mixer In the mixer bowl, combine the sponge, salt, rum, and 1 cup of the flour. Using the mixer paddle, beat on medium-low speed for 2 minutes. Add the butter, then gradually add the remaining flour ¼ cup at a time until the dough begins to pull away from the side of the bowl. Change to the dough hook. Continue to add flour 1 tablespoon at a time until the dough just begins to clean the bowl. Knead 4 to 5 minutes on medium-low.

First rise Put the dough in an oiled bowl and turn to coat the entire ball of dough with oil. Cover with a tightly woven towel and let rise until doubled, about one hour.

Shape Turn the dough out onto a lightly oiled work surface and pat to a thickness of ½ inch. Let the dough rest 5 minutes, then cut into 2- or 3-inch rounds.

Second rise Cover with a tightly woven towel and let the rounds rise on the work surface for 40 minutes.

Preheat fat About 20 minutes before frying, begin heating fat in a 3- to 4-inch-deep pan to 350°F.

Fry Drop the Paczki into the hot oil, a few at a time, and fry until golden; turn, and cook until golden on the other side. Remove from the fat and place on paper towels to drain.

Filling Place the filling or jam in a pastry bag fitted with a tip large enough for the filling to go through. Make a ½ -inch slit in the side of each warm Paczki and squeeze in about 1 teaspoon of the filling with the pastry bag. If you don't have a pastry bag, make a 1-inch slit in the side of each Paczki and fill them with a teaspoon. Roll the Paczki in sugar and place on racks to cool. These are best eaten warm.

NOTE: Paczki do not freeze well.

Prune Filling

8 ounces (2 cups) pitted prunes, finely chopped

1 cup orange juice

¼ cup brown sugar, packed

2 teaspoons finely grated orange zest

Combine the prunes, juice, sugar, and zest in a medium saucepan. Bring the mixture to a boil, stirring often. Reduce the heat and simmer for 10 minutes. Remove from the heat and cool.

Kolache

The part of the world composed of Austria, Hungary, Bohemia, Moravia, Silesia, the Czech Republic, Slovakia, and Slovenia has changed names so many times over the years that it is almost impossible to track the true history of the breads from these areas. Like Potica, Kolache—also known as Kolac, Kolace, Kolachy, or Kolachi—is claimed by all these countries, each with a slight variation. The Bohemian style is flat circles, about 4 inches across, with the filling exposed. The Moravian style is to fold filling inside the dough, making small "pillows." Sometimes the dough is cut into squares, spread with a rich nut filling, and rolled up into a small cylinder.

In northeastern Moravia, Kolache is like a pizza spread with filling. Sometimes different fillings are placed in sections for an interesting look or to please several different taste preferences. In Slovakia, *kolache* has become a generic word for baked goods.

Kolache are festive breads that are baked for almost every special occasion. They are a must for Christmas, Easter, New Year's, christenings, confirmations, weddings, and funerals. In Ratiskovice (in the Czech Republic, southern Moravia), the older women of the village still gather each Thursday to make Kolache for village weddings and to socialize. It is customary for the bride to "help" with the baking of Kolache for her wedding.

In my research I met a delightful woman, Helene Baine Cincebeaux, who is the editor of *Morava Krasna,* a Moravian heritage newsletter, and *Slovakia,* a Slovak heritage newsletter. Both she and her mother, Helen Zemek Baine, shared some of the history and customs of Kolache. They have visited more than 2,000 villages in the former Czechoslovakia and sat around kitchen tables to share stories and sample foods with the villagers.

KOLACHE ARE NOT KNEADED, so there are no directions for using any machines, though a mixer is a big help. They can be shaped into flatbreads, or the dough can be wrapped around the filling to form a small pillow. Jam can be substituted for the filling. Traditional Kolache measure about 4 inches across. Since most folks don't have 4-inch cutters, I have changed the recipe to make smaller buns.

MAKES 36 TO 40 BUNS

FOR THE SPONGE

1 scant tablespoon or 1 (¼-ounce) package active dry yeast

¼ cup warm water (about 110°F)

½ cup (1 stick) unsalted butter, softened

3 large egg yolks

1½ cup warm sour cream (about 110°F)

1 cup unbleached all-purpose flour

3 large egg whites, stiffly beaten

FOR THE DOUGH

½ cup granulated sugar

1 teaspoon salt

3 to 4 cups unbleached all-purpose flour

TO BRUSH ON DOUGH

¼ cup (½ stick) unsalted butter, melted

Fillings (recipes follow)

Topping (recipe follows)

Prepare sponge Soften the yeast in the water and set aside. Beat the butter and yolks until very fluffy and light colored, about 5 minutes at medium speed in a mixer. Add the sour cream and yeast and stir to combine. Fold in the flour, then add the egg whites and fold just until the whites are incorporated.

First rise Cover with plastic wrap and let rise for one hour. The sponge will be light and airy.

Prepare dough Stir the sponge down and add the sugar, salt, and 1 cup of the flour. Gradually add just enough of the remaining flour, a little at a time, for a soft but not sticky dough.

Second rise Cover with a tightly woven towel or plastic wrap and let rise until doubled, about one hour.

Filling Prepare the filling of your choice while the dough is rising and let cool before using.

Shape Turn the dough out onto a lightly oiled work surface and roll the dough into a 15-inch square about ¼ inch thick. Cover with a towel and let the dough rest for 5 minutes. Using a 2½-inch cutter or glass, cut the dough into rounds and place on parchment-lined or well-greased baking sheets about 1 inch apart. Brush the top of each Kolache with melted butter. Dough scraps can be kneaded together and allowed to rest for 10 minutes before rerolling.

Second rise Cover with plastic wrap and let rise for 30 minutes.

Preheat oven About 10 minutes before baking, preheat the oven to 350°F.

Final preparation Press the center of each Kolache flat, leaving a ½-inch ridge around the outside. I press the centers with a ¼-cup measuring cup that measures 1½ inches

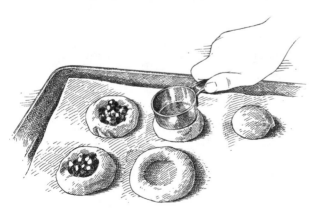

across the bottom. It fits perfectly. This can also be done with your fingers. Fill each indentation with a scant tablespoon of filling and spread it evenly. Sprinkle each Kolache with topping.

Bake and cool Bake for 20 minutes until lightly browned. Immediately remove from the baking sheet and place on a rack to cool.

NOTE: Kolache freeze nicely for up to 6 months. To serve, first thaw the buns, then reheat on a baking sheet in a 375°F oven for 5 to 7 minutes.

Poppy Seed Filling

1 cup poppy seeds

1 tablespoon unbleached all-purpose flour

½ cup heavy cream

½ cup honey

2 tablespoons unsalted butter

1 teaspoon vanilla extract

Combine the poppy seeds and flour in a saucepan. Add the cream and honey and mix well. Cook, stirring often, over medium heat until the mixture comes to a boil. Cook for one minute. Remove from the heat and stir in the butter and vanilla. Let cool completely before using.

Cheese Filling

2 tablespoons unsalted butter, softened

8 ounces cream cheese, softened

2 cups cottage cheese

4 large egg yolks, lightly beaten

¼ cup granulated sugar

½ cup golden raisins, finely chopped

Cream the butter and cream cheese until light and fluffy, about 5 minutes. Add the cottage cheese, yolks, sugar, and raisins and stir just until combined. Refrigerate for 30 minutes before using.

Prune Filling

1½ cups pitted prunes

½ cup brown sugar, packed

1 tablespoon finely grated lemon zest

1 tablespoon lemon juice

¾ cup water, apple juice, or orange juice

Combine all the ingredients in a saucepan. Bring the mixture to a boil. Reduce the heat to low and cook, stirring often, until the mixture is soft and thick, about 30 minutes. Remove from the heat and cool before using. Mash the mixture with a potato masher or fork.

Apricot Filling

1½ cups finely chopped dried apricots

½ cup granulated sugar

1 tablespoon finely grated orange zest

1 cup orange juice

1 tablespoon butter

Combine the apricots, sugar, zest, and juice in a saucepan over medium heat. Bring the mixture to a boil. Reduce the heat and cook until the mixture is soft and thick, about 30 minutes. Remove from the heat and stir in the butter. Cool before using.

Topping

½ cup granulated sugar

½ cup unbleached all-purpose flour

¼ cup (½ stick) unsalted butter, cold

In a bowl, combine the sugar and flour. With a pastry cutter or 2 knives, cut the butter into the sugar mixture until it looks like grains of rice.

Krofi

Slovenian folktales tell about the Kurent, a demon who chases winter away and ushers in spring. Kurentovanje began as an ancient pagan rite and is now tied to Carnival, the celebration before the forty days of Lent and a period of exaggerated eating. Among the favorite foods during Carnival are Krofi, jam-filled doughnuts. During the first days of Lent and Holy Week, food containing fat, meat, and milk is destroyed and the dishes are washed thoroughly. When Lent is over and Easter begins, all food restrictions come to an end.

During Kurentovanje, people dress in elaborate sheepskin costumes with leather masks that have big horns, large noses, and long tongues, plus cowbells hanging from their belts. During the eleven days prior to Lent, hundreds of these demons come from outlying villages to exorcise the winter spirits. Years ago only a few chosen young men were selected to be Kurenti, but today anyone can be one, as long as they can afford the handmade costume and the essential belt of huge brass cowbells imported from Austria. They must also be able to cavort for hours at a time in the hot costume that weighs around one hundred pounds.

During Kurentovanje, children dressed in costumes go from door to door, singing and showing off their festive attire. They are rewarded with Krofi and sometimes money.

When I was doing research for this book, I contacted the Slovenian Embassy for information. They put my request on a Slovenian website. Anja Hajdinjak responded with helpful information and this recipe. She also sent darling pictures of her grandson in his Kurent costume.

MAKES ABOUT 36

FOR THE SPONGE

(NOTE: The sponge uses no water.)

1 scant tablespoon or 1 (¼-ounce) package active dry yeast

⅓ cup warm milk (about 110°F)

2 teaspoons granulated sugar

½ cup unbleached all-purpose flour

FOR THE DOUGH

⅔ cup warm milk (about 110°F)

2 tablespoons canola oil

1 tablespoon dark rum

1 tablespoon finely grated lemon zest

1 teaspoon salt

⅓ cup granulated sugar

3½ to 4½ cups unbleached all-purpose flour

FOR THE FILLING

About ¾ cup apricot, strawberry, or other favorite jam

FOR FRYING

Half butter and half oil

FOR THE TOPPING

Confectioners' sugar (optional)

Prepare sponge In a large bowl, sprinkle the yeast in the milk to soften. Add the sugar and flour and stir to combine. Cover and let rise for 20 minutes.

By hand Combine the sponge, milk, oil, rum, zest, salt, sugar, and 2 cups of the flour. Beat vigorously for 2 minutes. Gradually add the remaining flour ¼ cup at a time until the dough begins to pull away from the side of the bowl. Turn the dough out onto a floured work surface. Knead, adding flour a little at a time, until the dough is smooth and elastic.

By mixer In the mixer bowl, combine the sponge, milk, oil, rum, zest, salt, sugar, and 2 cups of the flour. Using the mixer paddle, beat on medium-low speed for 2 minutes. Gradually add the remaining flour ¼ cup at a time until the dough begins to pull away from the side of the bowl. Change to the dough hook. Continue to add flour 1 tablespoon at a time until the dough just begins to clean the bowl. Knead 4 to 5 minutes on medium-low.

By food processor Combine the sponge, milk, oil, and rum. In the bowl of the food processor fitted with the dough blade, combine the zest, salt, sugar, and 3½ cups flour with 4 or 5 pulses. With the food processor running, add the liquid ingredients as fast as the dry ingredients will accept them. If you hear a sputtering sound, pour the liquid slower. As soon as all the liquid is added, turn the processor off. Check the liquid-to-flour ratio (see page 28). Pulse until the dough forms a ball, then process exactly 60 seconds.

By bread machine Put the sponge, milk, oil, and rum in the bread pan. Add the zest, salt, sugar, and 3½ cups flour, then sprinkle with the yeast. Select the Dough cycle and press Start. While the dough is mixing, check the liquid-to-flour ratio (see page 29). The machine stops after the kneading cycle. You may let the dough rise in the bread machine or a bowl.

First rise Put the dough in an oiled bowl and turn to coat the entire ball of dough with oil. Cover with a tightly woven towel and let rise until doubled, about one hour.

Shape Turn the dough out onto a lightly oiled work surface and pat ½ inch thick. Cover and let rest 5 minutes. Using a 2-inch cutter or glass, cut as many circles as possible. Place the circles on a floured towel and cover. Knead the dough scraps into a ball, cover, and let rest 10 minutes. Reroll and cut as directed.

Second rise Cover with a tightly woven towel and let rise for 30 minutes.

Preheat fat About 10 minutes before baking, preheat about 3 inches butter and oil in a Dutch oven to 375°F.

Fry and fill Place several circles in the pan, being careful not to crowd them. Fry until golden, then turn and fry the other side until golden. Remove with a slotted spoon and place on paper towels to drain. Make a 1-inch slit in the side of each bun and put about 1 teaspoon jam through the slit into the center. Dust with confectioners' sugar if desired.

NOTE: This bread does not freeze well and is best eaten fresh.

Korovai

F all and the period after Christmas are the major seasons for courtship and weddings in the Ukraine, with many parties and social events where the young people can meet and court. At one time the matrimonial ritual was always set in motion by the groom, who would select the girl he wished to marry and inform his parents of his intent.

The groom's parents invited two respected elders to act as *starosty,* or emissaries, who would visit the girl's parents to persuade them that this was a good match. As a token of good faith, they brought with them a loaf of bread and a bottle of Horilka, a caraway- and lemon-infused whiskey. If the girl's parents felt the suitor was her equal in social position and desirable to the girl herself, they expressed their "humble" surprise and joy at the proposal.

An exchange of breads sealed the contract, and the girl was allowed to join the meeting. She would give the *starosty* embroidered ritual cloths, which they tied diagonally across their chests as emblems of the agreement. Horilka flowed as toasts were proposed to honor the union.

Now the groom would invite the bride, her parents, the *starosty,* and the bridesmaids to a formal dinner hosted by his parents. The groom would present the bride with a beautiful scarf—a symbol of her womanhood—and she, in turn, would give him an embroidered linen shirt. The bride's parents reciprocated the groom's hospitality by increasing the girl's dowry. Afterward the couple ate their first Korovai, wedding bread, in which two hard-boiled eggs, representing fertility, were baked. Now the engagement was official, a date was set, and wedding preparations began. The length of the engagement was usually short, but the minimum time was one week, which was the amount of time needed for cooking and other preparations.

Today, courtship rituals may be more relaxed, but some wedding traditions remain. Three or four days before the wedding, Korovai is baked. At one time, the wedding bread had to be prepared by seven happily married young women, each of whom, according to custom, brought flour from wheat grown in seven fields. They also brought water from seven different locations, eggs from seven different hens, and butter from seven different sources in order to assure good fortune for the wedding couple. The good-luck loaf is braided and formed by the bride's friends, and decorated with rosettes and other flower shapes. The friends sculpt nesting doves and cupid's hearts.

The day before the wedding ceremony the civil marriage contract is signed. Later in the day the bride and her helpers braid wreaths and a ritual tree or branch to grace the table during the wedding. Also on that day, the *divych vechir* or maiden evening, where the bride bids farewell to her friends, used to be celebrated by the bride, her bridesmaids, and other female relatives. The women sang folk songs, told stories, played games, and joked about the wedding. Later in the evening, the groom and his attendants came and gave gifts to the bride's mother, her attendants, and all other guests. This custom has become a wedding shower where everyone brings gifts to the bride and groom.

Bread continues to play a major role in the wedding festivities. On the wedding day—always a Sunday—the bride and groom receive blessings at their own homes from their parents. Gifts of small breads such as pretzels, bagels, or rolls in the shape of pine cones may be given as favors to the guests. After the ceremonies, there is music and dancing, and then dinner is served. The great Korovai, wedding bread, covered with two crossed cloths with a pine bough laid over the top, is the centerpiece on the main table. The decorative dough sculptures on top of the bread are saved for the newlyweds. Then the Korovai is cut and offered to all the guests, who in turn contribute money for the newlyweds. The next morning there is a ceremonial breakfast for the bridal couple. In olden days this meal was accompanied by proof of the bride's virginity.

KOROVAI IS considered an indispensable ritual bread for weddings. It is customary to hold the piece of bread with a napkin out of respect, since it is considered holy.

Korovai is decorated with symbolic ornaments, which include birds, pine cones, moons, suns, and other shapes. Favorites are doves, symbolizing love and fidelity, and pine cones, symbolizing fertility. The Korovai has no set form or design, and each region and person creates their own. Some are large, round breads covered with acorns, others with birds. Some have hollow centers and some are intertwined with gilt and periwinkle.

MAKES 1 LARGE LOAF

FOR THE SPONGE

1 scant tablespoon or 1 (¼-ounce) package active dry yeast

¼ cup warm water (about 110°F)

¾ cup warm light cream (about 110°F)

2 tablespoons granulated sugar

1 cup unbleached all-purpose flour

FOR THE DOUGH

½ cup granulated sugar

¼ cup (½ stick) unsalted butter, softened

2 large eggs, beaten

1 teaspoon vanilla extract

1 tablespoon finely grated lemon zest

1 teaspoon salt

3 to 4 cups unbleached all-purpose flour

FOR THE GLAZE

1 large egg

1 tablespoon cold water

FOR THE DECORATIONS

Whole cloves for decorating doves

Two 18-inch-long very thin twigs

Floral tape

Fresh myrtle, periwinkle, or herbs

Prepare sponge In a large bowl, sprinkle the yeast in the water to soften. Add the cream, sugar, and flour to the yeast and mix well. Cover with plastic wrap and let rise for one hour.

By hand Add the sugar, butter, eggs, vanilla, zest, salt, and 1 cup of the flour to the sponge. Beat vigorously for 2 minutes. Gradually add the remaining flour ¼ cup at a time until the dough begins to pull away from the side of the bowl. Turn the dough out onto a floured work surface. Knead, adding flour a little at a time, until the dough is smooth and elastic.

By mixer In the mixer bowl, add the sugar, butter, eggs, vanilla, zest, salt, and 1 cup of the flour to the sponge. Using the mixer paddle, beat on medium-low speed for 2 minutes. Gradually add the remaining flour ¼ cup at a time until the dough begins to pull away from the side of the bowl. Change to the dough hook. Continue to add flour 1 tablespoon at a time until the dough just begins to clean the bowl. Knead 4 to 5 minutes on medium-low.

By food processor Combine the sponge, eggs, vanilla, and zest. In the bowl of the food processor fitted with the dough blade, combine the butter, sugar, salt, and 3 cups flour with 4 or 5 pulses. With the food processor running, add the liquid ingredients as fast as the dry ingredients will accept them. If you hear a sputtering sound, pour the liquid slower. As soon as all the liquid is added, turn the processor off. Check the liquid-to-flour ratio (see page 28). Pulse until the dough forms a ball, then process exactly 60 seconds.

By bread machine Put the sponge, butter, eggs, vanilla, and zest in the bread pan. Add the sugar, salt, and 3 cups flour. Select the Dough cycle and press Start. While the dough is mixing, check the liquid-to-flour ratio (see page 29). The machine stops after the kneading cycle. You may let the dough rise in the bread machine or a bowl.

First rise Put the dough in an oiled bowl and turn to coat the entire ball of dough with oil. Cover with a tightly woven towel and let rise until doubled, about 1½ hours.

Shape Turn the dough out onto a lightly oiled work surface. Remove about one-third of the dough and set it aside covered.

Remove a piece of dough about the size of a tangerine from the remaining dough and roll it into a 7-inch-long rope. Coil the rope and place it in the center of a 10- or 12-inch round baking pan or a large Dutch oven. (Don't worry if it tries to uncoil; when you put the braid from the next step into place, you can reshape it.) Divide the rest of the larger piece into thirds. Roll each piece into a 28-inch-long rope. Lay the ropes side by side on the work surface. Starting in the center of the ropes, place the right rope over the middle rope (note that the right rope has now become the middle rope), then place the left rope over the middle, the right over the middle, left over the middle, and so on. Continue this process until the ropes are too short to braid. Pinch the ends together.

To braid the other end, place the middle rope over the right rope, then the rope that is now in the middle over the left, middle over the right, middle over the left, and so on, until the ends are too short to braid. Pinch the ends together. Loosely coil the braid in the 10-inch pan around the piece of dough coiled in the center.

Take the remaining dough and remove one-third of it. Cover the larger piece and set it aside to use for decorations. Divide the smaller piece in half and roll each piece into a 28-inch-long rope. Starting in the middle, twist the 2 ropes together tightly all the way to the end. Repeat with the other end of the ropes. Lay the twist on top of the braid on the outside edge next to the side of the pan.

Second rise Cover with a tightly woven towel and let rise for 50 minutes.

Prepare the glaze Beat the egg with the cold water and brush lightly over the top of the loaf.

Shape decorations While the loaf is rising, shape the decorations. Korovai is covered with decorations of birds, pinecones, and rosettes. Use the remaining dough for these shapes. To decorate the loaf, form at least 5 birds, at least 3 pinecones, and 3 rosettes. Use the remaining dough to shape more birds, pinecones, or rosettes as you desire.

Decorations do not need rising time. They are shaped, glazed, and baked.

To form pinecones, squeeze off a piece of dough about the size of a small egg. Roll it into a flat strip about 8 inches long and 2 inches wide at one end and 1 inch wide at the other. With scissors or a knife, cut into the strip at ¼-inch intervals to about ½ inch from the straight edge. Holding the strip by the uncut edge, begin coiling the dough at the wider end (moving down about ¼ inch as you coil to form a spiral.) When you get to the end, tuck the dough under the bottom and smooth it slightly so it will sit straight. Spread the scales apart to resemble a pinecone and place on a parchment-lined or well-greased baking sheet. Brush each cone with glaze and bake for 10 minutes. Remove from the oven and brush once again with glaze. Return to the oven and bake for 5 minutes until golden brown.

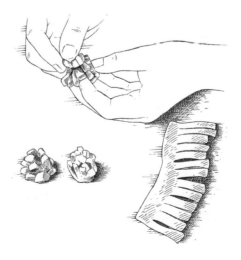

To form birds, squeeze off a piece of dough about the size of a small egg and divide it in half. Roll each half into a 4-inch rope. Lay 1 rope on a parchment-lined baking sheet at least 3 inches from the edge of the pan or another bird. Lay the other rope across the first rope about one-third of the way down. Take the ends from the bottom rope and cross them over the top rope. Flatten the ends of the crossed rope slightly. Also flatten the long end of the other rope. Using a knife or scissors, cut the ends of the wings and the tail to form feathers. Lift the head slightly and pinch the dough to form a beak. Use whole cloves for the eyes of the bird. Brush each bird with glaze and bake for 10 minutes. Remove from the oven and brush once again with glaze. Return to the oven and bake for 5 minutes until golden brown.

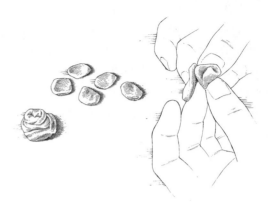

To form rosettes, pinch off pieces of dough between your thumb and forefinger so the pieces are about the size and thickness of a nickel. You will need 7 pieces to form a rosette. Hold one piece dough at the bottom so that the top is free. Overlap the first piece of dough with the second piece of dough and pinch it together at the bottom. Roll the top edge out slightly to give the petal form. Take the third piece of dough and overlap it to cover the edge where the second piece ended. Slightly roll the top edge. Continue overlapping the pieces of dough and slightly rolling the tops until all 7 pieces are used. Flatten the bottom of the rosette and place on a parchment-lined or well-greased baking sheet. Brush each rosette with glaze and bake for 8 minutes. Remove from the oven and brush once again with glaze. Return to the oven and bake for 5 minutes until golden brown.

Preheat oven About 10 minutes before baking, preheat the oven to 375°F.

Final preparation Brush glaze lightly over the loaf.

Bake and cool Bake the loaf for 25 minutes; remove from the oven, and brush the top of the loaf once again with glaze. Bake 25 minutes longer until the internal temperature of the bread reaches 190°F. Immediately remove the bread from the pan and place on a rack to cool.

Assemble Remove the bark from the twigs. Soak the twigs in warm water for 30 minutes to make them pliable. Join the thinner ends of the twigs with floral tape. Cover the joined twigs with myrtle, periwinkle, or fresh herbs, leaving about 1½ inches free at each end. To make the handle, insert each end of the twigs about 1½ inches into the loaf just inside the twist that forms the top edge of the loaf. Insert toothpicks into the bottom of each bird about ½ inch deep, then position 2 birds facing each other in the center of the loaf (lovebirds for the bride and groom). Using toothpicks, anchor the rosettes around the lovebirds, then place pinecones around the rosettes and add more birds.

NOTE: This bread does not freeze well.

Mandryky

The Feast of Saints Peter and Paul falls in July and marks the height of summer in the Ukraine. In the high mountain plains of western Ukraine, as the land is not suitable for farming, sheep and cattle are raised. On the Feast of Saints Peter and Paul, the villagers honor the head shepherds and assistants for keeping the communal flocks safe and healthy with gifts of clothing, tools, and food.

An important part of this celebration is the special baked rolls called Mandryky, from the word *mandruvaty,* meaning "to wander." According to legend, the apostles Peter and Paul were sustained by these rolls while traveling on their missions.

THESE SMALL ROUNDS of filled bread are perfect to serve as a light lunch with soup or salad, as picnic fare, or as finger food for a party.

MAKES 18 FILLED BREADS

FOR THE SPONGE

1 scant tablespoon or 1 (¼-ounce) package active dry yeast

¼ cup warm water (about 110°F)

1 tablespoon granulated sugar

1 cup unbleached all-purpose flour

⅔ cup warm milk (about 100°F)

FOR THE DOUGH

2 large eggs, beaten

1 teaspoon salt

3 to 4 cups unbleached all-purpose flour

Cheese or Cabbage Filling (recipes follow)

Prepare sponge In a large bowl, sprinkle the yeast in the water to soften. Stir the sugar, flour, and milk into the yeast. Cover and let rise for 30 minutes.

By hand Add the eggs, salt, and 2 cups of the flour to the sponge. Beat vigorously for 2 minutes. Gradually add the remaining flour ¼ cup at a time until the dough begins to pull away from the side of the bowl. Turn the dough out onto a floured work surface. Knead, adding flour a little at a time, until the dough is smooth and elastic.

By mixer In the mixer bowl, add the eggs, salt, and 2 cups of the flour to the sponge. Using the mixer paddle, beat on medium-low speed for 2 minutes. Gradually add the remaining flour ¼ cup at a time until the dough begins to pull away from the side of the bowl. Change to the dough hook. Continue to add flour 1 tablespoon at a time until the dough just begins to clean the bowl. Knead 4 to 5 minutes on medium-low.

By food processor In the bowl of the food processor fitted with the dough blade, combine the salt and 3 cups flour with 4 or 5 pulses. Combine the eggs and sponge, and add to the dry ingredients. Pulse until the mixture comes together into a ball. Check the liquid-to-flour ratio (see page 28). Pulse until the dough forms a ball, then process exactly 60 seconds.

By bread machine Put the sponge and eggs in the bread pan. Add the salt and 3 cups flour to the bread pan. Select the Dough cycle and press Start. While the dough is mixing, check the liquid-to-flour ratio (see page 29). The machine stops after the kneading cycle. You may let the dough rise in the bread machine or a bowl.

First rise Put the dough in an oiled bowl and turn to coat the entire ball of dough with oil. Cover with a tightly woven towel and let rise until doubled, about one hour.

Prepare filling While the dough is rising, make the filling.

Shape Turn the dough out onto a lightly oiled work surface and roll ¼ inch thick. Using a 3-inch cutter or the rim of a glass about the same size, cut the dough into rounds. Gather the dough scraps into a ball, cover with a towel, and let rest 10 minutes before rerolling and cutting as directed. With the edge of your finger and your thumb, pinch the edge of the rounds to create a decorative rim to hold the filling in place. Spread the filling of your choice over each round and place on parchment-lined or well-greased baking sheets.

Second rise Cover with a tightly woven towel and let rise for 45 minutes.

Preheat oven About 10 minutes before baking, preheat the oven to 375°F.

Bake and cool Bake for 20 minutes until the Mandryky are lightly browned. Immediately remove from the baking sheets and place on a rack to cool.

NOTE: This bread does not freeze well and is best eaten fresh. It can be made up to 2 days in advance and reheated on a baking sheet in a 375°F oven for 5 minutes.

Cheese Filling

½ cup finely chopped onion

2 tablespoons unsalted butter

2 cups cottage cheese or farmer's cheese

1 large egg, beaten

2 teaspoons snipped fresh dill

1 teaspoon salt

Put the onion and butter in a small saucepan and cook over medium heat until the onion is transparent. In a medium bowl, stir the onion, cheese, egg, dill, and salt together.

Cabbage Filling

2 cups finely shredded cabbage

¼ cup finely chopped onion

2 tablespoons unsalted butter

Pinch caraway seeds

Salt and pepper to taste

Put the cabbage, onion, butter, and caraway seeds in a saucepan and cook over medium heat until the cabbage is limp and slightly transparent. Season with salt and pepper.

Kalyra ✦ *Pampushky*

In the Ukraine, the Feast of Saint Catherine on December 7 and the Feast of Saint Andrew on December 13 are celebrated after all the crops are gathered and put up for the year. During these feasts many socials are planned to give young people a chance to get together, become better acquainted, and perhaps find a mate.

These parties take place in private homes. The young men bring firewood, mead, and fruit-flavored spirits to the party, while the young women bring the food. These social events are chaperoned, and everyone must be on their best behavior or they are asked to leave.

Saint Catherine is the patron saint of girls and women and is responsible for their fortune. Saint Andrew the Apostle blessed the hills around Kiev where the first Ukrainian kingdom was established in the ninth century. His feast day is shared with the ancient festival of the sun god. Kalyra—a flat round bread with four holes, glazed with honey and sprinkled with poppy seeds—symbolizes the sun.

Many games are linked to Kalyra. The most popular game is played by hanging Kalyra from a ceiling beam by a red ribbon. The young men "ride" around the room on sticks, pretending to be on horses. Then they jump up and bite the bread without using their hands. As the boys ride their steeds, the girls encourage them with much teasing and laughter. Whoever wins becomes Saint Andrew, and master of the games, for the rest of the night.

After an evening of games, a late meal is served. Since these parties take place during Advent, no meat dishes are served. A favorite bread for these late dinners is Pampushky, a small fried bread tossed with fresh garlic and salt.

Kalyra

THESE ATTRACTIVE LITTLE BREADS can also be used as decorations. Tie a bright red ribbon through one of the holes and hang it from a pine bough, or use a group of them on a buffet table between other dishes of food.

MAKES 8 FLATBREADS

FOR THE DOUGH

1 scant tablespoon or 1 (¼-ounce) package active dry yeast

¾ cup warm water (about 110°F)

2 tablespoons honey

2 tablespoons lard or vegetable shortening

1 teaspoon salt

2¼ to 3¼ cups unbleached all-purpose flour

FOR THE TOPPING

¼ cup warm honey

¼ teaspoon salt

Poppy seeds for sprinkling

By hand In a large bowl, sprinkle the yeast in the water to soften. Add the honey, lard, salt, and 1 cup of the flour to the yeast. Beat vigorously for 2 minutes. Gradually add the remaining flour ¼ cup at a time until the dough begins to pull away from the side of the bowl. Turn the dough out onto a floured work surface. Knead, adding flour a little at a time, until the dough is smooth and elastic.

By mixer In the mixer bowl, sprinkle the yeast in the water to soften. Add the honey, lard, salt, and 1 cup of the flour to the yeast. Using the mixer paddle, beat on medium-low speed for 2 minutes. Gradually add the remaining flour ¼ cup at a time until the dough begins to pull away from the side of the bowl. Change to the dough hook. Continue to add flour 1 tablespoon at a time until the dough just begins to clean the bowl. Knead 4 to 5 minutes on medium-low.

By food processor In a cup or small bowl, sprinkle the yeast in the water to soften. In the bowl of the food processor fitted with the dough blade, combine the honey, lard, salt, and 2¼ cups flour with 4 or 5 pulses. With the food processor running, add the yeast as fast as the dry ingredients will accept it. If you hear a sputtering sound, pour the yeast slower. As soon as all the yeast is added, turn the processor off. Check the liquid-to-flour ratio (see page 28). Pulse until the dough forms a ball, then process exactly 60 seconds.

By bread machine Put the water, honey, lard and salt in the bread pan. Add 2¼ cups flour to the bread pan, then sprinkle with the yeast. Select the Dough cycle and press Start. While the dough is mixing, check the liquid-to-flour ratio (see page 29). The machine stops after the kneading cycle. You may let the dough rise in the bread machine or a bowl.

First rise Put the dough in an oiled bowl and turn to coat the entire ball of dough with oil. Cover with a tightly woven towel and let rise until doubled, about one hour.

Shape Turn the dough out onto a lightly oiled work surface and divide into 8 equal pieces. Round each piece into a ball, cover with the towel, and let rest for 10 minutes.

Roll each ball into a 7-inch circle. With a ½-inch cutter, thimble, or small cap, cut 4 holes in each circle about ½ inch from the edge. Visualize the dough as the face of a clock and cut the holes at 12, 3, 6, and 9 o'clock. Place the rounds on parchment-lined or well-greased baking sheets.

Second rise Cover with tightly woven towels and let rise for 20 minutes.

Preheat oven About 10 minutes before baking, preheat the oven to 400°F.

Final preparation Combine the honey and salt and brush onto each round. Sprinkle liberally with poppy seeds.

Bake and cool Bake for 15 minutes until golden. Immediately remove the breads from the baking sheets and place on a rack to cool.

NOTE: This bread freezes nicely for up to 6 months. To serve, first thaw the bread, then reheat on a baking sheet or directly on the oven rack in a 400°F oven for 5 minutes.

Pampushky

FRIED GARLIC PUFFS

THIS IS A BATTER, not a kneaded dough, and does not mix well in a bread machine. Serve the puffs as an appetizer or with soups, stews, or salads. Commercial garlic salt can be substituted for fresh garlic salt, but it is not as good. In many Central European countries and Russia, cooks add baking powder or vinegar to the oil before heating it to help prevent the dough from absorbing oil. The vinegar will grumble and roar but will not hurt you. Use an open pan when frying to prevent condensation. One of my testers used her electric fryer with a lid, and condensation gathered on the lid of the fryer. When the drops fell into the hot oil, it spattered and popped.

MAKES ABOUT 36

FOR THE DOUGH

1 scant tablespoon or 1 (¼-ounce) package active dry yeast

1 cup warm water (about 110°F)

¼ cup canola oil

2 tablespoons granulated sugar

1 teaspoon salt

1 teaspoon baking powder

3 to 3½ cups unbleached all-purpose flour

FOR FRYING

Oil for frying

1 tablespoon white or wine vinegar, optional

FOR THE TOPPING

4 cloves garlic

2 tablespoons fine sea salt

By hand Heat the water and oil to 110°F and add it to the yeast along with the sugar, salt, baking powder, and 2 cups of the flour. Beat vigorously for 2 minutes. Gradually add the remaining flour ¼ cup at a time until the dough begins to pull away from the side of the bowl.

By mixer Heat the water and oil to 110°F and add it to the yeast along with the sugar, salt, baking powder, and 2 cups of the flour. Using the mixer paddle, beat on medium-low speed for 2 minutes. Gradually add the remaining flour ¼ cup at a time until the dough begins to pull away from the side of the bowl.

By food processor In a cup or small bowl, sprinkle the yeast in the water to soften. Heat the oil to 100°F and add it to the yeast. To the bowl of the food processor fitted with the dough blade, add the sugar, salt, baking powder, and 3 cups flour. Add the yeast mixture and pulse until thoroughly combined.

First rise Put the dough in an oiled bowl and turn to coat the entire ball of dough with oil. Cover with a tightly woven towel and let rise until doubled, about one hour.

Prepare topping Either crush the garlic with a garlic press or chop very fine. Combine with the salt. Spread on a plate and leave at room temperature to dry.

Shape Turn the dough out onto a lightly oiled work surface and divide into 36 equal pieces about the size of a walnut.

Second rise Cover with a tightly woven towel and let rest on the work surface for 15 minutes.

Preheat oil About 10 minutes before frying, add 2 inches oil to a Dutch oven. Add the vinegar if using to the cold oil and heat to 375°F.

Fry and cool Add the dough balls to the hot oil and fry on all sides. Do not crowd. Remove from the oil with a slotted spoon and drain on paper towels. Place the garlic mixture in a plastic bag, breaking it up if it has clumped together. Add the warm puffs to the bag and shake to coat. Serve warm.

NOTE: These puffs are at their best eaten immediately.

Paska

Ukrainians regard the Easter season as a new beginning. Villagers who have been inside during the winter months are eager to be outdoors and help with the thorough cleaning of the village. Any debris is removed and burned, each home is whitewashed or painted, and many houses are decorated with folk motifs.

In central Ukraine one of the old traditions was that on the first day of Lent, called *poloskozub,* people rinsed their teeth with whiskey to remove all traces of forbidden meats and dairy foods. About halfway through the Lenten season, women baked a heavy bread made completely from rye that was marked with a cross on top. This inedible loaf was taken to the fields as a good-luck totem when farmers sowed the first crops of poppy and wheat.

Good Friday is a day of mourning, when Christians remember the suffering of Jesus Christ and his death on the cross. It is also the day Ukrainian women begin their ritual of baking Paska. I found forty different recipes. In the past, some Paska contained up to 120 egg yolks and reached a meter in height. Some were colored with saffron to produce the intense yellow color of the sun. The perfect Paska was at least a foot tall.

The generosity and wealth of the village women were proved by the amount of eggs in the dough—the bigger the bread, the more generous the family. For years the competition was intense. In this contest, the Paska could be so large that it had to be carried by wagon to the church. Sometimes the bread rose so high in the oven that the oven had to be dismantled to save the bread. Although there is still competition to make the most beautiful bread, the really huge Paska loaves are a thing of the past.

On Easter Eve everyone turns out for midnight church services. The women pack baskets with their best breads and foods for the breakfast to be blessed. There are rows and rows of baskets lighted with candles decorating the lawn of the church. Priests chant prayers and blessings over the Easter breads, while the choir and congregation sing traditional hymns.

After the church service, there is great anticipation for the Easter morning meal that breaks the fast. The meal always contains Paska, hard-boiled eggs—both plain and baked in various dishes—fresh pork roast, ribs, sausages, ham, a roast piglet, pâtés, relishes, cheesecakes, tortes, and pastries.

PASKA MOLDS are somewhere between the height of a soufflé dish and a 3-pound coffee can. If you use a soufflé dish, the dough will "mushroom" slightly over the top of the dish; if you use a can, your Paska will have straight sides. Making a collar for the soufflé dish usually doesn't work since the strong dough pushes the collar in all the wrong places. Please note that the milk is heated to 100°F for all the methods; this differs from most of the other recipes in this book.

MAKES 2 LOAVES

FOR THE DOUGH

1 scant tablespoon or 1 (¼-ounce) package active dry yeast

¼ cup warm water (about 110°F)

½ cup warm milk (about 100°F)

8 large egg yolks, beaten

¼ cup (½ stick) unsalted butter, melted

¼ cup granulated sugar

1 tablespoon finely grated lemon zest

2 teaspoons finely chopped candied ginger

1 teaspoon salt

4 to 5 cups unbleached all-purpose flour

FOR THE PANS

Vegetable shortening or butter

1 cup dried bread crumbs

FOR THE TOPPING

1 large egg

1 tablespoon cold water

By hand In a large bowl, sprinkle the yeast in the water to soften. Add the milk, yolks, butter, sugar, zest, ginger, salt, and 2 cups of the flour. Beat vigorously for 2 minutes. Gradually add the remaining flour ¼ cup at a time until the dough begins to pull away from the side of the bowl. Turn the dough out onto a floured work surface. Knead, adding flour a little at a time, until the dough is smooth and elastic.

By mixer In the mixer bowl, sprinkle the yeast in the water to soften. Add the milk, yolks, butter, sugar, zest, ginger, salt, and 2 cups of the flour. Using the mixer paddle, beat on medium-low speed for 2 minutes. Gradually add the remaining flour ¼ cup at a time until the dough begins to pull away from the side of the bowl. Change to the dough hook. Continue to add flour 1 tablespoon at a time until the dough just begins to clean the bowl. Knead 4 to 5 minutes on medium-low.

By food processor In a large measuring cup or bowl, sprinkle the yeast in the water to soften. Add the milk, yolks, and butter. In the bowl of the food processor fitted with the dough blade, combine the sugar, zest, ginger, salt, and 4 cups flour with 4 or 5 pulses. Add the yeast mixture and pulse to combine. With the food processor running, add the liquid ingredients as fast as the dry ingredients will accept them. If you hear a sputtering sound, pour the liquid slower. As soon as all the liquid is added, turn the processor off. Check the liquid-to-flour ratio (see page 28). Pulse until the dough forms a ball, then process exactly 60 seconds.

By bread machine Put the water, milk, yolks, and butter in the bread pan. Add the sugar, zest, ginger, salt, and 4 cups flour, then sprinkle with the yeast. Select the Dough cycle and press Start. While the dough is mixing, check the liquid-to-flour ratio (see page 29). The machine stops after the kneading cycle. You may let the dough rise in the bread machine or a bowl.

First rise Put the dough in an oiled bowl and turn to coat the entire ball of dough with oil. Cover with a tightly woven towel and let rise until doubled, 1 to 1½ hours.

Prepare pans Heavily grease two 3-pound coffee cans or 8-inch soufflé dishes. Sprinkle the sides and bottoms of the molds with bread crumbs.

Shape Turn the dough out onto a lightly oiled work surface. Remove about one-fourth of the dough and cover it. Divide the remaining dough in half and shape each piece into a smooth ball. Place the dough in the prepared molds. Divide the remaining piece of dough into 4 equal pieces and roll each one into a short rope equal to the diameter of the molds. Snip the ends of each rope about 1 inch. Lay 2 ropes at right angles to each other on each loaf and curl the ends outward.

Second rise Cover with tightly woven towels and let rise for 45 minutes.

Preheat oven About 10 minutes before baking, preheat the oven to 375°F.

Final preparation Beat the egg with the cold water and brush over the top of each loaf.

Bake and cool Bake for 25 minutes until the internal temperature of the bread reaches 190°F. Immediately remove the bread from the molds and place on a rack to cool.

NOTE: This bread freezes nicely for up to 6 months. To serve, first thaw the bread, then reheat on a baking sheet or directly on the oven rack in a 375°F oven for 7 to 10 minutes.

9

The Eastern Mediterranean

Christopsomo

Greek Christians, like those in Egypt, rely on the Julian calendar rather than the Gregorian calendar used by Roman Catholics and most Protestants. They celebrate the birth of Jesus during the first or second week of January rather than December 25. Christmas is the second most important holiday in Greece, surpassed only by Easter.

Saint Nicholas is an entirely different character in Greece than in other parts of the world. The Greek Saint Nick is the patron saint of sailors and is traditionally shown with his clothing drenched in brine, his beard dripping with seawater, and his face covered with perspiration, since he has been working hard against the waves and rough seas to rescue sinking ships. No jolly fat man here! No Greek ship sails without some icon of Saint Nicholas on board.

On Christmas Eve children stroll through the streets of their town or village singing *kalanda,* Greek Christmas carols, announcing the birth of Christ. The children often accompany their singing with musical triangles and clay drums. They are rewarded for sharing the good news by neighbors and shopkeepers with treats of sweets and fruit.

Though Christmas trees are gaining favor in Greece, the main symbol of the season is a shallow wooden bowl with a piece of wire suspended across the rim from which hangs a wooden cross wrapped with fresh basil. There is a small amount of holy water in the bowl to keep the basil fresh. The holy water is sprinkled in each room of the house every day to ward off the *killantzaroi,* mythical creatures who emerge from the center of the earth attracted by the jollity of the season. These small creatures appear only during the twelve-day celebration of Christmas and are always wreaking havoc by stealing holiday goodies, souring the cream, braiding horses' tails, putting out fires, and making any other mischief they can find. Since it is believed that they arrive via the chimney, roaring fires are kept going day and night throughout the Christmas season to keep them out of the house.

Christmas Day is quietly celebrated in churches and with family and close friends. After the forty-day fast, the Christmas feast is greatly anticipated. Freshly slaughtered pigs are on almost every table, though stuffed turkeys are becoming popular with the younger generation. There is always Christopsomo, Christ's bread, on the holiday table to complete the celebration.

THE TOP OF THIS ROUND LOAF is decorated with the Greek cross. Glacé cherries or walnut halves are placed in the curled ends of the cross. In centuries past the top of the loaf was decorated in some way to reflect the family's profession. Mastic is a natural resin or gum from the acacia tree used throughout Greece and the Middle East. It has a faint licorice flavor. You can substitute anise seeds for a similar flavor.

MAKES 1 LARGE LOAF

FOR THE DOUGH

1 scant tablespoon or 1 (¼-ounce) package active dry yeast

¼ cup warm water (about 110°F)

¾ cup milk

¼ cup honey

¼ cup (½ stick) unsalted butter, softened

2 large eggs, beaten

1 large egg yolk

1 teaspoon salt

1½ teaspoons mastic or 1 teaspoon anise seeds

4 to 5 cups unbleached all-purpose flour

FOR THE TOP

4 glacé cherries, cut in half, or 8 small walnut halves

1 large egg white

By hand In a large bowl, sprinkle the yeast in the water to soften. Heat the milk to 110°F and add it to the yeast along with the honey, butter, eggs, yolk, salt, mastic or anise and 2 cups of the flour. Beat vigorously for 2 minutes. Gradually add the remaining flour ¼ cup at a time until the dough begins to pull away from the side of the bowl. Turn the dough out onto a floured work surface. Knead, adding flour a little at a time, until the dough is smooth and elastic.

By mixer In the mixer bowl, sprinkle the yeast in the water to soften. Heat the milk to 110°F and add it to the yeast along with the honey, butter, eggs, yolk, salt, mastic or anise and 2 cups of the flour. Using the mixer paddle, beat on medium-low speed for 2 minutes. Gradually add the remaining flour ¼ cup at a time until the dough begins to pull away from the side of the bowl. Change to the dough hook. Continue to add flour 1 tablespoon at a time until the dough just begins to clean the bowl. Knead 4 to 5 minutes on medium-low.

By food processor In a large measuring cup or bowl, sprinkle the yeast in the water to soften. Heat the milk to 100°F and add it to the yeast along with the honey, eggs, and yolk. In the bowl of the food processor fitted with the dough blade, combine the butter, salt, mastic or anise, and 4 cups flour with 4 or 5 pulses. With the food processor running, add the liquid ingredients as fast as the dry ingredients will accept them. If you hear a sputtering sound, pour the liquid slower. As soon as all the liquid is added, turn the processor off. Check the liquid-to-flour ratio (see page 28). Pulse until the dough forms a ball, then process exactly 60 seconds.

By bread machine Put the water, milk, honey, butter, eggs, and yolk in the bread pan. Add the salt, mastic or anise, and 4 cups flour, then sprinkle with the yeast. Select the Dough cycle and press Start. While the dough is mixing, check the liquid-to-flour ratio (see page 29). The machine stops after the kneading cycle. You may let the dough rise in the bread machine or a bowl.

First rise Put the dough in an oiled bowl and turn to coat the entire ball of dough with oil. Cover with a tightly woven towel and let rise until doubled, about one hour.

Shape Turn the dough out onto a lightly oiled work surface. Remove a tennis-ball-sized piece of dough (about ½ cup) and set aside. Shape the remaining dough into a large ball and place it on a parchment-lined or well-greased baking sheet. Slightly flatten the center of the ball so that the loaf is about 3 inches high. Divide the remaining dough in half and roll each piece into an 8-inch rope. Lay the 2 ropes on the center of the loaf to form a cross. With scissors make a 3-inch cut in the end of each rope and curl the ends back to form circles. Place a cherry or walnut half in each circle at the ends of the cross.

Bake and cool Bake for 25 minutes until the internal temperature of the bread reaches 190°F. Immediately remove the bread from the baking sheet and place on a rack to cool.

VARIATION: The day before baking, scald the milk and add 6 dried figs. Remove from the heat, cover, and let sit at room temperature for 8 to 12 hours. Remove the figs from the milk and finely chop. Add the figs to the recipe with the eggs. Measure the fig-flavored milk and add more milk to measure ¾ cup; use this milk in the recipe.

Second rise Cover with a tightly woven towel and let rise for 45 minutes.

Preheat oven About 10 minutes before baking, preheat the oven to 375°F.

Final preparation Beat the egg white until foamy and brush over the loaf.

NOTE: This bread freezes nicely for up to 6 months. To serve, first thaw the bread, then reheat on a baking sheet or directly on the oven rack in a 375°F oven for 7 to 10 minutes.

Loukoumades

Chanukah, the Festival of Lights, commemorates the Jewish victory under the leadership of the five Maccabee brothers over King Antiochus of Syria. The king ordered the Jews to reject their God, their religion, their customs, and their beliefs.

In their battle for freedom, the Maccabees drove the Syrians out of Israel and reclaimed the Temple in Jerusalem. They wanted to cleanse the Temple and remove the hated symbols and statues of King Antiochus. Religious ritual required that oil be lit and burned continually. With only enough sacred oil to light the menorah for one day, a miracle occurred; the oil lasted for eight days, just long enough to rededicate the Temple.

One of the traditions of Chanukah is the lighting of candles each evening—one candle is lit on the first night, two on the second, and so on—to commemorate the miracle at the Temple. Jews throughout the world light the Chanukah candles on the 25th of Kislev, usually in early or mid-December.

There are many types of bread cooked in oil to commemorate the miracle of the oil at Chanukah. Greek Jewish women claim their Loukoumades resemble the very same cakes the Maccabees ate.

THIS IS A YEASTED BATTER and just mixed together; therefore, I've streamlined the method to just a bowl and whisk. Make certain the walnuts for the coating are ground very fine so they stick to the bread. The grains should be about the size of sesame seeds.

MAKES ABOUT 36

FOR THE DOUGH

1 scant tablespoon or 1 (¼-ounce) package active dry yeast

1¼ cups warm water (about 110°F)

1 teaspoon salt

3 cups unbleached all-purpose flour

FOR THE SYRUP

½ cup water

½ cup granulated sugar

1 cup honey

1 tablespoon lemon juice

Oil for frying

FOR THE COATING

Ground cinnamon

Toasted sesame seeds and/or finely chopped walnuts

Prepare the dough In a large bowl, sprinkle the yeast in the water to soften. Add the salt and flour and beat vigorously for 2 minutes.

Rise Cover the bowl with plastic wrap and let rise one hour. *Do not deflate the dough.*

Prepare syrup Combine the water, sugar, honey, and lemon juice in a large saucepan over medium-high heat. Bring the mixture to a rolling boil. Reduce the heat and simmer for 15 minutes. Remove from the heat.

Preheat oil About 10 minutes before frying, start heating 3 to 4 inches oil in a Dutch oven to 375°F. For safety's sake there should be about 2 inches between the oil and the top of the pan.

Fry Drop the dough by the tablespoonful into the hot oil; do not crowd. When the Loukoumades rise to the top of the oil (about 2 minutes) and have turned a golden color, turn them and fry them on the other side for about one minute until evenly colored. Remove from the oil with a slotted spoon and drain on paper towels.

To serve Dip warm Loukoumades in hot syrup and immediately sprinkle with cinnamon and sesame seeds or walnuts.

NOTE: Loukoumades do not freeze well and are best served fresh.

Tsoureki

Easter is the most important holiday for the Greek Orthodox Church, which devotes one hundred days to Easter—fifty days before Easter Sunday dedicated to strengthening members' faith, and fifty days after, dedicated to the belief that God is with all people all of the time.

On Good Friday all Greek Orthodox Christians go to church. After the service, the church bells are rung loudly, and a funeral procession, known as the *epitaphios,* winds through the streets around the church. People carrying lighted candles follow the facsimile of Christ's bier in the procession.

On the eve of Easter, everyone attends midnight mass. Again the church bells are rung loudly and people light candles. Each person walks home with a lit candle, and, once there, makes the sign of a cross on the door with the soot of the burning candle.

During their traditional Easter meal, Greeks eat Tsoureki, a sumptuous bread flavored with orange and anise, said to recall the sweetness of life. This lovely bread is braided and either left in a long braid or shaped in a wreath to symbolize the circle of life. Bright red hard-cooked eggs are tucked in the folds of the braid to symbolize the blood and suffering of Christ upon the cross.

Tsoureki, or Lambropsomo (which means "Easter bread"), has bright red eggs tucked in it. If you have access to a Middle Eastern store, you can purchase the special dye used for these eggs. This dye is nothing like American Easter egg dye and makes the eggs a very intense deep red. If you cannot find this special dye, you can use commercial red clothing dye. Dissolve 1 packet of dye in 6 tablespoons vinegar. Place up to 12 eggs in a large pan in one layer and cover with enough water to come at least 1 inch above the eggs. Add the dye solution, cover, and quickly bring the water to a full boil. Remove from the heat and let stand covered for 15 minutes. Immediately place the eggs in iced water for 5 minutes to stop the cooking. Remove from the water, dry, and rub with oil to give the eggs a deep shine. The eggs may be eaten.

MAKES I LARGE LOAF

FOR THE DOUGH

1 scant tablespoon or 1 (¼-ounce) package active dry yeast

¼ cup warm water (about 110°F)

½ cup milk

½ cup (1 stick) unsalted butter

½ cup honey

2 large eggs, beaten

1 large egg yolk

1 teaspoon vanilla extract

1 tablespoon finely grated orange zest

1 teaspoon salt

½ teaspoon anise seeds

4 to 5 cups unbleached all-purpose flour

Hard-boiled eggs dyed bright red (1 or 2 for each person)

FOR THE TOPPING

1 large egg white

1 tablespoon cold water

3 tablespoons sesame seeds

By hand In a large bowl, sprinkle the yeast in the water to soften. Heat the milk, butter, and honey to 110°F and add it to the yeast along with the eggs, yolk, vanilla, zest, salt, anise seeds, and 2 cups of the flour. Beat vigorously for 2 minutes. Gradually add the remaining flour ¼ cup at a time until the dough begins to pull away from the side of the bowl. Turn the dough out onto a floured work surface. Knead, adding flour a little at a time, until the dough is smooth and elastic.

By mixer In the mixer bowl, sprinkle the yeast in the water to soften. Heat the milk, butter, and honey to 110°F and add it to the yeast along with the eggs, yolk, vanilla, zest, salt, anise seeds, and 2 cups of the flour. Using the mixer paddle, beat on medium-low speed for 2 minutes. Gradually add the remaining flour ¼ cup at a time until the dough begins to pull away from the side of the bowl. Change to the dough hook. Continue to add flour 1 tablespoon at a time until the dough just begins to clean the bowl. Knead 4 to 5 minutes on medium-low.

By food processor In a cup or small bowl, sprinkle the yeast in the water to soften. Heat the milk, butter, and honey to 100°F and add it to the yeast along with the eggs, yolk, and vanilla. In the bowl of the food processor fitted with the dough blade, combine the zest, salt, anise seeds, and 4 cups flour with 4 or 5 pulses. With the food processor running, add the liquid ingredients as fast as the dry ingredients will accept them. If you hear a sputtering sound, pour the liquid slower. As soon as all liquid is added, turn the processor off. Check the liquid-to-flour ratio (see page 28). Pulse until the dough forms a ball, then process exactly 60 seconds.

By bread machine Put the water, milk, butter, honey, eggs, yolk, and vanilla in the bread pan. Add the zest, salt, anise seeds, and 4 cups flour, then sprinkle with the yeast. Select the Dough cycle and press Start. While the dough is mixing, check the liquid-to-flour ratio (see page 29). The machine stops after the kneading cycle. You may let the dough rise in the bread machine or a bowl.

First rise Put the dough in an oiled bowl and turn to coat the entire ball of dough with oil. Cover with a tightly woven towel and let rise until doubled, about one hour.

Shape Turn the dough out onto a lightly oiled work surface and divide in half. Roll each half into a 30-inch-long rope. Lay the ropes side by side. Starting in the middle, loosely twist the ropes together. Bring the ends together. To make it look like a continuous twist, pinch the end that comes over the top on the right side to the bottom on the left side. Take the bottom on the right side and lay it across the part where you pinched the dough together. Gently stretch the top end on the left and tuck it under the dough.

Second rise Cover with a tightly woven towel and let rise for 30 minutes.

Add eggs Gently spread the dough at equal places around the circle. Carefully lay an egg lengthwise in each space, letting the dough snuggle above the eggs slightly to keep them in place.

Third rise Cover and let the dough rise for 20 minutes.

Preheat oven About 10 minutes before baking, preheat the oven to 375°F.

Final preparation Beat the egg white until frothy. Add the water and beat to combine. Brush the egg white over the bread, being careful not to let it puddle in the crevices. Do not brush the eggs. Sprinkle with the sesame seeds.

Bake and cool Bake for 25 minutes until the internal temperature of the bread reaches 190°F. Immediately remove the bread from the baking sheet and place on a rack to cool.

NOTE: Because of the eggs used as decoration, this bread does not freeze well. It is best eaten fresh.

Vasilopita
SAINT BASIL'S BREAD

$\mathcal{V}$asilopita is a Greek New Year's bread made to honor Saint Basil, the great father of the early Church. This caring priest knew the poor members of his church were proud people who would not receive charity. Wanting to ensure that they had enough for life's necessities, he came up with a plan to have the ladies of his church prepare sweet breads with coins baked into them. He declared that the person receiving the coin would be especially blessed for the year. He also guaranteed that those in want would be taken care of without receiving charity.

As the clock strikes midnight on New Year's Eve, families divide their Saint Basil's bread. The first piece of bread is reserved for the saint, the second piece is set aside for the poor, and the third piece goes to the eldest person in the family, then the head of the house, his spouse, and so on, according to age, boys before girls, until everyone has a slice. (The coin is cleaned and baked in the bread for good luck.) Once each person receives a share of bread, it is dipped into a bowl of wine and the words are uttered, "This is for our grandfather, Saint Basil."

VASILOPITA, which uses the Syrian and Turkish spice mahlab, was introduced to Greece by Hellenes who lived in Constantinople to honor Saint Vasilio (Saint Basil). The wonderful spice that gives Vasilopita its unique taste goes by a number of names: mahlab, malepi, mahlepi, and mahlep, just to name a few. I refer to the spice as mahlab, since that is the way it is listed in the catalog where I purchase it (see Sources on page 331).

Mahlab is made from the pits of sour cherries and adds a sweet-and-sour nutty taste when used in baked goods. It is the favored flavoring for Vasilopita, but anise seeds can be substituted and impart an entirely different, but pleasant, flavor. The traditional bread is baked in a round pan called a *tapsi*. The dough should be extremely sticky and soft at the end of the mixing process and is not kneaded, and is refrigerated 8 to 24 hours.

MAKES 1 LARGE LOAF

FOR THE DOUGH

1 scant tablespoon or 1 (¼-ounce) package active dry yeast

¼ cup warm water (about 110°F)

½ cup cold milk

4 large eggs, room temperature

1 tablespoon finely grated lemon zest

1 teaspoon salt

1 teaspoon mahlab or anise seeds

½ cup granulated sugar

3½ cups unbleached all-purpose flour

1 cup (2 sticks) unsalted butter, softened

TO PLACE IN SHAPED DOUGH

Coin, washed and wrapped in foil (see Notes)

FOR THE TOPPING

1 large egg, beaten

1 tablespoon cold water

2 tablespoons sesame seeds

¼ cup finely chopped walnuts

By hand In a large bowl, sprinkle the yeast in the water and let sit for 10 minutes until foamy. Add the milk, eggs, zest, salt, mahlab, sugar, and 2 cups of the flour to the yeast. Beat vigorously for 2 minutes. Add the butter 1 tablespoon at a time, beating well after each addition. Gradually add the remaining flour ¼ cup at a time until fully incorporated. The dough will be extremely sticky.

By mixer In the mixer bowl, sprinkle the yeast in the water and let sit for 10 minutes until foamy. Add the milk, eggs, zest, salt, mahlab, sugar, and 2 of the cups flour to the yeast. Using the mixer paddle, beat on medium-low speed for 2 minutes. Add the butter 1 tablespoon at a time, beating well after each addition. Gradually add the remaining flour ¼ cup at a time until fully incorporated. The dough will be extremely sticky.

By food processor In a large measuring cup or bowl, sprinkle the yeast in the water to soften. Add the milk and eggs. In the bowl of the food processor fitted with the dough blade, combine the zest, salt, mahlab, sugar, and 3½ cups flour with 4 or 5 pulses. With the food processor running, add the liquid ingredients as fast as the dry ingredients will accept them. If you hear a sputtering sound, pour the liquid slower. As soon as all the liquid is added, turn the processor off. Cut the butter into 8 equal pieces. Place 4 pieces evenly spaced on the top of the dough. Pulse the processor just until the butter is incorporated. Add the remaining 4 pieces of butter and pulse to incorporate.

By bread machine Put the water, milk, and eggs in the bread pan. Add the zest, salt, mahlab, sugar, and 3½ cups flour, then sprinkle with the yeast. Select the Dough cycle and press Start. Once the ingredients have mixed, drop in the butter 1 tablespoon at a time, letting the dough mix about 20 seconds between additions. The dough will be extremely sticky. The machine stops after the kneading cycle. You may let the dough rise in the bread machine or a bowl.

First rise Put the dough in an oiled bowl and turn to coat the entire ball of dough with oil. Cover with a tightly woven towel and let rise for two hours. The dough may not double in size.

Shape Punch down the dough to remove most of the air. Press the coin into the dough so that it is hidden. Turn the dough into a well-greased 10-inch round pan. Press the dough into the pan so that it is completely flat. If there is any hint of where the coin is, press it deeper into the dough.

Second rise Cover with plastic wrap and a tightly woven towel and refrigerate for 8 to 24 hours.

Preheat oven About 10 minutes before baking, preheat the oven to 375°F.

Final preparation Remove the dough from the refrigerator. Mix the beaten egg with the cold water and brush on top of the loaf. Sprinkle with the sesame seeds and walnuts.

Bake and cool Bake for 35 minutes until the internal temperature of the bread reaches 190°F. Immediately remove the bread from the pan and place on a rack to cool.

NOTES: A whole almond with the skin still on it can be substituted for the coin. Many people recommend using a blanched almond in place of the coin, but testers who used blanched almonds never found them in the baked bread.

This bread freezes nicely for up to 6 months. To serve, first thaw the bread, then reheat on a baking sheet or directly on the oven rack in a 375°F oven for 7 to 10 minutes.

10

The Middle East

Sufganiyot

Two very popular foods prepared for Chanukah are fried in oil to symbolize the miracle of the oil in the Temple—potato pancakes, called latkes; and Sufganiyot (or Soofganiot), or jelly doughnuts. These are so popular in Israel that during the holiday season they are sold at most grocery stores, supermarkets, kiosks, cafés, and espresso bars.

JEWISH DIETARY LAWS forbid the consumption of animal products and dairy products in the same meal. The pareve (parve) margarine called for in this recipe contains no derivatives of meat or milk. If you don't follow Jewish dietary laws, substitute butter for the margarine. Though it isn't traditional, I prefer using milk instead of water to produce a lighter doughnut. (If you use butter or milk in the recipe, observant Jews will not be able to eat these with a meat-based meal.) Since this dough is not kneaded, I have not included instructions for the bread machine. The amount of oil you need for frying will depend on the size pot you use.

MAKES 24 TO 30 JELLY-FILLED DOUGHNUTS

FOR THE DOUGH

1 scant tablespoon or 1 (¼-ounce) package active dry yeast

¾ cup warm water (about 110°F)

2 large eggs

2 egg yolks

½ cup pareve margarine, softened

1 teaspoon salt

1 teaspoon ground cinnamon or 1 teaspoon finely grated lemon zest

3½ to 4 cups unbleached all-purpose flour

FOR THE FILLING

About ½ cup apricot, strawberry, blueberry, or other favorite jam or preserves

2 egg whites, beaten until frothy

FOR THE TOPPING

Granulated or confectioners' sugar

By hand In a large bowl, sprinkle the yeast in the water to soften. Combine the yeast mixture, eggs, yolks, margarine, salt, cinnamon or zest, and 2 cups of the flour. Beat vigorously for 4 minutes. Gradually add the remaining flour ¼ cup at a time until the dough begins to pull away from the side of the bowl. This dough is not kneaded but should be very thick.

By mixer In the mixer bowl, sprinkle the yeast in the water to soften. Add the eggs, yolks, margarine, salt, cinnamon or zest, and 2 cups of the flour to the yeast mixture. Using the mixer paddle, beat on medium-low speed for 4 minutes. Gradually add the remaining flour ¼ cup at a time until the dough begins to pull away from the side of the bowl. This dough is not kneaded but should be very thick.

By food processor In a medium measuring cup or bowl, sprinkle the yeast in the water to soften. Add the eggs and yolks to the yeast mixture. In the bowl of the food processor fitted with the dough blade, combine the margarine, salt, cinnamon or zest, and 3½ cups flour with 4 or 5 pulses. With the food processor running, add the liquid ingredients as fast as the dry ingredients will accept them. If you hear a sputtering sound, pour the liquid slower. As soon as all the liquid is added, turn the processor off and scrape the sides of the processor bowl. Process for 60 seconds.

First rise Put the dough in an oiled bowl and turn to coat the entire ball of dough with oil. Cover with a tightly woven towel and let rise until doubled, about one hour.

Second rise Punch all the air out of the dough by pressing your fist in the center of the dough all the way to the bottom of the bowl. Take the dough from the sides of the bowl, stretch it to the center, and press the dough to the bottom. Continue until all the dough is deflated. Cover again with the towel and let rise for 30 minutes.

Shape Turn the dough out onto a lightly oiled work surface and roll ¼ inch thick. Let the dough rest 5 minutes. Using a 2- to 2½-inch cutter or tumbler, cut the dough into circles. Reroll the scraps. (The doughnuts from the rerolled dough will not be as puffy and tender as the others.) Place ½ teaspoon jam in the center of a circle. Brush around the jam with the beaten egg white all the way to the outside edge. Place another circle over the jam and securely pinch the edges together with your thumb and forefinger (seal it tightly to prevent the jam from coming out during frying). Repeat until all the circles are filled. Place about 1 inch apart on baking sheets or the work surface.

Third rise Cover with a tightly woven towel and let rise for 30 minutes.

Preheat oil About 10 minutes before frying, preheat about 2 inches oil in a large deep pan or Dutch oven to 375°F.

Fry Gently place 3 or 4 doughnuts in the oil and fry until golden, about 3 minutes. Turn and fry the other side until golden, about 2 minutes. Drain on paper towels and repeat with the remaining doughnuts. Be especially careful; should some of the filling ooze out, the oil will splatter.

Finish Place the sugar in a shallow bowl and coat the doughnuts one at a time with the sugar. Place on a rack until the jam has a chance to cool slightly, about 5 minutes. Serve immediately.

NOTE: Sufganiyot must be served fresh. They do not freeze well.

Mannaeesh

MANAEESH

In Arabic countries bread is made fresh daily and accompanies every meal. In fact, since bread is sacred, it is a disgrace to have no bread on the table. Not only does bread fill the stomach but it is also a celebration of the soul, a gift from God that is treated with complete reverence. There is no single celebration that calls for Mannaeesh, but because bread is a daily celebration of life, I've included this recipe.

Should a piece of bread fall upon the floor, it is picked up and kissed, a short prayer is uttered, and then it is placed on the table again. Bread is never discarded. What is not eaten is put upon a windowsill or ledge to share with anyone who is hungry and happens to pass by. Arabic breads are almost always round, forming the eternal circle, and they are broken by hand, never cut.

THIS BREAD IS COATED WITH ZATAR (za'tar, zaatar, zahtar), which rhymes with batter. There are many versions of the mixture, but my favorite is a mixture of sumac, thyme, sesame, and salt (see Sources on page 331). You can make your own or purchase it commercially.

MAKES 12 FLATBREADS

FOR THE DOUGH

1 scant tablespoon or 1 (¼-ounce) package active dry yeast

1 cup warm water (about 110°F)

¼ cup olive oil

1 teaspoon salt

4 to 5 cups unbleached all-purpose flour

FOR THE TOPPING

Olive oil

¼ cup zatar (see Note)

By hand In a large bowl, sprinkle the yeast in the water to soften. Add the oil, salt, and 2 cups of the flour. Beat vigorously for 2 minutes. Gradually add the remaining flour ¼ cup at a time until the dough begins to pull away from the side of the bowl. Turn the dough out onto a floured work surface. Knead, adding flour a little at a time, until the dough is smooth and elastic.

By mixer In the mixer bowl, sprinkle the yeast in the water to soften. Add the oil, salt, and 2 cups of the flour. Using the paddle, beat on medium-low speed for 2 minutes. Gradually add the remaining flour ¼ cup at a time until the dough begins to pull away from the side of the bowl. Change to the dough hook. Continue to add flour 1 tablespoon at a time until the dough just begins to clean the bowl. Knead 4 to 5 minutes on medium-low.

By food processor In a cup or small bowl, sprinkle the yeast in the water to soften. Put the oil, salt, and 4 cups flour in the food processor fitted with the dough blade. Pulse 3 or 4 times to combine. With the food processor running, add the liquid ingredients as fast as the dry ingredients will accept them. If you hear a sputtering sound, pour the liquid slower. As soon as all liquid is added, turn the processor off. Check the liquid-to-flour ratio (see page 28). Pulse until the dough forms a ball, then process exactly 60 seconds.

By bread machine Put the water, oil, and salt in the bread pan. Add 4 cups flour and sprinkle with the yeast. Select the Dough cycle and press Start. While the dough is mixing, check the liquid-to-flour ratio (see page 29). The machine stops after the kneading cycle. You may let the dough rise in the bread machine or a bowl.

First rise Put the dough in an oiled bowl and turn to coat the entire ball of dough with oil. Cover with a tightly woven towel and let rise until doubled, about one hour.

Preheat oven About 45 minutes before baking, place a baking stone on a shelf in the lower third of the oven. Preheat the oven to 450°F. If you don't have a stone, preheat a heavy baking sheet.

Shape Turn the dough out onto a lightly oiled work surface and divide it into 12 equal pieces. Roll each piece of dough into a 5-inch circle. Brush each round of dough with olive oil and sprinkle evenly with zatar. Roll the dough again so that each round is about 6 inches in diameter with the herbs and seeds embedded in the dough.

Second rise Turn the rounds over on the work surface. Cover with tightly woven towels and let rest for 20 minutes.

Bake and cool Bake a few rounds at a time, herb side up, on the stone or baking sheet. Bake for 8 minutes until lightly browned. Immediately remove the bread from the baking stone and wrap in a tightly woven towel to cool.

NOTE: Here is a quick topping that can be substituted for zatar. Although it isn't quite as aromatic and woodsy tasting as the real thing, it's certainly delicious. Combine 3 tablespoons chopped fresh thyme or 1 tablespoon dried thyme, 3 tablespoons chopped fresh marjoram or 1 tablespoon dried marjoram, 3 tablespoons sesame seeds, and 1 tablespoon kosher salt.

Ka'ak
KAHK, KAAHK

In Syria these small crisp rings are a must for breaking the fast of Esther, the day before Purim. Purim commemorates the deliverance of the Jews in the Persian Empire under Artaxerxes (also known as Ahashuarus), as recounted in the Scroll of Esther.

Ka'ak are so small that *motzi,* the blessing of the bread, need not be recited before they are eaten. The round shape symbolizes the circle of life.

KA'AK ARE FLAVORED with a Middle Eastern spice called mahlab (see page 186).

MAKES 32 RINGS

FOR THE SEED MIXTURE

½ teaspoon anise seeds

½ teaspoon cumin seeds

¼ teaspoon caraway seeds

¼ teaspoon mahlab

FOR THE DOUGH

1 scant tablespoon or 1 (¼-ounce) package active dry yeast

2 tablespoons warm water (about 110°F)

½ cup milk

¼ cup (½ stick) unsalted butter, melted

½ teaspoon salt

2 teaspoons granulated sugar

2 to 3 cups unbleached all-purpose flour

FOR THE TOPPING

1 large egg

2 tablespoons cold water

1 cup sesame seeds

Prepare seeds Combine the anise, cumin, caraway, and mahlab in a mortar or spice grinder. Crush with a pestle or grind to a coarse powder. You can also crush this mixture with a hammer on a cutting board.

By hand In a large bowl, sprinkle the yeast in the water to soften. Heat the milk to 110°F and add it to the yeast along with the butter, salt, sugar, and 1½ cups flour. Beat vigorously for 2 minutes. Add the seed mixture and then the remaining flour ¼ cup at a time until the dough begins to pull away from the side of the bowl. Turn the dough out onto a floured work surface. Knead, adding flour a little at a time, until the dough is smooth and elastic.

By mixer In the mixer bowl, sprinkle yeast in the water to soften. Heat the milk to 110°F; add to the yeast with the butter, salt, sugar, and 1½ cups flour. Using the paddle, beat on medium-low speed for 2 minutes. Add the seeds, then the remaining flour ¼ cup at a time until the dough begins to pull away from the side of the bowl. Change to the dough hook. Continue to add flour 1 tablespoon at a time until the dough just begins to clean the bowl. Knead 4 minutes on medium-low.

By food processor In a cup or small bowl, sprinkle the yeast in the water to soften. Heat milk to 100°F; add to the yeast with the butter. In a food processor fitted with the dough blade, combine the salt, sugar, seeds, and 2 cups flour with 4 or 5 pulses. With the processor running, add the liquid ingredients as fast as the dry ingredients will accept them. If you hear a sputtering sound, pour the liquid slower. As soon as all the liquid is added, turn the processor off. Check the liquid-to-flour ratio (see page 28). Pulse until the dough forms a ball, then process exactly 60 seconds.

By bread machine Put the water, milk, and butter in the bread pan. Add the salt, sugar, seeds, and 2 cups flour, then sprinkle with the yeast. Select the Dough cycle and press Start. While the dough is mixing, check the liquid-to-flour ratio (see page 29). The machine stops after the kneading cycle. You may let the dough rise in the machine or a bowl.

First rise Put the dough in an oiled bowl and turn to coat the entire ball of dough with oil. Cover with a tightly woven towel and let rise until doubled, about one hour.

Shape Turn the dough out onto a lightly oiled work surface and divide into 32 equal pieces. Roll each piece into a 10-inch-long rope. Bring the ends of 1 rope together, overlapping them slightly, and press together to seal. Repeat with the remaining ropes.

Second rise Cover with a tightly woven towel and let rest on the work surface for 20 minutes.

Preheat oven About 10 minutes before baking, preheat the oven to 375°F.

Final preparation Beat the egg and cold water together in a shallow bowl. Sprinkle the sesame seeds in another shallow bowl. Dip a ring in the egg mixture, then coat with the seeds on both sides. Place about 1 inch apart on parchment-lined or well-greased baking sheets. You may need to arrange your oven racks in the top third and bottom third. Put 2 baking sheets in the oven at one time and rotate them halfway through the baking time.

Bake and cool Bake for 15 to 18 minutes until lightly browned. Immediately remove the rings from the baking sheets and place on racks to cool.

NOTE: These rings freeze nicely for up to 6 months.

Kubaneh

Kubaneh, or Kubneh, is a Yemenite bread prepared for Shabbat, the Jewish Sabbath. Since Jewish law prevents work of any kind on the Sabbath, this unusual bread is prepared the day before, making it perfect for the Shabbat breakfast or brunch.

The bread is coiled in a special Kubaneh pan or Dutch oven, baked at a low temperature for 2 hours, the heat reduced, covered, and baked overnight. The bread, semi-steamed in the tight-fitting pot, has a unique soft texture with a very thick brown crust. Traditionally eggs are cooked along with the dough and later served with the finished bread (instructions follow). Hilbeh (recipe follows), a spicy sauce, usually accompanies the Kubaneh; however, some serve it with sprinkled sugar, or butter and jam.

TRADITIONALLY, HARD-BOILED EGGS are wrapped in foil and placed on top of the bread as it bakes. The eggs become slightly bitter, which is the way they should be. They come out brown after cooking so long and are nothing like how one would expect a hard-boiled egg to taste. If you prefer eggs that are cooked less, you can either soft-boil or coddle them. Because of the lengthy rising and baking times, you will need to start this bread 13 to 15 hours before you wish to serve it.

MAKES 1 LARGE LOAF

FOR THE SPONGE

1 scant tablespoon or 1 (¼-ounce) package active dry yeast

1¼ cups warm water (about 110°F)

2 cups unbleached all-purpose flour

FOR THE DOUGH

1 teaspoon salt

¼ cup honey

2 to 3 cups unbleached all-purpose flour

½ cup (1 stick) unsalted butter, melted

6 to 8 hard-boiled eggs in their shells, individually wrapped in foil, optional

Prepare sponge In a large bowl, sprinkle the yeast in the water to soften. Add the flour and stir to combine. Cover with plastic wrap and let sit for one hour.

By hand Add the salt, honey, and 1 cup of the flour to the sponge. Beat vigorously for 2 minutes. Gradually add the remaining flour ¼ cup at a time until the dough begins to pull away from the side of the bowl. Turn the dough out onto a floured work surface. Knead, adding flour a little at a time, until the dough is smooth and elastic.

By mixer In the mixer bowl, add the salt, honey, and 1 cup of the flour to the sponge. Using the mixer paddle, beat the mixture on medium-low speed for 2 minutes. Gradually add the remaining flour ¼ cup at a time until the dough begins to pull away from the side of the bowl. Change to the dough hook. Continue to add flour 1 tablespoon at a time until the dough just begins to clean the bowl. Knead 4 to 5 minutes on medium-low.

By food processor In the bowl of the food processor fitted with the dough blade, combine the sponge, salt, honey, and 2 cups flour with 4 or 5 pulses. Check the liquid-to-flour ratio (see page 28). Pulse until the dough forms a ball, then process exactly 60 seconds.

By bread machine Put the sponge, salt, honey, and 2 cups flour in the bread pan. Select the Dough cycle and press Start. While the dough is mixing, check the liquid-to-flour ratio (see page 29). The machine stops after the kneading cycle. You may let the dough rise in the bread machine or a bowl.

First rise Put the dough in an oiled bowl and turn to coat the entire ball of dough with oil. Cover with a tightly woven towel and let rise until doubled, about one hour.

Shape Turn the dough out onto a lightly oiled work surface and roll into an 18 by 22-inch rectangle. Spread the butter evenly over the dough. Roll the dough into a 22-inch-long cylinder. Coil the dough in a spiral, starting at the center of a well-greased Dutch oven. Cover with the lid.

Second rise Let rise for 30 minutes.

Bake and cool Place the pan in a *cold* oven. Set the heat at 250°F and bake 2 hours. Reduce the heat to 200°F. Place the foil-wrapped eggs on top of the dough. Cover and bake for 8 to 10 hours (overnight). Remove the bread and eggs from the pan and place on a rack to cool slightly. No need to use a thermometer after baking the bread this long; the loaf is definitely done.

NOTE: This bread does not freeze well and is best eaten immediately.

Hilbeh

THIS SAUCE has a flavor that sneaks up on you. It should be extremely spicy and hot, but you can adjust the heat by the amount of chiles. When you first make the sauce, it will be spicy hot, but the heat mellows as the sauce sits. Dip Kubaneh into the sauce and serve with the peeled baked eggs.

MAKES 1½ CUPS

2 teaspoons fenugreek seeds

½ cup cold water

½ teaspoon salt

½ teaspoon caraway seeds

¼ teaspoon freshly ground black pepper

3 cloves garlic, peeled

1 to 4 small fresh chiles, seeded

¾ cup fresh chopped cilantro

2 tablespoons fresh lemon juice

3 medium tomatoes, peeled, seeded, and quartered

Soak the fenugreek seeds in the cold water for 12 to 18 hours. They should develop a translucent jellylike coating. Drain on paper towels. Place the fenugreek seeds, salt, caraway, and pepper in a food processor. With the machine running, drop in the garlic and process until finely chopped. Add the chiles and process until they are finely chopped. (A mortar and pestle can be used to pulverize this mixture, but it is a lot of work.) Scrape the sides of the container. Add the cilantro, lemon juice, and tomatoes and pulse until the tomatoes are coarsely chopped. Transfer to a glass container, tightly cover, and let sit for at least 1 hour for the flavors to blend. Keeps refrigerated for one week. Serve at room temperature.

11

Russia and Asia

Blini

*L*ate in February many Russians celebrate a lively festival called Maslen-itsa. The name comes from the word *maslo,* which means "butter." It is also the name of a pagan deity who ruled over the winter season. The ancient Slavs were sun worshipers, so the revelry around the festival centered on the return of the sun.

Originally Maslenitsa had nothing to do with Christian holidays; the ancient Russian folk rituals were incorporated into many of the Christian rituals soon after the Russians adopted Christianity in 988. The weeklong festival now precedes Lent. Maslenitsa, known as the overeating holiday, is the wildest, merriest celebration of the year. Everything is decorated in bright colors to usher out the darkness of winter and welcome the warmth of spring.

Blini, the most sought-after food of the festival, symbolize the sun itself. They are served with a wide choice of condiments, usually caviar or some type of fish, and then bathed in melted butter with a large dollop of sour cream. Everyone, rich or poor, male or female, child or adult, eats many blini.

Stories of wealthier Russian celebrations describe a vicious cycle of overeating and overdrinking: After consuming copious quantities of vodka, they would eat numerous blini drowned in butter and sour cream to counteract the effects of the alcohol. Then they'd need more vodka to counteract all the rich, buttery blini. . . .

BLINI, small, thin buckwheat pancakes, are topped with caviar or fish to accompany copious amounts of vodka, or with jam or preserves when served for tea. Leftover pancakes are stacked with filling between layers and served as blini pie.

MAKES ABOUT 36

1 tablespoon granulated sugar

1 scant tablespoon or 1 (¼-ounce) package active dry yeast

2 cups warm milk (about 110°F)

1 teaspoon salt

¼ cup (½ stick) unsalted butter, melted

3 large egg yolks, beaten

1 cup buckwheat flour

1 cup unbleached all-purpose flour

3 large egg whites, stiffly beaten

Toppings: Red or black caviar; smoked salmon, mackerel, sturgeon, or herring; pickled smelts, sardines, or salt herring; jam or preserves; lots of melted butter, sour cream, and dill sprigs

By hand In a large bowl, combine the sugar and yeast. Gradually whisk in the milk and let sit for 5 minutes. Add the salt, butter, egg yolks, buckwheat flour, and all-purpose flour. Beat vigorously for 10 minutes (the secret to great blini is in the beating). Gently fold in the egg whites just until the ingredients are combined.

By mixer In the mixer's bowl, combine the sugar and yeast. Gradually blend in the milk and let sit for 5 minutes. Add the salt, butter, egg yolks, buckwheat flour, and all-purpose flour. Beat vigorously for 5 minutes (the secret to great blini is in the beating). Gently fold in the egg whites just until the ingredients are combined.

First rise Cover with plastic wrap and let rise 45 minutes until light and airy. Do not deflate.

Cook Generously butter a heavy skillet and place it over medium heat. Using about 2 tablespoons per blini, drop the batter about 1 inch apart in the pan. Cook the blini on one side until lightly browned, about 2 minutes, then turn them over and cook the other side about 1 minute. Keep the cooked blini warm in a 200°F oven, covered loosely with foil so they don't dry out, while cooking the rest.

Serve Serve warm. Drizzle each pancake generously with melted butter, ¼ teaspoon caviar or small bits of fish, garnish with dill sprigs, and dollop with sour cream. Or, if serving for tea or dessert, drizzle each pancake generously with melted butter, spread with jam or preserves, and dollop with sour cream.

NOTE: Blini do not freeze well and are at their best eaten immediately. Blini make a wonderful breakfast slathered with butter and generously doused with syrup. Not traditional but extremely yummy!

Khachapuri

Khachapuri, cheese-filled bread, comes from the Republic of Georgia. It is made by both Protestants and Jews to celebrate Pentecost.

The Protestant feast of Pentecost commemorates the resurrection of Jesus Christ and the descent of the Holy Spirit on the disciples with tongues of fire and rushing winds, giving them the power to speak so that people of all languages could understand them. The Christian feast of Pentecost is observed as the birthday of the church and the feast of the Holy Spirit.

The Jewish feast of Pentecost, Shavout (or Shavouth), is one of three pilgrimage festivals and celebrates the end of the spring grain harvest that began formally at Passover, fifty days prior.

THE RUSSIAN CHEESES used for Khachapuri are nearly impossible to find in America. My testers and I checked almost every cheese source for *immeruli, suluguni,* and *bryndza,* to no avail. However, I have received many substitutions from families who've made Khachapuri for years. The combination of Muenster and feta cheeses is my favorite, but you could also try a mixture of Cheddar and goat cheese, or mozzarella mixed with either goat cheese or Roquefort. This bread needs an hour or more to set up before cutting or the cheese will run out.

MAKES 1 LARGE LOAF

FOR THE SPONGE

1 scant tablespoon or 1 (¼-ounce) package active dry yeast

¾ cup warm milk (about 110°F)

½ teaspoon granulated sugar

1 cup unbleached all-purpose flour

FOR THE DOUGH

1 teaspoon salt

1 tablespoon granulated sugar

½ cup (1 stick) unsalted butter, softened

2 to 3 cups unbleached all-purpose flour

For the Filling

1 pound Muenster cheese, shredded

8 ounces feta cheese, crumbled

1 large egg, lightly beaten

For Brushing the Loaf

2 tablespoons unsalted butter, melted

Prepare sponge In a large bowl, sprinkle the yeast in the milk to soften. Add the sugar and flour and beat until smooth. Cover with plastic wrap and let rise 30 minutes.

By hand Combine the sponge, salt, sugar, butter, and 1 cup of the flour. Beat vigorously for 2 minutes. Gradually add the remaining flour ¼ cup at a time until the dough begins to pull away from the side of the bowl. Turn the dough out onto a floured work surface. Knead, adding flour a little at a time, until the dough is smooth and elastic.

By mixer In the mixer bowl, combine the sponge, salt, sugar, butter, and 1 cup of the flour. Using the mixer paddle, beat the mixture on medium-low speed for 2 minutes. Gradually add the remaining flour ¼ cup at a time until the dough begins to pull away from the side of the bowl. Change to the dough hook. Continue to add flour 1 tablespoon at a time until the dough just begins to clean the bowl. Knead 4 to 5 minutes on medium-low.

By food processor In the bowl of the food processor fitted with the dough blade, combine the salt, sugar, butter, and 2 cups flour with 4 or 5 pulses. With the food processor running, add the sponge as fast as the dry ingredients will accept it. If you hear a sputtering sound, pour the liquid slower. As soon as all the liquid is added, turn the processor off. Check the liquid-to-flour ratio (see page 28). Pulse until the dough forms a ball, then process exactly 60 seconds.

By bread machine Put the sponge in the bread pan. Add the salt, sugar, butter, and 2 cups flour. Select the Dough cycle and press Start. While the dough is mixing, check the liquid-to-flour ratio (see page 29). The machine stops after the kneading cycle. You may let the dough rise in the bread machine or a bowl.

First rise Put the dough in an oiled bowl and turn to coat the entire ball of dough with oil. Cover with a tightly woven towel and let rise until doubled, about one hour.

Prepare filling In a large bowl, toss the Muenster, feta, and egg to combine.

Shape Turn the dough out onto a lightly oiled work surface and roll into a 22-inch circle. Lightly dust the dough with flour and fold into quarters. Carefully lift the dough and place it in a well-greased 9-inch springform pan. Unfold the dough, draping the edge evenly over the side of the pan. Spoon the filling into the pan. Cover the filling with the dough, pleating it as you go. Twist the pleated dough to form a topknot.

Second rise Cover with a tightly woven towel and let rise for 30 minutes.

Preheat oven About 10 minutes before baking, preheat the oven to 375°F.

Bake and cool Bake for 30 minutes. Remove the side of the springform pan and return the bread to the oven. Bake 5 minutes longer until the side of the bread is golden brown. An instant-read thermometer will not work because of the thick cheese filling. Place the bread on a rack to cool for at least one hour before cutting. Brush the top and sides of bread with melted butter while warm. Leave the bread on the bottom of the pan while it cools; this bread is extremely fragile, and if it splits, the cheese runs out.

NOTE: This bread does not freeze well.

Kolach

Many Eastern European countries, especially those along the western edge of what was once the Union of Soviet Socialist Republics, have breads similar to Kolach or Kalach. The name is taken from the word *kolo,* which means "wheel." The circle is an ancient symbol of eternity and good fortune. The people of Saint Petersburg assert that Kolach originated in their city, and a true Kolach is made only from the water of the Moskva River.

In Russia there are special breads for every occasion—marriage, birth, death, and every conceivable holiday in between. One of my favorite Kolach rituals is that of greeting guests at the door (or a bride and groom in their new home) with bread and salt. As guests enter they are presented a tray of fresh bread with a small mound of salt that is to be sprinkled over the bread and eaten. The tradition is a way of saying "Even if all we have is bread and salt, you are welcome to share what we do have. Here's to wishes that you and your family will never want."

After the 1917 revolution, religious celebrations were forbidden, and Christmas became a winter festival with no connection to the birth of Jesus Christ. Many families secretly worshiped and kept their traditions. Since the fall of Communism in Eastern Europe, Christianity has been openly practiced, and the rich traditions of the Christmas season that were whispered for so long are now coming back.

For Christmas Eve supper, two cloths adorn the table—one for deceased family members and another for the living. Hay is scattered on the floor and tabletop as a reminder of the birth of Jesus in a manger. A large loaf of Kolach is placed in the center of the table with a single candle next to it. The supper is served in twelve courses, representing the twelve apostles.

KOLACH, OR KALACH, is showy bread shaped in a 4-strand loaf that is brought together in a circle. Although this is the traditional shape for the Christmas holidays, it can also be left in the shape of a long slender braid, as is done here. Just tuck the ends of the loaf under to give it a better shape.

MAKES I LARGE BRAIDED CIRCLE

FOR THE SPONGE

1 scant tablespoon or 1 (¼-ounce) package active dry yeast

¼ cup warm water (about 110°F)

1 teaspoon granulated sugar

FOR THE DOUGH

¾ cup milk

2 large eggs

6 tablespoons (¾ stick) unsalted butter, melted

½ cup granulated sugar

1 teaspoon salt

4 to 5 cups unbleached all-purpose flour

FOR THE TOPPING

1 large egg

1 tablespoon cold water

Poppy seeds, optional

Prepare sponge Combine the yeast, water, and sugar in a large bowl. Whisk until smooth. Let sit for 10 minutes until the mixture has doubled in size; note that there is no flour in this sponge.

By hand Heat the milk to 110°F and add it to the yeast along with the eggs, butter, sugar, salt, and 2 cups of the flour. Beat vigorously for 2 minutes. Gradually add the remaining flour ¼ cup at a time until the dough begins to pull away from the side of the bowl. Turn the dough out onto a floured work surface. Knead, adding flour a little at a time, until the dough is smooth and elastic.

By mixer Heat the milk to 110°F and add it to the yeast along with the eggs, butter, sugar, salt, and 2 cups of the flour. Using the mixer paddle, beat the mixture on medium-low speed for 2 minutes. Gradually add the remaining flour ¼ cup at a time until the dough begins to pull away from the side of the bowl. Change to the dough hook. Continue to add flour 1 tablespoon at a time until the dough just begins to clean the bowl. Knead 4 to 5 minutes on medium-low.

By food processor Heat the milk to 100°F and add it to the yeast along with the eggs and butter. In the bowl of the food processor fitted with the dough blade, combine the sugar, salt, and 4 cups flour with 4 or 5 pulses. With the food processor running, add the liquid ingredients as fast as the dry ingredients will accept them. If you hear a sputtering sound, pour the liquid slower. As soon as all liquid is added, turn the processor off. Check the liquid-to-flour ratio (see page 28). Pulse until the dough forms a ball, then process exactly 60 seconds.

By bread machine Put the yeast mixture, milk, eggs, and butter in the bread pan. Add the sugar, salt, and 4 cups flour to the bread pan. Select the Dough cycle and press Start. While the dough is mixing, check the liquid-to-flour ratio (see page 29). The machine stops after the kneading cycle. You may let the dough rise in the bread machine or a bowl.

First rise Put the dough in an oiled bowl and turn to coat the entire ball of dough with oil. Cover with a tightly woven towel and let rise until doubled, about one hour.

Shape Turn the dough out onto a lightly oiled work surface and divide into 4 equal pieces. Shape each piece into a 30-inch-long rope.

STEP 1: Pinch the end of the ropes together at the top and spread the ropes apart.

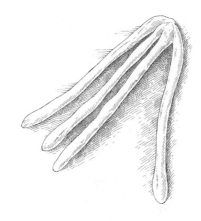

STEP 2: Take the rope on the far left and lay it over 2 ropes.

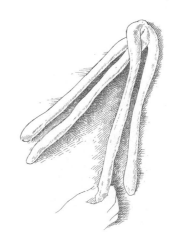

STEP 3: Lay the second rope from the left over the second rope from the right.

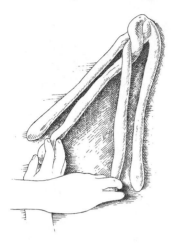

STEP 4: Take the rope on the far right and lay it over 2 ropes.

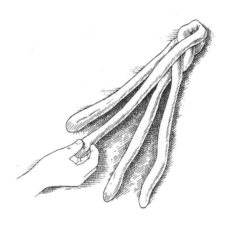

STEP 5: Take the second rope from the right and lay it over the second rope from the left.

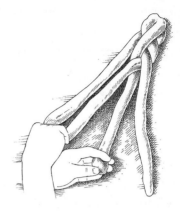

STEP 6: Go back to step 2 and continue this process until the ropes are too short to work with. Pinch the 4 ends together on each end and tuck under. Carefully lift the braid and place on a parchment-lined or well-greased baking sheet.

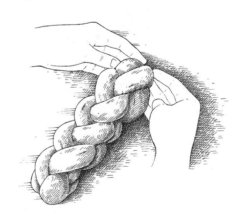

Second rise Cover with a tightly woven towel and let rise for 45 minutes.

Preheat oven About 10 minutes before baking, preheat the oven to 375°F.

Final preparation Beat the egg and cold water together and brush the loaf with the glaze, taking care not to let the glaze in the crevices of the loaf. Let sit 3 minutes and brush again. Sprinkle the loaf with poppy seeds if desired.

Bake and cool Bake for 30 minutes until the internal temperature of the bread reaches 190°F. Immediately remove the bread from the baking sheet and place on a rack to cool.

NOTE: This bread freezes nicely for up to 6 months. To serve, first thaw the bread, then reheat on a baking sheet or directly on the oven rack in a 375°F oven for 7 to 10 minutes.

Krendl

K rendl is a large pretzel-shaped sweet bread filled with fruit. It can also be shaped into a figure eight rather than a pretzel. Krendl is a Russian bread that is served on birthdays or name days with candles placed along the fat curve.

Name days are the feast days of the saint for whom a person is named or to celebrate the day on which a person is christened. Flowers are often given as gifts to celebrate name days (but there must be an even number; an odd number of flowers is for funerals).

THE FILLING for Krendl contains a mixture of fresh apples and dried fruits. You may vary the dried fruits to suit your taste, but the fresh apples are a must. I love to use tart apples like Granny Smiths because they keep their shape when baked. Make certain the fruit is finely chopped or the loaf will be misshapen.

MAKES 1 LARGE LOAF

FOR THE DOUGH

1 scant tablespoon or 1 (¼-ounce) package active dry yeast

¼ cup warm water (about 110°F)

¾ cup milk

3 large egg yolks, beaten

1 teaspoon vanilla extract

½ teaspoon almond extract

½ cup (1 stick) unsalted butter, softened

½ cup finely chopped candied orange peel (see Notes)

¼ cup granulated sugar

1 teaspoon salt

½ teaspoon ground cardamom

4 to 5 cups unbleached all-purpose flour

FOR THE FILLING

1 cup finely chopped fresh apples

1 cup finely chopped almonds

½ cup finely chopped pitted prunes

½ cup finely chopped dried apricots

½ cup brown sugar, packed

½ teaspoon ground cinnamon

¼ cup (½ stick) unsalted butter, melted

1 large egg yolk

1 teaspoon vegetable oil

2 teaspoons cold water

3 to 4 tablespoons sliced almonds

2 tablespoons granulated sugar

By hand In a large bowl, sprinkle the yeast in the water to soften. Heat the milk to 110°F and add it to the yeast along with the yolks, vanilla extract, almond extract, butter, orange peel, sugar, salt, cardamom, and 2 cups of the flour. Beat vigorously for 2 minutes. Gradually add the remaining flour ¼ cup at a time until the dough begins to pull away from the side of the bowl. Turn the dough out onto a floured work surface. Knead, adding flour a little at a time, until the dough is smooth and elastic.

By mixer In the mixer bowl, sprinkle the yeast in the water to soften. Heat the milk to 110°F and add it to the yeast along with the yolks, vanilla extract, almond extract, butter, orange peel, sugar, salt, cardamom, and 2 cups of the flour. Using the mixer paddle, beat the mixture on medium-low speed for 2 minutes. Gradually add the remaining flour ¼ cup at a time until the dough begins to pull away from the side of the bowl. Change to the dough hook. Continue to add flour 1 tablespoon at a time until the dough just begins to clean the bowl. Knead 4 to 5 minutes on medium-low.

By food processor In a large measuring cup or bowl, sprinkle the yeast in the water to soften. Heat the milk to 100°F and add it to the yeast along with the yolks, vanilla extract, butter, and almond extract. In the bowl of the food processor fitted with the dough blade, combine the butter, orange peel, sugar, salt, cardamom, and 4 cups flour with 4 or 5 pulses. With the food processor running, add the liquid ingredients as fast as the dry ingredients will accept them. If you hear a sputtering sound, pour the liquid slower. As soon as all the liquid is added, turn the processor off. Check the liquid-to-flour ratio (see page 28). Pulse until the dough forms a ball, then process exactly 60 seconds.

By bread machine Put the water, milk, yolks, vanilla extract, almond extract, butter, and orange peel in the bread pan. Add the sugar, salt, cardamom, and 4 cups flour to the bread pan, then sprinkle with the yeast. Select the Dough cycle and press Start. While the dough is mixing, check the liquid-to-flour ratio (see page 29). The machine stops after the kneading cycle. You may let the dough rise in the bread machine or a bowl.

First rise Put the dough in an oiled bowl and turn to coat the entire ball of dough with oil. Cover with a tightly woven towel and let rise until doubled, about one hour.

Prepare filling In a medium bowl, toss the apples, almonds, prunes, apricots, brown sugar, and cinnamon together to combine. Set aside.

Shape *To shape in a pretzel,* turn the dough out onto a lightly oiled work surface and roll into a *shape* about 36 inches long and 10 inches wide in the middle with the ends tapering to about 4 inches wide. Brush with the melted butter, leaving a ½-inch border at one long edge. The butter-free edge ensures that the dough will adhere to itself when you pinch to seal it. Spread the filling evenly over the butter and roll up into a 36-inch roll. Shape into a U. Twist the ends together twice and tuck them into the center of the U. Place on a parchment-lined or well-greased baking sheet.

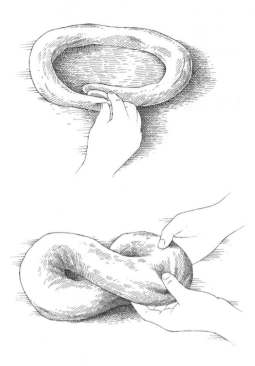

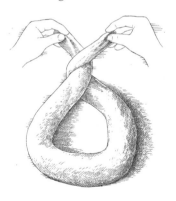

To shape a figure eight, turn the dough out onto a lightly oiled work surface and roll into a rectangle 10 by 30 inches. Brush with the melted butter, leaving a ½-inch border at one long edge. Spread the filling evenly over the butter and roll up into a 30-inch roll. Bring the ends together and pinch to seal. Twist the dough over the part where the dough is pinched so you don't see where it is joined. Place on a parchment-lined or well-greased baking sheet.

Second rise Cover with a tightly woven towel and let rise for 45 minutes.

Preheat oven About 10 minutes before baking, preheat the oven to 375°F.

Final preparation Whisk the yolk, oil, and cold water together. Brush lightly over the loaf, wait 5 minutes, and brush once more. Sprinkle with the sliced almonds, then with the sugar.

Bake and cool Bake 25 minutes until the internal temperature of the bread reaches 190°F. Immediately remove the bread from the baking sheet and place on a rack to cool.

NOTES: If you prefer to make your own candied peel, see page 326.

This bread freezes nicely for up to 6 months. To serve, first thaw the bread, then reheat on a baking sheet in a 375°F oven for 7 to 10 minutes.

Kulich ◆ Paskha

Russian Easter, the Christianization of an old Slavic tradition of celebrating the arrival of spring, is the biggest event in the spiritual life of a Christian and the height of the religious year. No other holiday in the Russian Orthodox calendar revolves so completely around food.

Holy Week, the days preceding Christ's ascension into heaven, begins with Maundy Thursday, the day of spiritual purification and prayer. It is also the day when *pysanki,* the beautiful intricately decorated eggs, are painted. Good Friday is the day that Jesus was crucified and died, followed by Holy Saturday, the day of sorrow.

On Saturday afternoon, the Easter table is set and left for the whole week. In the evening everyone heads off to church; even those who don't regularly attend turn out for the Easter midnight mass. During part of the service the priest blesses baskets of food containing eggs, Kulich (a rich spiced bread), Paskha (a creamy, sweetened cheese), and *kolbasa* (or kielbasa).

After church the blessed foods are taken home and placed on the table amid garlands and flowers. In the center of the table is a lamb molded from butter, symbolizing Jesus, the Lamb of God. For the feast after mass, eggs are the first food to break the fast and symbolize the renewal of life.

Next a slice of Kulich with a wedge of Paskha is served. Kulich is the first bread and Paskha the first cheese to be eaten after the Lenten fast. The top of the Kulich dome is draped with white icing to represent the round domes of Russian churches covered with snow. Traditionally a single red rose is laid on top of the glazed bread, representing the blood of Christ shed for all Christians.

Finally the kielbasa is eaten. Since this sausage is made from several types of meat and spices, it represents all the meat that was forbidden during Lent.

On Easter Sunday men go visiting, while women stay home to receive guests and regale them with the abundance of their tables. Since the women have spent many days baking in preparation for this time of visiting, there is always a fresh Kulich on the table for the next set of guests. On Easter Monday women go visiting. Guests roam from house to house greeting all by saying, "Christ is risen," followed with the reply, "Indeed he has!"

Kulich

THOUGH KULICH IS A ROBUST BREAD, it is traditionally cooled on its side on a soft pillow to prevent the loaf from becoming misshapen. Once the bread has cooled, it should stand as a tall cylinder. This saffron-scented bread is topped with a mushroom-type crown said to represent the snow-covered round domes of the Russian churches. The crown is first cut off the top, then the loaf is sliced horizontally. The crown is always replaced after slicing so that the loaf doesn't dry out and keeps its beautiful appearance.

MAKES 2 TALL LOAVES

FOR THE DOUGH

1 scant tablespoon or 1 (¼-ounce) package active dry yeast

¼ cup warm water (about 110°F)

½ cup milk

¼ teaspoon or 1 large pinch saffron

4 large eggs, beaten

½ teaspoon ground cardamom

1 teaspoon salt

1 teaspoon vanilla extract

1 tablespoon finely grated lemon zest

½ cup granulated sugar

¾ cup (1½ sticks) unsalted butter, cold

4 to 5 cups unbleached all-purpose flour

½ cup slivered almonds, toasted

1 cup golden raisins

¼ cup finely chopped candied orange peel (see Notes)

FOR THE ICING

1 cup confectioners' sugar

2 to 4 tablespoons heavy cream

Nonpareils (tiny multicolored candies) to sprinkle on top

By hand In a large bowl, sprinkle the yeast in the water to soften. Heat the milk to 110°F and add the saffron. Let sit 5 minutes. Add the milk, eggs, cardamom, salt, vanilla, zest, and sugar to the yeast. Using a pastry blender, cut the butter into 2 cups of the flour until the butter resembles small grains of rice. Add to the yeast mixture and beat vigorously for 2 minutes. Add the almonds, raisins, and orange peel and stir to combine. Gradually add the remaining flour ¼ cup at a time until the dough begins to pull away from the side of the bowl. Turn the dough out onto a floured work surface. Knead, adding flour a little at a time, until the dough is smooth and elastic.

By mixer In the mixer bowl, sprinkle the yeast in the water to soften. Heat the milk to 110°F and add the saffron. Let sit 5 minutes. Add the milk, eggs, cardamon, salt, vanilla, zest, and sugar to the yeast. Using a pastry blender, cut the butter into 2 cups of the flour until the butter resembles small grains of rice. Add the butter mixture to the yeast. Using the mixer paddle, beat the mixture on medium-low speed for 2 minutes. Add the almonds, raisins, and orange peel, then gradually add the remaining flour ¼ cup at a time until the dough begins to pull away from the side of the bowl. Change to the dough hook. Continue to add flour 1 tablespoon at a time until the dough just begins to clean the bowl. Knead 4 to 5 minutes on medium-low.

By food processor In a large measuring cup or bowl, sprinkle the yeast in the water to soften. Heat the milk to 110°F and add the saffron. Let sit 5 minutes. Add the milk, eggs, cardamom, salt, vanilla, and zest to the yeast and stir to combine. In the bowl of the food processor fitted with the metal blade, combine the sugar, butter, and 4 cups flour. Pulse until the butter resembles small grains of rice. With the food processor running, add the yeast mixture as fast as the dry ingredients will accept it. If you hear a sputtering

sound, pour the liquid slower. As soon as all the liquid is added, turn the processor off. Check the liquid-to-flour ratio (see page 28). Pulse until the dough forms a ball, then process exactly 60 seconds.

By bread machine Put the water, milk, saffron, eggs, and vanilla in the bread pan. Cut the butter into ¼-inch pieces and add to the bread pan. If your machine has an Add Fruit cycle, add the almonds, raisins, and orange peel when prompted; if not, add them with the butter. Add the cardamom, salt, zest, sugar, and 4 cups flour to the bread pan, then sprinkle with the yeast. Select the Dough cycle and press Start. While the dough is mixing, check the liquid-to-flour ratio (see page 29). The machine stops after the kneading cycle. You may let the dough rise in the bread machine or a bowl.

First rise Put the dough in an oiled bowl and turn to coat the entire ball of dough with oil. Cover with a tightly woven towel and let rise until doubled, about three hours.

Shape Turn the dough out onto a lightly oiled work surface and divide in half. Knead each piece into a smooth ball, then stretch the dough slightly so that they fit in 2 well-greased 3-pound coffee cans, measuring about 5½ inches high and 4 inches wide.

Second rise Cover with a tightly woven towel and let rise for 45 minutes.

Preheat oven Since the loaves will be in tall cans or molds, place the rack in the lower third of the oven to give plenty of room for rising, and remove the top rack. About 10 minutes before baking, preheat the oven to 375°F.

Bake and cool Bake for 35 minutes until the internal temperature of the bread reaches 190°F. Let the bread cool in the cans for 5 minutes, then remove the bread from the cans and place on a rack to cool for 20 to 30 minutes.

Finish Combine the confectioners' sugar with enough heavy cream to reach the consistency of honey. Pour over the top of each loaf and sprinkle with nonpareils.

NOTES: If you prefer to make your own candied peel, see page 326.

This bread freezes nicely for up to 6 months. If freezing the bread, do not ice it until you're ready serve it. To serve, first thaw the bread and wrap it in foil. Reheat in a 375°F oven for 10 minutes. Finish with icing as directed.

Paskha

PASHKA is always served with Kulich. It is traditionally shaped into a pyramid with the letters *XB* on the sides. Old molds in Russia have the letters pressed into the sides of the mold. For those who don't have the proper mold, use a 6-inch flowerpot with a hole in the bottom (it doesn't matter if it is plastic or clay; it's the drainage hole that's most important). You can form the *XB* with fruit or nuts. Many from the old country do not like almonds in the Paskha because they feel it should be very creamy, not gritty; I agree.

MAKES ENOUGH TO ACCOMPANY
2 KULICH LOAVES

3 cups small-curd cottage or wet farmer's cheese

8 ounces cream cheese

¾ cup granulated sugar

3 large hard-cooked egg yolks

1 teaspoon vanilla extract

¾ cup heavy cream

½ cup finely chopped almonds, toasted, optional

¼ cup finely chopped candied orange peel (see Notes)

½ cup raisins

¼ cup coarsely chopped candied cherries (see Notes) or well-drained maraschino cherries

Additional almonds, raisins, and cherries for decoration

Make cheese In a food processor or blender, combine the cottage cheese, cream cheese, sugar, yolks, and vanilla. Process to combine. If your processor or blender is small, divide the mixture in half and work with 2 batches. With the food processor running, gradually add the cream in a thin stream and process until combined. Turn the mixture into a large bowl and fold in the almonds if using, orange peel, raisins, and cherries.

Prepare container Line a Paskha mold, 6-inch flowerpot, or tall cylindrical 4-cup container with holes in the bottom with 2 layers of damp cheesecloth, allowing the excess cloth to hang over the sides. Spoon the cheese mixture into the pot and pleat the excess cloth evenly over the top.

Press Now the cheese needs to be compressed to squeeze out the excess liquid. I cut a round from a cardboard box the same size as the top of my mold and wrap it in foil. You can also use a large plastic lid cut to size or a small plate. Place this on top of the cheese and place a weight of some kind—a brick, several cans of food, a large rock—on top. Put the mold on a rack over a bowl to collect the liquid as it seeps out and refrigerate for 12 hours.

Unmold Remove the weights, unfold the cheesecloth covering the top of the cheese, and invert the mold onto a plate. Carefully remove the cheesecloth. Use additional fruit and nuts to decorate the cheese. Traditionally the letters *XB* are imprinted into the side of the cheese as a symbol that "Christ has risen." Allow the cheese to sit for 30 minutes at room temperature before serving with Easter Kulich.

NOTE: If you prefer to make your own candied peel, see page 326. For your own candied fruit, see page 325.

Zwieback

Most Americans know Zwieback (the word is German for "twice-baked") as a rusk-type bread that is first baked as a loaf, then sliced and toasted. Many of us gave these crisp breads to our teething babies or ate them soaked in warm milk for an upset tummy. However, Russian Mennonites know Zwieback as the traditional tall, soft, double-stacked bun—a small bun on the bottom with an even smaller bun placed on top—that is served at all festive occasions.

Zwieback are essential for weddings and funerals in Russia. For a traditional Mennonite wedding, the bride's family treated guests to a full meal the evening before the wedding, a full meal at noon on the wedding day, and then *faspa*—a late afternoon or evening snack—plus another full meal later in the evening.

Since weddings were well attended—often three hundred to five hundred guests—and the bride's family couldn't possibly bake for this many guests, it was customary for the village women to help out. They contributed butter, eggs, and cream. They helped mix the dough, then divided it up to be baked in their own homes. There were so many Zwieback baked for these large occasions that one whole room was cleaned and spread with fresh hay, so the women would have somewhere to spread the buns for cooling.

Funerals were often even more of a social gathering than weddings. After the burial ceremony, all family and friends gathered for coffee and Zwieback. This *faspa* hour was a time to comfort the family and say farewell to the departed. Funeral Zwieback were smaller than regular Zwieback, and, once again, all the village women shared in contributing ingredients as well as doing the actual baking.

ZWIEBACK are traditionally shaped by squeezing off a ball of dough between the thumb and index finger and placing it on a baking sheet. A smaller dough ball is pinched off and pressed deeply into the larger ball so that it doesn't topple off during baking. If the top leans or slides off, those Zwieback are referred to as "lazy Zwieback," and if the top comes off completely, you can expect company to drop in after church. There is a strict rule that says you may not spread butter or jam or anything else on Zwieback, since they already are baked with everything you need in them. However, they can be dunked into coffee and sprinkled with a little sugar before eating.

MAKES 30 BUNS

FOR THE SPONGE

1 scant tablespoon or 1 (¼-ounce) package active dry yeast

¼ cup warm water (about 110°F)

¾ cup warm milk (about 110°F)

1 tablespoon granulated sugar

1 cup unbleached all-purpose flour

FOR THE DOUGH

½ cup mashed potatoes, unseasoned

¼ cup lard or vegetable shortening

½ cup (1 stick) unsalted butter, softened

1 teaspoon salt

3 to 4 cups unbleached all-purpose flour

FOR THE TOPPING

¼ cup (½ stick) unsalted butter, melted

Prepare sponge In a medium bowl, sprinkle the yeast in the water to soften. Add the milk, sugar, and flour and whisk to combine. Cover with plastic wrap and let sit at room temperature for 45 minutes.

By hand In a large bowl, combine the potatoes, lard, butter, and salt. Add the sponge and beat until smooth. Gradually add the flour ¼ cup at a time until the dough begins to pull away from the side of the bowl. Turn the dough out onto a floured work surface. Knead, adding flour a little at a time, until the dough is smooth and elastic.

By mixer In the mixer bowl with the paddle, combine the potatoes, lard, butter, and salt. Add the sponge and beat until smooth. Gradually add the flour ¼ cup at a time until the dough begins to pull away from the side of the bowl. Change to the dough hook. Continue to add flour 1 tablespoon at a time until the dough just begins to clean the bowl. Knead 4 to 5 minutes on medium-low.

By food processor In the bowl of the food processor fitted with the dough blade, combine the potatoes, lard, butter, salt, and 3 cups flour with 4 or 5 pulses. Add the sponge and pulse until combined. Check the liquid-to-flour ratio (see page 28). Pulse until the dough forms a ball, then process exactly 60 seconds.

By bread machine Put the potatoes, lard, butter, and sponge into the bread pan. Add the salt and 3 cups flour. Select the Dough cycle and press Start. While the dough is mixing, check the liquid-to-flour ratio (see page 29). The machine stops after the kneading cycle. You may let the dough rise in the bread machine or a bowl.

First rise Put the dough in an oiled bowl and turn to coat the entire ball of dough with oil. Cover with a tightly woven towel and let rise until doubled, about one hour.

Shape Turn the dough out onto a lightly oiled work surface. Divide the dough into 2 pieces, using one-third of the dough for one piece and two-thirds of the dough for the other. Divide each piece into 30 smaller pieces and shape them into balls. Place the larger balls about 2 inches apart on parchment-lined or well-greased baking sheets. You will need to use 2 baking sheets to ensure that the buns do not touch while rising and baking. Flatten these balls to about 1 inch thick.

Flatten the smaller balls so that they are just slightly smaller than the larger balls on the baking sheet. Center a small ball on each of the larger balls. Oil your index finger and press your finger into the center of the top ball all the way through the bottom ball to the baking sheet.

Second rise Cover with tightly woven towels and let rise for 45 minutes.

Preheat oven About 10 minutes before baking, preheat the oven to 375°F.

Bake and cool Bake for 20 minutes until the buns are very lightly browned. Immediately remove the buns from the baking sheets and place on a rack.

Finish Brush the buns with melted butter while they are still warm.

NOTE: These buns freeze nicely for up to 6 months. To serve, first thaw and wrap in foil, then reheat in a 375°F oven for 10 to 12 minutes.

Steamed Buns

*T*he tiny island of Cheung Chau off Hong Kong hosts the world's only annual Bun Festival. It is held in the fourth Chinese lunar month, usually around the end of April or first part of May.

Legend tells of the powerful god Pak Tai, who drove away wicked pirates who were launching attacks on Cheung Chau. The island was plagued by a series of misfortunes thought to be caused by the spirits of the pirates' victims. A Taoist priest advised islanders to placate the restless wandering spirits by making offerings to them each year.

Originally the Bun Festival paid homage to the gods and placated the haunting spirits. Today the celebration is also intended to apologize to the ghosts of any animals or fish that have been killed for food. In honor of these creatures, the priest at the Pak Tai Temple reads a decree on the first night of the festival stating that no animal or fish will be killed or eaten on the island during the three-day festival. The decree is honored by everyone on the island—even those who are not Chinese.

Days before the festival, scaffolding is erected and decorated with bright paper flowers and written prayers for good luck and health, offerings of thanks for the god's blessings, and the names of contributors (in the hopes that they will receive extra consideration!).

On the square outside the Pak Tai Temple, three gigantic bamboo "bun towers," each about 50 feet tall, are erected. Thousands of puffy white buns filled with lotus paste decorate these towers. Each bun is marked in deep pink with a Chinese character wishing good fortune.

During the week there are celebrations and presentations in the temple square, with entertainment by martial arts performers, folk dancers, and Chinese opera companies. The children are brightly costumed as Chinese heroes, fairies, demons, scholars, beauties, and celebrities.

At dusk on the last night of the festival, dozens of "nether feasts" are prepared. The spirits are called from the cemetery with burning incense and prayers to eat their fill. After the last spirit finishes his dinner, he is chased off in the hope that all the spirits are well fed and will stay away for another year.

At fifteen minutes before midnight, the rite is brought to its climax when a paper effigy of the King of Ghosts is set on fire. The culmination of the festival is one of the most colorful and beautiful parades in the world. Beginning in the square of Pak Tai Temple, it is led by lion dancers and dragons, followed by kung fu club members with their banners held high, storybook characters walking far above the group on extremely tall stilts, and Taoist priests in their traditional dress. There is much merrymaking, with fireworks and dancing.

The most spectacular entries in the parade are the Piaose, a selected group of young children in bright costumes and very heavy makeup. These apparitions seem to "float" above the crowds. If you look very closely, you can see the cunningly concealed system of wires and rods holding them above the crowds.

The parade ends back at the Pak Tai Temple square, where several men climb the immense bun towers to "harvest" the buns. The buns are collected in large bamboo baskets and distributed to the villagers, who believe the buns bring good luck, especially those from the top of the heap. The more buns one can claim, the more luck one will experience.

THE AUTHENTIC RECIPE for these steamed buns has no salt. I find the buns flavorless without it, so I add a teaspoon to bring out the flavors of the other ingredients. For the festival, the dough is marked with special Chinese characters for good fortune.

Lotus paste filling is a combination of lotus seeds and lye water boiled and blended into a paste. Lotus seeds are small oval seeds with a slight hint of almond. Since adding peanut oil and cooked glutinous rice flour results in a sticky paste, I prefer substituting a can of commercially prepared lotus paste. All the ingredients here are available in Asian markets or through Internet sources.

To steam the buns, you'll need a stacking bamboo steamer, or you can rig a steamer by using a large pot. Place a round cake rack or round thin piece of wood, about an inch smaller than the diameter of your pot, on an upturned cup. This allows the steam to circulate through the cooker. Put about 1 inch of water in the bottom of the pot. The rack or wood round should be about 1 inch above the water, and there should be at least 2 inches of space between the buns and the lid of the pot. You will probably have to steam in several batches (place the buns for later batches in the refrigerator to retard their rising). Note that the filling should sit overnight before you use it.

MAKES 24 BUNS

FOR THE FILLING

3½ cups lotus seeds

1½ tablespoons lye water (kan sui)

2 to 3 tablespoons cold water

1¼ cups peanut oil

2 cups granulated sugar

1 tablespoon maltose

1 tablespoon cooked glutinous rice flour (kao fun)

FOR THE SPONGE

1 teaspoon granulated sugar

1 cup warm water (about 110°F)

1 scant tablespoon or 1 (¼-ounce) package active dry yeast

1 cup unbleached all-purpose flour

FOR THE DOUGH

1 teaspoon salt

¼ cup granulated sugar

2 tablespoons lard, vegetable shortening, or chicken fat

3 to 4 cups unbleached all-purpose flour

FOR THE GLAZE

1 large egg

1 tablespoon cold water

Prepare filling Combine the seeds and lye water. Mix well and let sit for 20 minutes. Pour in enough boiling water to cover the seeds; allow an extra inch of water for expansion. Let sit for 20 to 30 minutes. Strain and wash the lotus seeds well to remove the skins.

Cover the lotus seeds with fresh water and bring to a boil over medium-high heat. Cook until the seeds are soft, about 20 minutes. Put the seeds in a blender with 1 tablespoon cold water and blend to a thick paste. Add additional water if necessary to make a thick paste about the consistency of peanut butter.

Heat ¼ cup of the oil and ½ cup of the sugar in a wok or large skillet. Cook over medium heat until the sugar turns light brown; add the lotus paste and the remaining 1½ cups sugar. Stir until smooth. Add the remaining 1 cup oil 1 tablespoon at a time, stirring well after each addition, until the paste is thick. After all the oil is absorbed, add the maltose and stir well.

Press the *kao fun* through a sieve and stir it into the paste. Cover and let sit overnight at room temperature before using.

Prepare sponge In a large bowl, dissolve the sugar in the water. Sprinkle the yeast in the water to soften. Add the flour and beat until smooth. Cover with plastic wrap and let sit for 30 minutes.

By hand Add the salt, sugar, fat, and 1 cup flour to the sponge. Beat vigorously for 2 minutes. Gradually add the remaining flour ¼ cup at a time until the dough begins to pull away from the side of the bowl. Turn the dough out onto a floured work surface. Knead, adding flour a little at a time, until the dough is smooth and elastic.

By mixer In the mixer bowl, add the salt, sugar, fat, and 1 cup flour to the sponge. Using the mixer paddle, beat the mixture on medium-low speed for 2 minutes. Gradually add the remaining flour ¼ cup at a time until the dough begins to pull away from the side of the bowl. Change to the dough hook. Continue to add flour 1 tablespoon at a time until the dough just begins to clean the bowl. Knead 4 to 5 minutes on medium-low.

By food processor In the bowl of the food processor fitted with the dough blade, combine the salt, sugar, fat, and 3 cups flour with 4 or 5 pulses. With the food processor running, add the sponge as fast as the dry ingredients will accept it. If you hear a sputtering sound, pour the sponge slower. As soon as all the sponge is added, turn the processor off. Check the liquid-to-flour ratio (see page 28). Pulse until the dough forms a ball, then process exactly 60 seconds.

By bread machine Put the sponge and fat in the bread pan. Add the salt, sugar, and 3 cups flour. Select the Dough cycle and press Start. While the dough is mixing, check the liquid-to-flour ratio (see page 29). The machine stops after the kneading cycle. You may let the dough rise in the bread machine or a bowl.

First rise Put the dough in an oiled bowl and turn to coat the entire ball of dough with oil. Cover with a tightly woven towel and let rise for two hours.

Shape Turn the dough out onto a lightly oiled work surface and knead for 2 minutes until the dough is tight and elastic again. Divide the dough in half and roll each half into a 12-inch-long cylinder. Using a serrated or extra-sharp knife, slice each cylinder into 12 equal pieces. Press each piece of dough into a 3-inch round with the outer edge being thinner than the center. Place about 1 table-spoon filling in the center of each round. Bring the edges of the dough together over the filling, pleating to make the dough fit. Twist together to seal. Place on a lightly floured work surface.

Second rise Cover with a tightly woven towel and let rest for 25 minutes.

Preheat About 10 minutes before steaming, place water in the bottom of the steamer and bring to a boil. Reduce the heat to low.

Final preparation Beat the egg and water together and brush over the top and sides of each bun.

Steam Place as many buns as will fit in a single layer about 1 inch apart on the steamer basket or rack. Cover and steam for 20 minutes. Refrigerate the uncooked buns for later batches. Take care not to burn your-self when removing buns from the steamer.

Cool Place the buns on a tightly woven towel to cool.

NOTE: This bread does not freeze well. The buns are best served warm. To reheat them, steam them for a couple of minutes.

12

Scandinavia

Kringle

Kringle is a favorite bread to serve at Christmas, Easter, anniversary celebrations, or any special occasion in Denmark. The bread was developed in the 1800s when Danish bakers went on strike to receive wages rather than just their customary room and board. Bakery owners rebelled and brought in bakers from Austria instead. The Austrian bakers had a unique method of folding light yeast dough with layers of butter to produce a flaky crust. When the strike was finally settled, the Danish bakers were so impressed with the Viennese bread that they adopted the technique themselves.

Many Danes settled in Wisconsin in the late 1800s and brought with them their craft of making Kringle and other Danish pastries. Originally Kringle was made into a pretzel shape, but customers complained that there wasn't enough filling in the overlapping areas of dough. The current horseshoe shape was developed in Wisconsin and spread back to Denmark.

DON'T THROW OUT THE EGG WHITES—all will be used before you finish. Kringle dough is mixed, not kneaded, so a bread machine is not recommended. The dough must be made a day ahead and refrigerated overnight. The almond filling is the most traditional, but fruit and nut fillings are gaining popularity.

MAKES 2 HORSESHOE-SHAPED LOAVES

FOR THE DOUGH

1 scant tablespoon or 1 (¼-ounce) package active dry yeast

¼ cup warm water (about 110°F)

¾ cup heavy cream

3 large egg yolks

1 large egg white

3 tablespoons granulated sugar

1 teaspoon salt

1 teaspoon ground cardamom

3½ cups unbleached all-purpose flour

1 cup (2 sticks) unsalted butter, very cold

Fillings (recipes follow)

FOR THE TOPPING

1 large egg white

Sliced almonds

2 tablespoons granulated sugar

Prepare dough In a large measuring cup or medium bowl, sprinkle the yeast in the water to soften. Heat the cream to 100°F and add it to the yeast along with the egg yolks and egg white. Whisk to combine.

In a large bowl, combine the sugar, salt, cardamom, and flour. Using a pastry blender or 2 knives, cut the butter into the flour mixture until it is the size of tiny peas. This process also can be done easily in a food processor. Add the yeast mixture to the dry ingredients and stir just until combined. Do not mix too much, because you do not want to soften the cold butter. You should see small flour-coated pieces of butter throughout the dough.

Overnight rise Put the dough in an oiled bowl and turn to coat the entire ball of dough with oil. Cover with a piece of plastic wrap and a tightly woven towel and refrigerate 12 hours or overnight.

Prepare fillings Prepare the fillings just before using. Each recipe will fill one loaf (half of the dough). If you do not want an assortment, the filling recipes are easily doubled to fill both loaves.

Shape Turn the dough out onto a lightly oiled work surface and divide in half. Roll each half into a 24-inch square. Fold the dough in half from top to bottom, then fold the dough in half from side to side to make a 12-inch square. Cover with a towel and let rest 10 minutes.

Working with 1 square of dough at a time, roll the dough into a 12 by 24-inch rectangle. Spread 1 recipe of filling evenly over two-thirds of the dough, filling an area of 8 by 24 inches. Fold the portion of dough that has no filling onto the center third of filled dough, then fold the other third of dough to the center, forming a 4 by 24-inch rectangle. Pinch the long edge to seal.

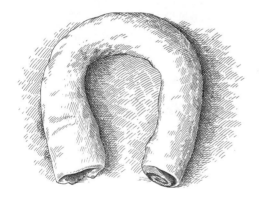

Place the dough seam side down on a parchment-lined or well-greased baking sheet. Bring the ends of the dough almost together (about 4 inches apart) to form a horseshoe. Repeat with the second piece of dough. If you cannot get both Kringles on a baking sheet, cover the second one and put it in the refrigerator until the first Kringle finishes baking, then bake as below.

Second rise Cover with tightly woven towels and let rise for one hour.

Preheat oven About 10 minutes before baking, preheat the oven to 375°F.

Final preparation For the topping, beat the egg white with a whisk or fork until frothy and brush over the loaves. Sprinkle with sliced almonds and then granulated sugar.

Bake and cool Bake for 25 minutes until the internal temperature of the bread reaches 190°F. Immediately remove the bread from the baking sheet and place on a rack to cool.

NOTE: This bread freezes nicely for up to 6 months. To serve, first thaw the bread, then reheat on a baking sheet in a 375°F oven for 7 to 10 minutes.

Almond Filling

2 tablespoons unsalted butter, softened

½ cup granulated sugar

1 (7- or 8-ounce) can almond paste

1 large egg white

½ teaspoon almond extract

In a mixer or medium bowl, combine the butter, sugar, almond paste, egg white, and almond extract and beat until smooth and creamy. Use to fill one loaf.

Apple Pecan Filling

I'M PARTIAL to Granny Smith apples because I like their tart flavor and they keep their shape during baking.

½ cup light brown sugar, packed

1 cup finely chopped, peeled, and cored apples

½ cup finely chopped pecans

2 tablespoons unsalted butter, melted

1 teaspoon ground cinnamon

In a medium bowl, stir the sugar, apples, pecans, butter, and cinnamon together until well mixed. Use to fill one loaf.

Date Walnut Filling

½ cup light brown sugar, packed

1 cup finely chopped pitted dates

½ cup finely chopped walnuts

2 tablespoons unsalted butter, melted

In a medium bowl, stir the sugar, dates, walnuts, and butter together until well mixed. Use to fill one loaf.

Joululimppa

ikkujoulu is a relatively new Finnish tradition that began in the 1920s. The Christmas season begins sometime in October when the women of many church groups and organizations gather together for Pikkujoulu, or Little Christmas. They plan the holiday bazaars, make Christmas decorations, and listen to talks, Christmas programs, and music.

Advent, the penitent period preparing for the celebration of the birth of Christ, begins four Sundays before Christmas and officially starts the holiday. Many churches hold concerts featuring Volger's *Hosianna*. Children hang Advent calendars with small pockets or windows that hold small treats for each day until Christmas.

Families hang a horizontal wreath containing four Advent candles in a circle. One candle is lit on the first Sunday of Advent during an hour of contemplation and then extinguished. On the second Sunday, the first candle and another one are lit for an hour and then extinguished. This pattern continues each Sunday until Christmas.

Baking during the holidays is a Finnish tradition; it begins early and continues throughout the month. There's a different cake, cookie, or bread scent almost every day. Joululimppa, an orange rye bread, is one of the favorites for the holidays.

On Christmas Eve the family goes out and selects a beautiful spruce tree to be brought home and decorated by the children. The house is scrubbed from top to bottom, and the women begin cooking the lavish Christmas dinner to be served later in the evening.

One of the most important Christmas traditions for the Finns is the Christmas Eve sauna. The sauna is an essential part of Finnish life and is usually heated several times a week. The Christmas sauna is an affair for the whole family, including all the children. The sauna marks the end of the holiday rush and the beginning of the holiday itself.

Legend states that Father Christmas actually lives in the northern part of Finland in Korvatunturi, just north of the Arctic Circle. He visits each home in person on Christmas Eve while the children are awake. (Most often it is the father, older brother, neighbor, or relative in full costume.) When Father Christmas arrives, he yells as he enters the door, "Are there any good children here?" This, of course, receives an enthusiastic "Yes!"

Father Christmas brings the gifts in a large basket. The children sing songs for him, but, of course, he cannot spend too much time in any one place, since he has many homes to visit. He leaves his basket of gifts for the children to hand out. Once all the gifts have been distributed, the traditional Christmas dinner is served. After dinner many families visit cemeteries to leave candles on the graves of loved ones.

THIS SLIGHTLY SWEET, orange-flavored bread is served often throughout the Christmas holidays in Finland. The Finns prefer using dark rye for their breads—check the Sources on page 331—but light rye can be used if you cannot find the dark.

MAKES 2 LOAVES

FOR THE DOUGH

1 scant tablespoon or 1 (¼-ounce) package active dry yeast

¼ cup warm water (about 110°F)

1¼ cups buttermilk

¼ cup molasses

1 teaspoon salt

1 teaspoon caraway seeds

2 tablespoons finely grated orange zest

¾ cup rye flour

¾ cup whole-wheat flour

2½ to 3 cups unbleached all-purpose flour

FOR THE TOPPING

2 tablespoons hot water

1 tablespoon molasses

By hand In a large bowl, sprinkle the yeast in the water to soften. Heat the buttermilk to 110°F and add it to the yeast along with the molasses, salt, caraway, zest, rye flour, whole-wheat flour, and 1 cup of the all-purpose flour. Beat vigorously for 2 minutes. Gradually add the remaining all-purpose flour ¼ cup at a time until the dough begins to pull away from the side of the bowl. Turn the dough out onto a floured work surface. Knead, adding flour a little at a time, until the dough is smooth and elastic.

By mixer In the mixer bowl, sprinkle the yeast in the water to soften. Heat the buttermilk to 110°F and add it to the yeast along with the molasses, salt, caraway, zest, rye flour, whole-wheat flour, and 1 cup of the all-purpose flour. Using the mixer's paddle, beat the mixture on medium-low speed for 2 minutes. Gradually add the remaining all-purpose flour ¼ cup at a time until the dough begins to pull away from the side of the bowl. Change to the dough hook. Continue to add all-purpose flour 1 tablespoon at a time until the dough just begins to clean the bowl. Knead 4 to 5 minutes on medium-low.

By food processor In a medium measuring cup or bowl, sprinkle the yeast in the water to soften. Heat the buttermilk to 100°F and add it to the yeast along with the molasses. In the bowl of the food processor fitted with the dough blade, combine the salt, caraway, zest, rye flour, whole-wheat flour, and 2½ cups all-purpose flour with 4 or 5 pulse. With the food processor running, add the liquid ingredients as fast as the dry ingredients will accept them. If you hear a sputtering sound, pour the liquid slower. As soon as all the liquid is added, turn the processor off. Check the liquid-to-flour ratio (see page 28). Pulse until the dough forms a ball, then process exactly 60 seconds.

By bread machine Put the water, buttermilk, and molasses in the bread pan. Add the salt, caraway, zest, rye flour, whole-wheat flour, and 2½ cups all-purpose flour to the bread pan, then sprinkle with yeast. Select the Dough cycle and press Start. While the dough is mixing, check the liquid-to-flour ratio (see page 29). The machine stops after the kneading cycle. You may let the dough rise in the bread machine or a bowl.

First rise Put the dough in an oiled bowl and turn to coat the entire ball of dough with oil. Cover with a tightly woven towel and let rise until doubled, about 1½ hours.

Shape Turn the dough out onto a lightly oiled work surface and divide in half. Shape each half into a ball and place in well-greased 8-inch round pans. Flatten the center of the dough so it is slightly concave and the edge of the dough almost reaches the side of the pan.

Second rise Cover with a tightly woven towel and let rise for one hour.

Preheat oven About 10 minutes before baking, preheat the oven to 375°F.

Final preparation Combine the molasses with the hot water and brush over the top of each loaf.

Bake and cool Bake for 25 minutes until the internal temperature of the bread reaches 190°F. Immediately remove the bread from the pans and place on a rack to cool.

NOTE: This bread freezes nicely for up to 6 months. To serve, first thaw the bread and wrap in foil. Reheat in a 350°F oven for 12 to 15 minutes.

Pääsiäisleipä

In Finland "silent week" begins on Palm Sunday and ends on Easter Sunday. On Palm Sunday people greet friends and relatives by lightly hitting them with twigs. The custom symbolizes the people's greeting Jesus as he rode into Jerusalem on a donkey by swinging palm fronds. Since palm fronds are hard to come by in Finland, the Finns use twigs instead.

In olden days special restrictions were imposed during silent week. People dressed in dark clothing, and the children were on their best behavior. On Good Friday chores were banned. No one could build a cooking fire in the stove, the floor could not be swept, women were forbidden to spin, and no one was permitted to go visiting. Dining was allowed only after sunset. In some parts of Finland children were spanked early in the morning on Good Friday to remind them of Christ's suffering.

On Easter Eve children walked around their village carrying musical instruments, cowbells, or any kind of noisemaker they could find, creating a tremendous racket to end the silent week. Easter was celebrated by a large feast and a tobogganing event attended by the whole village. On Easter Sunday people could play and visit friends again.

Scandinavian legend has it that witches fly between Good Friday and Easter Sunday, the time when Jesus was still sealed in his tomb. The witches were old women who had sold themselves to the devil, and were much feared because they had the power to hurt people and pets. People would burn bonfires on Holy Saturday to scare away the witches. The witch with her cat and broomstick, part of children's Easter games, has become a familiar character, and pictures of witches are featured on Easter cards and letters much like Santa Claus at Christmas.

For the Easter season, the Finns make an interesting bread called Pääsiäisleipä—I have yet to see a pronunciation help for this word. Usually rye breads are savory with little to no sweetener added. However, this lovely lightly sweetened bread is enriched with cream, butter, eggs, raisins, almonds, cardamom, and citrus zest.

This Finnish Easter bread is usually baked in a large milking pail. I find a 3-pound coffee can a good substitute. Better yet, I prefer to divide the recipe and use three smaller cans (the kind that hold roughly 1 pound of coffee). The top of the bread is dull after baking. Though it isn't traditional to do so, I rub the loaf with melted butter for a nice shine.

Makes 1 large loaf or 3 smaller loaves

1 scant tablespoon or 1 (¼-ounce) package active dry yeast

¼ cup warm water (about 110°F)

¾ cup light cream or half-and-half

½ cup (1 stick) unsalted butter, melted

2 large eggs, beaten

1 teaspoon salt

1 teaspoon ground cardamom

1 teaspoon coarsely grated lemon zest

1 teaspoon coarsely grated orange zest

½ cup granulated sugar

1 cup rye flour

3 to 4 cups unbleached all-purpose flour

1 cup raisins

½ cup slivered almonds

By hand In a large bowl, sprinkle the yeast in the water to soften. Heat the cream to 110°F and add it to the yeast along with the butter, eggs, salt, cardamom, lemon and orange zests, sugar, rye flour, and 2 cups of the all-purpose flour. Beat vigorously for 2 minutes. Add the raisins and almonds. Gradually add the remaining flour ¼ cup at a time until the dough begins to pull away from the side of the bowl. Turn the dough out onto a floured work surface. Knead, adding flour a little at a time, until the dough is smooth and elastic.

By mixer In the mixer bowl, sprinkle the yeast in the water to soften. Heat the cream to 110°F and add it to the yeast along with the butter, eggs, salt, cardamom, lemon and orange zests, sugar, rye flour, and 2 cups of the all-purpose flour. Using the mixer paddle, beat the mixture on medium-low speed for 2 minutes. Gradually add the remaining flour ¼ cup at a time until the dough begins to pull away from the side of the bowl. Change to the dough hook. Add the raisins and almonds. Continue to add flour 1 tablespoon at a time until the dough just begins to clean the bowl. Knead 4 to 5 minutes on medium-low.

By food processor In a large measuring cup or bowl, sprinkle the yeast in the water to soften. Heat the cream to 100°F and add it to the yeast along with the butter and eggs. In the bowl of the food processor fitted with the dough blade, combine the salt, cardamon, lemon and orange zests, sugar, rye flour, and 3 cups all-purpose flour with 4 or 5 pulses. With the food processor running, add the liquid ingredients as fast as the dry ingredients will accept them. If you hear a sputtering sound, pour the liquid slower. As soon as all the liquid is added, turn the processor off. Check the liquid-to-flour ratio (see page 28). Pulse until the dough forms a ball, then process exactly 60 seconds. Turn the dough out onto a work surface and knead in the raisins and almonds.

By bread machine Put the water, cream, butter, and eggs in the bread pan. Add the salt, cardamon, lemon and orange zests, sugar, rye flour, and 3 cups all-purpose flour to the bread pan, then sprinkle with the yeast. If your machine has an Add Fruit cycle, add the raisins and almonds when prompted; if not, add them with the yeast. Select the Dough cycle and press Start. While the dough is mixing, check the liquid-to-flour ratio (see page 29). The machine stops after the kneading cycle. You may let the dough rise in the bread machine or a bowl.

First rise Put the dough in an oiled bowl and turn to coat the entire ball of dough with oil. Cover with a tightly woven towel and let rise until doubled, about 1½ hours.

Shape Turn the dough out onto a lightly oiled work surface and round into a ball. Traditionally this bread was baked in a large milking pail. A well-greased 3-pound coffee can or the equivalent is a good substitute. Ease the dough into the can. I prefer to use three 1-pound cans. Divide the dough in thirds, round into balls, and ease into well-greased cans. The dough can also be divided in half, shaped, and placed in 2 well-greased 8½ by 4½-inch loaf pans.

Second rise Cover with a tightly woven towel and let rise for 55 minutes.

Preheat oven About 10 minutes before baking, preheat the oven to 375°F.

Bake and cool Bake the single large loaf for 45 minutes and the smaller loaves for 25 minutes until the internal temperature of the bread reaches 190°F. Immediately remove the bread from the pan and place on a rack to cool.

NOTE: This bread freezes nicely for up to 6 months. It is most flavorful if served at room temperature.

Pulla

The lavish "coffee table" is a traditional Finnish way of entertaining. The more special the occasion, the more elaborate the table. There are always seven baked items served: pulla, a rich, slightly dense loaf of bread; a plain cake; a fancy decorated cake; and four types of cookies.

Pulla is shaped in a straight braid for the everyday coffee table but into a circle for celebrations. The Finns love to entertain, and there seems to be a coffee table for every occasion—after the sauna, after church, Christmas, Easter, birthdays, name days, weddings, anniversaries, christenings, funerals; in fact, any occasion that arises.

The coffee table is always set with one's finest dishes, and a vase of flowers is a must. In Beatrice Ojakangas's *Finnish Cookbook* she explains the ritual governing the coffee table: "With the first cup of coffee, guests take pulla, along with a cooky or two; with the second cup, the uniced cake and a cooky or two; with the third cup, as a grand finale and the last course, a piece of the filled, decorated cake. With the fourth cup of coffee it is permissible to sample the items missed, or you may simply sip the coffee through a lump of sugar, which you hold between your teeth. It is considered polite—and a great compliment to the hostess—to taste all of the items on the table."

THE FINNS SERVE PULLA plain without butter. For everyday eating or a simple "coffee table," shape the loaf into a straight braid, but for special occasions shape the braid into a circle.

Removing the hull and crushing cardamom with a mortar and pestle just before using it gives much more flavor than purchased ground cardamom. The Scandinavian *Pärlsocker,* or pearl sugar (small bright white pieces of sugar that are slightly larger than pretzel salt and do not melt during baking), really makes a difference on this bread. If you cannot find it locally, check page 331 for mail-order sources. *Pärlsocker* is a wonderful alternative to icing any sweet bread.

MAKES 1 LARGE LOAF

FOR THE DOUGH

1 scant tablespoon or 1 (¼-ounce) package active dry yeast

¼ cup warm water (about 110°F)

¾ cup light cream

2 large eggs, beaten

½ teaspoon salt

1 teaspoon whole cardamom seeds, crushed

½ cup granulated sugar

4 to 5 cups unbleached all-purpose flour

½ cup (1 stick) unsalted butter, melted

FOR THE TOPPING

1 large egg

1 tablespoon cold water

Pärlsocker *or coarsely crushed sugar cubes*

By hand In a large bowl, sprinkle the yeast in the water to soften. Heat the cream to 110°F and add it to the yeast along with the eggs, salt, cardamom, sugar, and 2 cups of the flour. Beat vigorously for 2 minutes. Add the butter and beat for 2 more minutes. Gradually add the remaining flour ¼ cup at a time until the dough begins to pull away from the side of the bowl. Turn the dough out onto a floured work surface. Knead, adding flour a little at a time, until the dough is smooth and elastic.

By mixer In the mixer bowl, sprinkle the yeast in the water to soften. Heat the cream to 110°F and add it to the yeast along with the eggs, salt, cardamom, sugar, and 2 cups of the flour. Using the mixer paddle, beat the mixture on medium-low speed for 2 minutes. Add the butter and beat for 2 more minutes. Gradually add the remaining flour ¼ cup at a time until the dough begins to pull away from the side of the bowl. Change to the dough hook. Continue to add flour 1 table-spoon at a time until the dough just begins to clean the bowl. Knead 4 to 5 minutes on medium-low.

By food processor In a large measuring cup or bowl, sprinkle the yeast in the water to soften. Heat the cream to 100°F and add it to the yeast along with the eggs and butter. In the bowl of the food processor fitted with the dough blade, combine the salt, cardamom, sugar, and 4 cups flour with 4 or 5 pulses. With the food processor running, add the liquid ingredients as fast as the dry ingredients will accept them. If you hear a sputtering sound, pour the liquid slower. As soon as all the liquid is added, turn the processor off. Check the liquid-to-flour ratio (see page 28). Pulse until the dough forms a ball, then process exactly 60 seconds.

By bread machine Put the water, cream, eggs, and butter in the bread pan. Add the salt, cardamom, sugar, and 4 cups flour to the bread pan, then sprinkle with the yeast. Select the Dough cycle and press Start. While the dough is mixing, check the liquid-to-flour ratio (see page 29). The machine stops after the kneading cycle. You may let the dough rise in the bread machine or a bowl.

First rise Put the dough in an oiled bowl and turn to coat the entire ball of dough with oil. Cover with a tightly woven towel and let rise until doubled, about one hour.

Shape Turn the dough out onto a lightly oiled work surface and divide into 3 equal pieces. Shape each piece into a 20-inch-long rope. Lay the ropes side by side on a parchment-lined or well-greased baking sheet. Starting in the center, place the right rope over the middle rope (note that the right rope has now become the middle rope), then the left rope over the middle, the right rope over the middle, left over the middle, and so on. Continue this process until the ropes are too short to braid. Do not pinch the ends together.

To braid the other end of the loaf, turn the baking sheet around so that the unbraided portion is facing you. Place the middle strand over the right strand, then the middle strand over the left, middle over the right, middle over the left, and so on, until the ends are too short to braid. Do not pinch the ends together.

Form the braid into a circle. Join the ends by connecting the outside left strand to the inside right strand, the two middle strands, then the inside left strand to the outside right strand.

Second rise Cover with a tightly woven towel and let rise for 45 minutes.

Preheat oven About 10 minutes before baking, preheat the oven to 375°F.

Final preparation Combine the egg with the cold water and brush over all exposed surfaces of the braid. Sprinkle the top liberally with *pärlsocker*.

Bake and cool Bake for 25 minutes until the internal temperature of the bread reaches 190°F. Immediately remove the bread from the baking sheet and place on a rack to cool.

NOTE: This bread freezes nicely for up to 6 months. To serve, first thaw the bread, then reheat on a baking sheet or directly on the oven rack in a 375°F oven for 7 to 10 minutes.

Laufabraud

Iceland is a remote island near the Arctic Circle; the growing season is extremely short. Icelanders must import much of their food, but storm-tossed seas prevent ships from delivering supplies during the winter months. Icelanders are very creative in making ingredients go as far as possible, exemplified by their famous Laufabraud, or leaf bread.

These traditional Christmas breads are rolled as thin as possible, decorated by cutting patterns of "leaves" in them, and then fried in tallow (sheep fat) or lard to give them a unique flavor. The decorating and frying of this famous leaf bread is an age-old Icelandic custom that involves the whole family. Literally hundreds of these intricately decorated deep-fried rounds are prepared for the holidays. In the old days, experts in design would travel from farm to farm to teach the craft of decorating these breads.

Following Icelandic tradition, the house must be cleaned from cellar to attic, then decorated inside and out, all presents bought and wrapped, and all the food for the Christmas dinner prepared by Saint Thorlakur's Day, December 23. On this day, the tree is decorated, and at six o'clock in the evening Christmas is officially "chimed" in when all church bells in the land ring in unison. All families light their holiday trees at one time.

MANY BAKERIES IN ICELAND sell ready-made Laufabraud dough—prekneaded and cut—that is ready to decorate and fry. These breads are decorated the same way we made snowflakes when I was a child. All of my testers preferred these sprinkled with powdered sugar (not traditional, but very tasty!).

MAKES 24 FLATBREADS

½ teaspoon salt

1 tablespoon baking powder

2 tablespoons granulated sugar

4 cups unbleached all-purpose flour (see Notes)

1½ cups milk

2 tablespoons butter

Fat for frying: sheep tallow or lard is used in Iceland, but shortening or peanut, corn, or canola oil can be used

Mix and knead In a large bowl, whisk the salt, baking powder, sugar, and flour together. Scald the milk. Add the butter and stir just until melted. Pour into the center of the flour mixture and mix. Turn out onto a work surface and knead until smooth and cool, 3 to 4 minutes. Divide the dough in half and shape each half into a 12-inch cylinder.

Rest Cover the dough with plastic wrap, then a damp towel. Let rest on the work surface for 30 minutes.

Shape Cut each cylinder into 12 pieces. Roll each piece into an 8-inch circle; the dough will be very thin. Layer the rounds between sheets of parchment or waxed paper. Place in a plastic bag and refrigerate for at least 30 minutes or as long as overnight.

Decorate Remove the dough from the refrigerator. Fold each round into quarters and cut the folded edges with a scissors or knife blade into snowflake patterns. Unfold, return to the papers, and keep covered with a towel while working.

Preheat fat In a pan 3 to 4 inches deep, heat 1 inch of fat to 375°F.

Fry Carefully drop one Laufabraud at a time into the hot fat, taking care that the bread doesn't fold. The dough sinks to the bottom of the pan, then rises to the top. As soon as it rises, turn and fry on the other side until golden, 1 to 2 minutes. Remove from the pan and drain on paper towels. If the bread does not lie flat, place a plate or something flat on it until it cools.

NOTES: You can replace all or part of the unbleached flour with whole-wheat or rye flour.

Stack breads in an airtight container and store in a cool place. They will last for several months in the container. They do not freeze well.

Julekake

The baking of Julekake (*Jule* means "Christmas"; *kake* means "cake") began in Norway in the eighteenth century when the Norwegians began to trade fish for rye flour with the Russians.

The original breads were extremely heavy and dense. The Norwegians brewed a special beer for Christmas. The wort and yeast from the brewing process was used to leaven the bread, and the only fruits available were prunes and raisins. The breads were shaped into large round loaves and baked in wood-fired bakery ovens.

As trading increased, wheat came into common use in Norway. People also began using butter, margarine, and sugar, which was imported from Europe. In 1845 they began producing cast-iron stoves, which made baking much easier. Eventually the rye flour was replaced by wheat flour; and fat, sugar, raisins, and candied fruits were added to the bread.

Christmas in Norway just isn't Christmas without Julekake to help usher in the season. Though some people serve Julekake with butter or jam, it is more often served with the Norwegian brown goat cheese, *gjetost*. In the countryside it is also served with salted meats.

THERE ARE MANY VERSIONS of this sweet bread in all Scandinavian countries, but all include an assortment of fruits, candied or dried, and a healthy measure of nuts. The addition of a large number of eggs for the liquid makes this Julekake extremely rich and golden colored. Grate the citrus peel using a coarse grater so that you have large pieces about ¼ by ½ inch in size. This gives much more flavor than grating the peel in small shreds.

MAKES 2 ROUND LOAVES

FOR THE DOUGH

1 scant tablespoon or 1 (¼-ounce) package active dry yeast

¼ cup warm water (about 110°F)

6 large eggs, beaten

½ cup (1 stick) unsalted butter, softened

1 teaspoon ground cardamom

1 teaspoon coarsely grated orange zest

1 teaspoon coarsely grated lemon zest

1 teaspoon salt

4 to 5 cups unbleached all-purpose flour

½ cup red candied cherries, coarsely chopped (see Notes)

½ cup green candied cherries, coarsely chopped (see Notes)

1 cup raisins

1 cup slivered almonds, toasted

FOR THE TOPPING

1 cup confectioners' sugar

2 tablespoons fresh orange juice

1 tablespoon fresh lemon juice

¼ cup thinly sliced or slivered almonds

By hand In a large bowl, sprinkle the yeast in the water to soften. Add the eggs, butter, cardamom, orange and lemon zests, salt, and 2 cups of the flour to the yeast. Beat vigorously for 2 minutes. Add the cherries, raisins, and almonds. Mix to combine. Gradually add the remaining flour ¼ cup at a time until the dough begins to pull away from the side of the bowl. Turn the dough out onto a floured work surface. Knead, adding flour a little at a time, until the dough is smooth and elastic.

By mixer In the mixer bowl, sprinkle the yeast in the water to soften. Add the eggs, butter, cardamom, orange and lemon zests, salt, and 2 cups of the flour to the yeast. Using the paddle, beat on medium-low speed for 2 minutes. Add the cherries, raisins, and almonds, and mix to combine. Gradually add the remaining flour ¼ cup at a time until the dough begins to pull away from the side of the bowl. Change to the dough hook. Continue to add flour 1 tablespoon at a time until the dough just begins to clean the bowl. Knead 4 to 5 minutes on medium-low.

By food processor In a cup or small bowl, sprinkle the yeast in the water to soften. Place 4 cups flour in the food processor fitted with the plastic blade. Add the yeast, eggs, butter, cardamom, orange and lemon zests, and salt, pulse 6 times. Add the cherries, raisins, and almonds. Pulse 4 to 5 more times to combine. Check the liquid-to-flour ratio (see page 28). Pulse until the dough forms a ball, then process exactly 60 seconds.

By bread machine Put the water, eggs, butter, cardamom, salt, and orange and lemon zests in the bread pan. Add 4 cups flour. Sprinkle the yeast over the flour. If your machine has an Add Fruit cycle, add the cherries, raisins, and almonds when prompted; if not, add them with the yeast. Select the Dough cycle and press Start. After the dough has mixed, check the liquid-to-flour ratio (see page 29). The machine stops after the kneading cycle. You may let the dough rise in the bread machine or a bowl.

First rise Put the dough in an oiled bowl and turn to coat the entire ball of dough with oil. Cover with a tightly woven towel and let rise until doubled, about 1½ hours.

Shape Turn the dough out onto a lightly oiled work surface and divide in half. Shape each half into an 8-inch round loaf and place on a parchment-lined or well-greased baking sheet. Press down on the center of the loaf so that it is slightly concave.

Second rise Cover with a tightly woven towel and let rise for 55 minutes.

Preheat oven About 10 minutes before baking, preheat the oven to 375°F.

Bake and cool Bake for 30 minutes until the internal temperature of the bread reaches 190°F. Immediately remove the bread from the baking sheets and place on a rack. Let cool 15 minutes.

Finish Combine the confectioners' sugar, orange juice, and lemon juice and drizzle the icing over the top of the bread. Sprinkle with the almonds.

NOTES: If you prefer to make your own candied cherries, see page 325.

This bread freezes nicely if properly wrapped for up to 6 months. If you are freezing the bread, do not drizzle with icing until ready to serve. Reheat the thawed bread in a 375°F oven for 7 to 10 minutes, then follow the directions for finishing the bread.

Doppbrød

In Sweden pigs are slaughtered in the autumn, when they are fattest. All the meat was once preserved in brine so it would keep throughout the year. However, one or two pigs were always saved for slaughter at Christmas, which was the only time of the year people ate fresh meat.

Today, fresh meat is available all year long, but pork is still the meat of choice for Christmas. In fact, Christmas wouldn't be right for many Swedes without ham, *brawn* (sausage made from the tasty bits of meat from the head of the pig), and sausages.

The Swedish Christmas celebration begins at midday on Christmas Eve, when the family gathers in the kitchen to share in a custom called *doppa I grytan,* "dipping in the kettle." Everyone sits around a pot filled with drippings from the ham and sausages that have been prepared for the dinner later in the evening. They dip Doppbrød, a dark, slightly sweet bread, into the drippings until the bread is completely soaked. Later, Christmas dinner is eaten, and the presents are shared on Christmas Eve rather than Christmas Day.

IN SWEDEN Doppbrød is also called Vort-brøt. The liquid used for this bread was a strong-flavored *vort,* beer mash from the local brewery. Today most people find a good dark ale or stout more convenient to use. Swedes use the zest of a bitter orange called *pomeransskal,* which gives a bit more zip than the oranges available in America.

MAKES 2 LOAVES

1 scant tablespoon or 1 (¼-ounce) package active dry yeast

¼ cup warm water (about 110°F)

1 cup ale or stout (the darker the better)

¼ cup granulated sugar

1 tablespoon finely grated orange zest

2 teaspoons anise seeds

2 teaspoons fennel seeds

1 teaspoon salt

1 cup rye flour

3 to 4 cups unbleached all-purpose flour

Melted butter to brush on loaves

By hand In a large bowl, sprinkle the yeast in the water to soften. Heat the beer to 110°F and add it to the yeast along with the sugar, zest, anise, fennel, salt, rye flour, and 1 cup of the all-purpose flour. Beat vigorously for 2 minutes. Gradually add the remaining flour ¼ cup at a time until the dough begins to pull away from the side of the bowl. Turn the dough out onto a floured work surface. Knead, adding flour a little at a time, until the dough is smooth and elastic.

By mixer In the mixer bowl, sprinkle the yeast in the water to soften. Heat the beer to 110°F and add it to the yeast along with the sugar, zest, anise, fennel salt, rye flour, and 1 cup of the all-purpose flour. Using the mixer paddle, beat the mixture on medium-low speed for 2 minutes. Gradually add the remaining flour ¼ cup at a time until the dough begins to pull away from the side of the bowl. Change to the dough hook. Continue to add flour 1 tablespoon at a time until the dough just begins to clean the bowl. Knead 4 to 5 minutes on medium-low.

By food processor In a medium measuring cup or bowl, sprinkle the yeast in the water to soften. Heat the beer to 100°F and add it to the yeast. In the bowl of the food processor fitted with the dough blade, combine the sugar, zest, anise, fennel, salt, rye flour, and 3 cups all-purpose flour with 4 or 5 pulses. With the food processor running, add the liquid ingredients as fast as the dry ingredients will accept them. If you hear a sputtering sound, pour the liquid slower. As soon as all the liquid is added, turn the processor off. Check the liquid-to-flour ratio (see page 28). Pulse until the dough forms a ball, then process exactly 60 seconds.

By bread machine Put the water, beer, and sugar in the bread pan. Add the zest, anise, fennel, salt, rye flour, and 3 cups all-purpose flour to the bread pan, then sprinkle with the yeast. Select the Dough cycle and press Start. While the dough is mixing, check the liquid-to-flour ratio (see page 29). The machine stops after the kneading cycle. You may let the dough rise in the bread machine or a bowl.

First rise Put the dough in an oiled bowl and turn to coat the entire ball of dough with oil. Cover with a tightly woven towel and let rise until doubled, about one hour.

Shape Turn the dough out onto a lightly oiled work surface and divide in half. Round each half into a ball, then roll back and forth to form an oval about 8 inches long and 5 inches wide. Place each oval on a parchment-lined or well-greased baking sheet.

Second rise Cover with tightly woven towels and let rise for 45 minutes.

Preheat oven About 10 minutes before baking, preheat the oven to 375°F.

Bake and cool Bake 25 minutes until the internal temperature of the bread reaches 190°F. Immediately remove the bread from the baking sheets and place on a rack to cool. Brush the tops of the loaves with melted butter.

NOTE: This bread freezes nicely for up to 6 months. To serve, first thaw the bread, then reheat on a baking sheet or directly on the oven rack in a 375°F oven for 7 to 10 minutes.

Saint Lucia's Cats or Crown

More than 1,000 years ago, King Canute of Sweden declared that Christmas celebrations would begin on December 13, Saint Lucia's Day. There are many versions of how Lucia became a revered figure in Swedish tradition.

Some stories say Vikings visiting Sicily brought home the celebration of the saint who was martyred in the year 304; others say it was missionaries. Some even believe Lucia herself visited Sweden.

Lucia means "light," and her feast day marks the return of the sun at the winter solstice. She is the patron saint of her home city of Syracuse and is also the patron saint of sight and of the blind.

Lucia came from a wealthy Sicilian family. During the days of Christian persecution, she carried food to Christians who hid in dark tunnels and caves. To light her way, she wore a wreath of candles on her head. Lucia vowed to remain a virgin and dedicate her life to serving the poor and the Christian church; however, her mother betrothed her to a pagan. Lucia rejected the young man, and he reported Lucia to the Roman authorities as a Christian. There followed a series of cruel tortures that included blinding; Lucia refused to renounce her faith to her death.

Saint Lucia brings hope during the darkest time of the year and has become the Swedish icon of winter. Two breads are made to celebrate Saint Lucia's Day: a crown with candles to represent the crown she wore; and Lucia Cats. The Norse goddess Freya drove a chariot pulled by the devil's cats. Through goodness and light, Lucia subdued the evil felines.

The Swedish people have turned Saint Lucia's Day into an especially charming festival. On the morning of December 13, a daughter of the household dons a long white dress with a crimson ribbon around her waist. On her head she wears an evergreen crown into which seven lighted candles are fitted; today these are battery-powered for safety's sake. The young girl goes throughout the house waking family members with saffron buns and the Lucia song.

SAFFRON is very expensive, for each little stigma must be hand-picked. There are only three stigmas per crocus flower, and it takes more than 14,000 to make an ounce of saffron. It can be purchased whole or powdered. I prefer the whole, since it loses flavor quickly once crushed. Luckily, a little goes a long way.

MAKES 24 CATS (BUNS)
OR 1 LARGE CROWN

FOR THE DOUGH

1 cup light cream

¼ teaspoon or 1 large pinch saffron threads

1 scant tablespoon or 1 (¼-ounce) package active dry yeast

¼ cup warm water (about 110°F)

1 large egg, beaten

1 large egg white

½ cup granulated sugar

1 teaspoon salt

4 to 5 cups unbleached all-purpose flour

¼ cup (½ stick) unsalted butter, melted

FOR THE GLAZE

1 large egg yolk

¼ cup milk

FOR THE DECORATIONS

Raisins or currants for cats, four 8-inch candles, whole cherries, and whole almonds for crown

Steep saffron Scald the cream and remove it from the heat. Add the saffron, cover, and cool to about 110°F. The cream will become a beautiful yellow color.

By hand In a large bowl, sprinkle the yeast in the water to soften. Add the cream, egg, egg white, sugar, salt, and 2 cups of the flour to the yeast. Beat vigorously for 2 minutes. Add the butter, then gradually add the remaining flour ¼ cup at a time until the dough begins to pull away from the side of the bowl. Turn the dough out onto a floured work surface. Knead, adding flour a little at a time, until the dough is smooth and elastic.

By mixer In the mixer bowl, sprinkle the yeast in the water to soften. Add the cream, egg, egg white, sugar, salt, and 2 cups of the flour to the yeast. Using the mixer paddle, beat the mixture on medium-low speed for 2 minutes. Add the butter, then gradually add the remaining flour ¼ cup at a time until the dough begins to pull away from the side of the bowl. Change to the dough hook. Continue to add flour 1 tablespoon at a time until the dough just begins to clean the bowl. Knead 4 to 5 minutes on medium-low.

By food processor In a large measuring cup or bowl, sprinkle the yeast in the water to soften. Add the cream, egg, and egg white to the yeast. In the bowl of the food processor fitted with the dough blade, combine the sugar, salt, and 4 cups flour with 4 or 5 pulses. Add the butter and pulse 4 or 5 times. With the food processor running, add the liquid ingredients as fast as the dry ingredients will accept them. If you hear a sputtering sound, pour the liquid slower. As soon as all the liquid is added, turn the processor off. Check the liquid-to-flour ratio (see page 28). Pulse until the dough forms a ball, then process exactly 60 seconds.

By bread machine Put the cream, water, egg, egg white, and butter in the bread pan. Add the sugar, salt, and 4 cups flour to the bread pan, then sprinkle with the yeast. Select the Dough cycle and press Start. While the dough is mixing, check the liquid-to-flour ratio (see page 29). The machine stops after the kneading cycle. You may let the dough rise in the bread machine or a bowl.

First rise Put the dough in an oiled bowl and turn to coat the entire ball of dough with oil. Cover with a tightly woven towel and let rise until doubled, about one hour. Punch the dough with your fist to deflate it. Fold the sides of the dough to the center, then turn it over.

Second rise Recover the dough with a tightly woven towel and let rise one hour.

Shape Turn the dough out onto a lightly oiled work surface.

To shape the cats, divide the dough into 48 equal pieces and roll each piece into an 8-inch rope. Curl the ends of each rope and arrange 2 pieces together as shown in the illustration. Place the cats about 3 inches apart on parchment-lined or well-greased baking sheets. Press a raisin in the center of each coil.

To shape the crown, remove approximately one-third of the dough and cover it with a towel. Divide the larger piece of dough into 3 equal pieces. Roll each piece into a 25-inch-long rope. Starting in the center of the ropes, place the right rope over the middle rope (note that the right rope has now become the middle rope), then the left rope over the middle, the right rope over the middle, left over the middle, and so on. Continue this process until the ropes are too short to braid.

To braid the other end of the loaf, turn the baking sheet around so that the unbraided portion is facing you. Place the middle rope over the right rope, then the middle rope over the left, middle over the right, middle over the left, and so on, until the ends are too short to braid.

Bring the ends together to form a wreath. Connect the right outside end to the left inside end and pinch to seal. Connect the middle ends from each side and pinch to seal. Connect the left outside end to the right inside end. Lift the wreath and place it on a parchment-lined or well-greased baking sheet.

Divide the remaining dough into thirds and roll each piece of dough into a 20-inch-long rope. Follow the directions for braiding and making a wreath as directed. Place on a parchment-lined or well-greased baking sheet, cover with a towel, and refrigerate until the first braid is baked. When the other braid has baked, remove the smaller one and bake it immediately.

Second rise Cover the cats and first braid with a tightly woven towel and let rise for 45 minutes.

Preheat oven About 10 minutes before baking, preheat the oven to 375°F.

Final preparation Beat the egg yolk with the milk and brush lightly over each crown or cat, taking care not to let the mixture puddle in the crevices.

Bake and cool Bake the cats for 18 minutes until golden, or crowns for 25 minutes until the internal temperature of the bread reaches 190°F. Immediately remove the bread from the baking sheet and place on a rack to cool.

Finish crown Cut four ½-inch-deep indentations the size of the candle base evenly spaced in the top of the smaller wreath. Place the smaller wreath on top of the larger one. Put candles in the prepared holes and arrange cherries and almonds decoratively in the space between the small wreath and the larger one and over the top.

NOTE: This bread freezes nicely for up to 6 months and after thawing can easily be reheated in a 375° oven. Wrap the cats in foil and reheat on a baking sheet for 7 to 10 minutes. Place the unwrapped crown directly on a baking sheet and reheat for 7 to 10 minutes.

Shrove Tuesday Buns

Sweden has not been under the influence of the Catholic Church since the 1500s. However, the Swedes have retained the custom of using the excess butter and eggs in some types of rich bread to rid their homes of the forbidden foods on Shrove Tuesday, or Fat Tuesday, the day before the forty-day Lenten fast begins. They love to feast on special buns called Semlor (Shrove Tuesday Buns).

Shrove Tuesday Buns became legendary in 1771, when the Swedish King Adolf Frederick died after eating a meal of oysters, lobster, meat with turnips, caviar, smoked Baltic herring, copious amounts of Champagne, and Semlor for dessert. Since Semlor was the last thing he ate, the Swedes figured it must have been the bun that "did him in." The buns were immediately banned.

Originally, Shrove Tuesday Buns came from Germany, where they were simple caraway buns made from finely ground wheat flour. By the early 1800s the buns began showing up in southern Sweden in local bakeries for Shrove Tuesday. Over the years this simple bun changed into a rich bun, without caraway seeds, that is filled with almond paste and served in a puddle of hot milk.

THE PRESENTATION for this bun is most unusual. The tops of the baked buns are cut off, and the soft inside is removed, mixed with almond paste and heavy cream, and used to fill the buns. They are then covered with their lids, sprinkled with sugar, and placed in a bowl of hot milk. The last step is traditional, but not necessary.

MAKES 24 BUNS

FOR THE DOUGH

1 scant tablespoon or 1 (¼-ounce) package active dry yeast

¼ cup warm water (about 110°F)

¾ cup milk

½ cup (1 stick) unsalted butter, melted

2 large eggs, beaten

1 teaspoon salt

¼ cup granulated sugar

4 to 5 cups unbleached all-purpose flour

FOR THE FILLING

1 cup heavy cream

7 to 8 ounces almond paste

FOR THE PRESENTATION

½ cup hot milk for each bun served

Confectioners' sugar to sprinkle tops

By hand In a large bowl, sprinkle the yeast in the water to soften. Heat the milk to 110°F and add it to the yeast along with the butter, eggs, salt, sugar, and 2 cups of the flour. Beat vigorously for 2 minutes. Gradually add the remaining flour ¼ cup at a time until the dough begins to pull away from the side of the bowl. Turn the dough out onto a floured work surface. Knead, adding flour a little at a time, until the dough is smooth and elastic. *This dough should be kneaded for only about 2 minutes.*

By mixer In the mixer bowl, sprinkle the yeast in the water to soften. Heat the milk to 110°F and add it to the yeast along with the butter, eggs, salt, sugar, and 2 cups of the flour. Using the mixer paddle, beat the mixture on medium-low speed for 2 minutes. Gradually add the remaining flour ¼ cup at a time until the dough begins to pull away from the side of the bowl. Change to the dough hook. Continue to add flour 1 tablespoon at a time until the dough just begins to clean the bowl. Knead 2 minutes on medium-low.

By food processor In a large measuring cup or bowl, sprinkle the yeast in the water to soften. Heat the milk to 100°F and add it to the yeast along with the butter and eggs. In the bowl of the food processor fitted with the dough blade, combine the salt, sugar, and 4 cups flour with 4 or 5 pulses. With the food processor running, add the liquid ingredients as fast as the dry ingredients will accept them. If you hear a sputtering sound, pour the liquid slower. As soon as all the liquid is added, turn the processor off. Check the liquid-to-flour ratio (see page 28). Pulse until the dough forms a ball, then process exactly 30 seconds.

By bread machine Put the water, milk, butter, and eggs in the bread pan. Add the salt, sugar, and 4 cups flour to the bread pan, then sprinkle with the yeast. Select the Dough cycle and press Start. While the dough is mixing, check the liquid-to-flour ratio (see page 29). The machine stops after the kneading cycle. You may let the dough rise in the bread machine or a bowl.

First rise Put the dough in an oiled bowl and turn to coat the entire ball of dough with oil. Cover with a tightly woven towel and let rise until doubled, about one hour.

Shape Turn the dough out onto a lightly oiled work surface and divide into 24 equal pieces. The dough should be very soft. If it is too sticky, lightly oil your hands. Round the pieces of dough into balls and place about 2 inches apart on a parchment-lined or well-greased baking sheet.

Second rise Cover with a tightly woven towel and let rise for 45 minutes.

Preheat oven About 10 minutes before baking, preheat the oven to 375°F.

Bake and cool Bake for 15 minutes until the internal temperature of the bread reaches 190°F. Immediately remove the buns from the baking sheet and place on a rack to cool.

Prepare filling After the buns have cooled, remove a ½-inch slice off the top of each bun and set aside. Scoop out the inside of each bun, leaving a ¼-inch shell. Shred the insides and soak in ½ cup of the cream for 5 minutes. Crumble the almond paste into the crumb mixture and mix with the back of a fork until combined. Whip the remaining cream until thick. Fold the whipped cream into the crumb mixture. Cover and refrigerate until ready to serve.

Finish Spoon the filling into each hollowed-out bun and replace the tops. Place each bun in a bowl of hot milk and sprinkle lightly with confectioners' sugar.

NOTE: The unfilled buns freeze nicely for up to 6 months. Thaw and fill just before serving.

Western Europe

Kugelhopf

Kugelhopf is a buttery egg bread studded with raisins and nuts. There are five traditional ways to spell the name of this delectable treat: kugelhopf, kugelhupf, gugelhopf, gouglehopf, and kouglof. The bread originated with the defeat of the Turkish army in Vienna in the seventeenth century when Austrian bakers made it in the shape of a Turkish turban to commemorate the victory. However, Germany, Poland, and France also claim the bread originated in their countries.

In Austria, gugelhopf is rich and served at teatime. The bread is most often baked with yeast but can be made with baking powder. In Alsace and the Black Forest region of Germany, kugelhopf is a breakfast bread baked at home on Sunday, which is the baker's day off.

The French believe that kugelhupf was brought to Versailles by Empress Marie-Antoinette. The French village of Ribeauville holds an annual kugelhupf festival, Fête du Kugelhupf, on the second Sunday in June.

In Austria the bread has long been a measure for judging a home baker's culinary skills; though it can be bought commercially, it is baked at home as a matter of pride. Housewives carefully guard their special recipe and generally pass it on from mother to daughter or daughter-in-law. At many weddings, the new daughter-in-law is given a decorated earthenware mold by the groom's family along with the family recipe.

Kugelhopf is baked in a fluted, spiral-patterned mold, called a chimney mold, with a hollow post in the center to help the bread bake evenly in the middle.

When kugelhopf is first baked, it is light in the center and crispy on the outside, but it goes stale quickly. It is, however, outstanding toasted.

KUGELHOPF IS A BATTER BREAD. The ingredients are mixed, then beaten vigorously to put as much air as possible into the dough, since it will not be kneaded. I highly recommend using a mixer for this task, not a food processor or bread machine.

Kirschwasser is a clear cherry brandy that can be found in most liquor stores.

MAKES 1 LARGE LOAF

FOR THE DOUGH

1 scant tablespoon or 1(¼-ounce) package active dry yeast

¼ cup warm water (about 110°F)

¾ cup milk

¼ cup kirschwasser or dark rum

½ cup (1 stick) unsalted butter, melted

2 large eggs, beaten

3 large egg yolks, beaten

1 teaspoon almond extract

1 teaspoon salt

2 teaspoons finely grated lemon zest

½ cup granulated sugar

3½ cups unbleached all-purpose flour

1 cup golden raisins

½ cup slivered almonds

FOR THE PAN

2 tablespoons granulated sugar

½ cup ground almonds

2 tablespoons unsalted butter, softened

Mix In a large bowl, sprinkle the yeast in the water to soften. Heat the milk to 110°F and add it to the yeast along with the kirschwasser, butter, eggs, yolks, extract, salt, zest, sugar, and 2 cups flour. Beat vigorously for 2 minutes. Add the raisins and almonds, then add the remaining flour ¼ cup at a time, beating well after each addition. Beat the bread for 5 minutes. This is a batter bread and not kneaded.

Prepare pan Combine the sugar and almonds. Rub the inside of a 10-inch Kugelhopf pan with soft butter (you may also use a 10-inch Bundt or tube pan) and sprinkle with the almond mixture.

Rise Put the dough in the prepared pan. Cover with plastic wrap and let rise one hour. The dough may not double but will rise more in the oven.

Preheat oven About 10 minutes before baking, preheat the oven to 375°F.

Bake and cool Bake for 25 minutes until the internal temperature of the bread reaches 190°F. Immediately remove the bread from the pan and place on a rack to cool.

NOTE: This bread freezes nicely for up to 6 months. To serve, first thaw the bread, then reheat on a baking sheet or directly on the oven rack in a 375°F oven for 7 to 10 minutes. It is also outstanding toasted.

Krentenwegge

The Dutch are big on bread and eat at least two bread meals per day. Eastern Holland, around the region of Twente, preserves an old tradition, still very strong today. Whenever there is a birth, the neighbors work together and present a huge loaf of Krentenwegge, a delicately spiced but very hearty raisin bread, to the mother of the child. Since the loaf is so large, it must be baked in a bakery oven. Krentenwegge is so long it must be presented on a long piece of wood to prevent it from breaking. With this large loaf on hand, the new mother will not have to bake for several days, possibly weeks.

TRADITIONALLY, THIS RECIPE is huge—I mean really huge. In all my research, no one has been able to tell me why it is so large. Since the traditional loaf will not fit in a standard oven, I have adjusted the recipe. In Holland the smaller loaf would be about 32 inches long, 10 inches wide, and 4½ inches high. The largest version can measure up to 6 feet long.

MAKES 1 LARGE LOAF

FOR THE SPONGE

1 scant tablespoon or 1(¼-ounce) package active dry yeast

¼ cup warm water (about 110°F)

2 tablespoons granulated sugar

½ teaspoon cumin seeds

½ teaspoon caraway seeds

½ teaspoon anise seeds

1 cup unbleached all-purpose flour

1¼ cups milk (about 110°F)

2 large eggs, beaten

FOR THE DOUGH

1 teaspoon salt

1 teaspoon ground cinnamon

3 to 4 cups unbleached all-purpose flour

½ cup (1 stick) unsalted butter, softened

2 cups raisins or currants

½ cup finely chopped candied lemon peel (see Notes)

1 tablespoon finely grated orange zest

FOR THE GLAZE

1 large egg

2 tablespoons cold milk

Prepare sponge In a large bowl, sprinkle the yeast in the water to soften. Whisk the sugar, cumin, caraway, anise, and flour together. Add the flour mixture, milk, and eggs to the yeast. Beat until the mixture is smooth. Cover with plastic wrap and let sit for one hour at room temperature.

By hand Add the salt, cinnamon, 1 cup of the flour, the butter, raisins, lemon peel, and orange zest to the sponge and stir to combine. Gradually add the remaining flour ¼ cup at a time until the dough begins to pull away from the side of the bowl. Turn the dough out onto a floured work surface. Knead, adding flour a little at a time, until the dough is smooth and elastic.

By mixer In the mixer bowl with the paddle, add the salt, cinnamon, 1 cup of the flour, and the butter to the sponge and mix to combine. Gradually add the remaining flour ¼ cup at a time until the dough begins to pull away from the side of the bowl. Change to the dough hook. Add the raisins, lemon peel, and orange zest. Continue to add flour 1 tablespoon at a time until the dough just begins to clean the bowl. Knead 4 to 5 minutes on medium-low.

By food processor In the bowl of the food processor fitted with the dough blade, combine the salt, cinnamon, 3 cups flour, and the butter with 4 or 5 pulses. Add the sponge and pulse until the dough forms a ball. Check the liquid-to-flour ratio (see page 28), then process exactly 60 seconds. Turn the dough onto a work surface and add the raisins, lemon peel, and orange zest. Knead by hand to combine.

By bread machine Put the sponge, butter, salt, and cinnamon in the bread pan. Add 3 cups flour to the bread pan. If your machine has an Add Fruit cycle, add the raisins, lemon peel, and orange zest when prompted; if not, add them with the flour. Select the Dough cycle and press Start. While the dough is mixing, check the liquid-to-flour ratio (see page 29). The machine stops after the kneading cycle. You may let the dough rise in the bread machine or a bowl.

First rise Put the dough in an oiled bowl and turn to coat the entire ball of dough with oil. Cover with a tightly woven towel and let rise until doubled, about one hour.

Shape Turn the dough out onto a lightly oiled work surface and knead for a few turns to release the air. Form into an oval about 12 inches long and 5 inches across. Place on a parchment-lined or well-greased baking sheet.

Second rise Cover with a tightly woven towel and let rise for 45 minutes.

Preheat oven About 10 minutes before baking, preheat the oven to 375°F.

Final preparation Combine the egg with the milk and brush over the top and sides of the loaf. With a sharp serrated blade, cut a ½-inch-deep slit down the length of the loaf.

Bake and cool Bake 35 minutes until the internal temperature of the bread reaches 190°F. Immediately remove the bread from the baking sheet and place on a rack to cool.

NOTES: If you prefer to make your own candied peel, see page 326.

This bread freezes nicely for up to 6 months. To serve, first thaw the bread, then reheat on a baking sheet or directly on the oven rack in a 375°F oven for 7 to 10 minutes.

Oliebollen

*T*he Dutch spend New Year's Eve with family and friends playing games or watching television. At midnight fireworks are set off, Champagne is brought out, toasts are made, and the traditional platter of Oliebollen is served to bring in the New Year.

The name of these knobby little breads doesn't sound very inviting when translated—oil balls—but they are light and delicious. It's difficult not to stuff yourself, since these little treats go down so easily.

THE DOUGH for these wonderful little fried balls keeps in the refrigerator for up to three days, so you don't have to fry them all at one time unless you wish to. The recipe is easily divided as well.

MAKES 32 TO 40

FOR THE BATTER

1 scant tablespoon or 1 (¼-ounce) package active dry yeast

¼ cup warm water (about 110°F)

¼ cup (½ stick) unsalted butter, melted

2 large eggs, beaten

2 cups warm milk (about 110°F)

1 teaspoon salt

1 tablespoon finely grated lemon zest

2 tablespoons granulated sugar

4 cups unbleached all-purpose flour

1 cup raisins

1½ cups coarsely chopped peeled tart apples

FOR FRYING

1 quart canola or vegetable oil

FOR THE COATING

1 teaspoon ground cinnamon

¼ cup granulated or confectioners' sugar

By hand or mixer In a large bowl, sprinkle the yeast in the water to soften. Add the butter, eggs, and milk. Stir to combine. Add the salt, zest, sugar, and 3 cups of the flour and stir to combine. Add the raisins and apples and stir to combine. Stir in the remaining flour. The mixture should be a thick batter.

First rise Cover with plastic wrap and let rise until doubled, about one hour. Or cover the batter with plastic wrap and a tightly woven towel and refrigerate it overnight or up to 3 days.

Prepare dough About one hour before frying, remove the dough from the refrigerator.

Heat oil Pour the oil into a large Dutch oven or other large deep pot and heat to 375°F.

Fry With a standard serving spoon (larger than a tablespoon) or medium scoop, carefully drop dough into the oil. Do not crowd. Cook for 2 minutes on each side. Remove from the oil and drain on paper towels.

Coat Combine the cinnamon and sugar in a heavy-duty plastic bag. Add the hot Oliebollen and shake to coat. Serve immediately.

NOTE: Oliebollen are best served immediately. They do not keep or freeze well once they are fried.

Fougasse
La Pompe à l'Huile

Christmas in Provence is an intimate domestic holiday with emphasis on the religious aspects of the season. The celebration actually begins on the saint's day of Sainte Barbe, when wheat is sown on cotton or a dampened spongy material and placed on a plate. The wheat sprouts predict a good harvest. The dish is the table centerpiece throughout the holiday season.

The custom of some families is that *Le Gros Souper*—the traditional meatless Christmas Eve dinner—can be eaten before mass but must stop at the cheese course. Upon a family's return from mass, the meal continues with *Les Treize Desserts* (the thirteen desserts) of Christmas. The desserts symbolize Christ and his twelve disciples at the Last Supper. Traditionally, however, *Le Gros Souper* is eaten after mass.

The Christmas table is very simple and beautiful. The table is always laid with three white tablecloths representing the Holy Trinity, three candlesticks, and three dishes (one holding the sprouted grains, one with heads of garlic, and another filled with holly).

Of the thirteen desserts, tradition demands: dark and white nougat candy containing dried fruits and nuts to remind us of the colors of the robe of the monastic order, raisins to represent the Dominicans, hazelnuts to represent the Augustinians, dried figs to represent the Franciscans, almonds to represent the Carmelite nuns, and *la pompe à l'huile*. The name translates literally as "oil pump," but this is actually a sweet anise-and-orange-flavored Fougasse, a rectangular lattice-shaped loaf, made with olive oil. There are also fresh fruits, nuts, and other desserts that are the hostess's choice—often the number of desserts exceeds thirteen.

WHEN ANISE SEEDS are crushed, the oils are released and they are much more pungent than otherwise. I usually use a mortar and pestle to crush the seeds, but they can be placed in a heavy plastic bag and pounded with a mallet or rolling pin. The orange flower water imparts an unusual bitter orange taste that fresh oranges or orange extract just cannot duplicate.

MAKES 1 LARGE LOAF

FOR THE SPONGE

1 scant tablespoon or 1 (¼-ounce) package active dry yeast

¾ cup warm water (about 110°F)

1 tablespoon granulated sugar

1 cup unbleached all-purpose flour

FOR THE DOUGH

3 tablespoons granulated sugar

¼ cup olive oil

1 tablespoon orange flower water

1 teaspoon salt

1 teaspoon finely grated orange zest

1 teaspoon anise seeds, crushed

2½ to 3½ cups unbleached all-purpose flour

FOR THE TOPPING

Olive oil to brush over finished loaves

Confectioners' sugar to sprinkle over finished loaves

Prepare sponge In a large bowl, sprinkle the yeast in the water to soften. Add the sugar and flour and beat vigorously for 2 minutes. Cover with plastic wrap and let sit for 30 minutes.

By hand Add the sugar, oil, orange flower water, salt, zest, anise, and 1 cup of the flour to the sponge. Beat vigorously for 2 minutes. Gradually add the remaining flour ¼ cup at a time until the dough begins to pull away from the side of the bowl. Turn the dough out onto a floured work surface. Knead, adding flour a little at a time, until the dough is smooth and elastic.

By mixer Add the sugar, oil, orange flower water, salt, zest, anise, and 1 cup of the flour to the sponge in the mixer bowl. Using the mixer paddle, beat the mixture on medium-low speed for 2 minutes. Gradually add the remaining flour ¼ cup at a time until the dough begins to pull away from the side of the bowl. Change to the dough hook. Continue to add flour 1 tablespoon at a time until the dough just begins to clean the bowl. Knead 4 to 5 minutes on medium-low.

By food processor Add the oil and orange flower water to the sponge. In the bowl of the food processor fitted with the dough blade, combine the sugar, salt, zest, anise, and 2½ cups flour with 4 or 5 pulses. With the food processor running, add the liquid ingredients as fast as the dry ingredients will accept them. If you hear a sputtering sound, pour the liquid slower. As soon as all the liquid is added, turn the processor off. Check the liquid-to-flour ratio (see page 28). Pulse until the dough forms a ball, then process exactly 60 seconds.

By bread machine Put the sponge, oil, and orange flower water in the bread pan. Add the sugar, salt, zest, anise, and 2½ cups flour to the bread pan. Select the Dough cycle and press Start. While the dough is mixing, check the liquid-to-flour ratio (see page 29). The machine stops after the kneading cycle. You may let the dough rise in the bread machine or a bowl.

First rise Put the dough in an oiled bowl and turn to coat the entire ball of dough with oil. Cover with a tightly woven towel and let rise until doubled, about one hour.

Shape Turn the dough out onto a lightly oiled work surface and pat into a 10 by 14-inch rectangle with rounded corners. Carefully place on a parchment-lined or well-greased baking sheet, reshaping if necessary.

Second rise Cover with a tightly woven towel and let rise for 35 minutes. The dough will not double.

Final preparation Using a sharp knife or razor blade cut diagonal slits all the way through the dough, starting about 1 inch from the center of the loaf and ending about 1 inch from the outside edge. Gently spread the slits open to about 1 inch. Cover and let rise for 10 minutes.

Preheat oven About 10 minutes before baking, preheat the oven to 400°F.

Bake and cool Bake for 20 minutes until the internal temperature of the bread reaches 190°F. Immediately remove the bread from the baking sheet and place on a rack to cool. Brush with additional olive oil. Just before serving, sprinkle the Fougasse with confectioners' sugar.

VARIATION: Replace the orange flower water and anise seeds with 2 tablespoons herbes de Provence. It won't be the traditional Christmas bread, but it will be great!

NOTE: This bread freezes nicely for up to 6 months. To serve, first thaw the bread, then reheat on a baking sheet or directly on the oven rack in a 400°F oven for 7 to 10 minutes.

Hutzelbrot

ome Christmas time in Germany, most major towns and villages have *Christkindlemarkts,* Christ child markets. These markets are filled with row after row of concessionaires offering toys, nutcrackers, little people formed out of prunes, and holiday foods that permeate the air with wonderful smells. It seems that every other booth has its own version of *Gluhwein* (glow wine), a warm spiced wine that certainly gives one a wonderful glow. Holiday breads such as Hutzelbrot are standard fare during the Christmas season and big sellers at *Christkindlemarkts.*

Hutzelbrot—*hutzel* meaning dried up or wrinkled, because of the dried fruit—is one of the oldest German Christmas breads. Hutzelbrot originally was made without sugar or honey and had to be produced with the utmost care to keep the dough light yet strong enough to hold all the fruit and nuts. Each *hausfrau,* lady of the house, had her own special recipe for Hutzelbrot, which she prepared and would proudly take to the village bake house to be baked. Hutzelbrot was eaten on Christmas Eve with freshly churned butter. The master of the house always shared a slice with the cows, thereby assuring extra milk for the year. Pieces were even given to the dogs in thanks for their watchfulness.

Girls gave the *klözchenschörzel,* the heel or end slice of bread, to their lovers as a gift. If the surface was cut smooth, it meant the dough was well kneaded and predicted a perfect union. Should the slice not be cut smoothly, it would be the end of a relationship. The only time a girl was allowed to eat the heel was if she wanted twins.

Today Hutzelbrot is baked in advance of the Christmas holidays to allow time for the flavors to mellow.

HUTZELBROT is made with a combination of dried fruit and nuts. You can vary it by using what is in the cupboard or what you like personally. Often a bit of spirits—flavored schnapps or kirschwasser—is added as part of the hot liquid used to soften the pears.

MAKES 2 LOAVES

FOR THE FRUIT

3 cups boiling water

8 ounces (about 1½ cups) dried pears, coarsely chopped

FOR THE DOUGH

1 scant tablespoon or 1 (¼-ounce) package active dry yeast

¼ cup warm water (about 110°F)

½ cup honey

1 teaspoon salt

1 teaspoon ground ginger

1 teaspoon ground cinnamon

4 to 5 cups unbleached all-purpose flour

½ cup finely chopped candied lemon peel (see Notes)

½ cup finely chopped candied orange peel (see Notes)

1 cup coarsely chopped skinned hazelnuts

1 cup coarsely chopped blanched almonds

FOR THE TOPPING

Soft butter, optional

Prepare fruit Pour the boiling water over the pears, cover, and let soak for 12 hours or overnight at room temperature. Just before preparing the bread, drain the pears and reserve 1 cup of the liquid.

By hand In a large bowl, sprinkle the yeast in the water to soften. Heat the reserved liquid to 110°F and add it to the yeast along with the honey, salt, ginger, cinnamon, and 2 cups of the flour. Beat vigorously for 2 minutes. Add the candied peels and the nuts, then gradually add the remaining flour ¼ cup at a time until the dough begins to pull away from the side of the bowl. Turn the dough out onto a floured work surface. Knead, adding flour a little at a time, until the dough is smooth and elastic.

By mixer In the mixer bowl, sprinkle the yeast in the water to soften. Heat the reserved liquid to 110°F and add it to the yeast along with the honey, salt, ginger, cinnamon, and 2 cups of the flour. Using the mixer paddle, beat the mixture on medium-low speed for 2 minutes. Gradually add the remaining flour ¼ cup at a time until the dough begins to pull away from the side of the bowl. Change to the dough hook. Add the candied peels and the nuts. Continue to add flour 1 tablespoon at a time until the dough just begins to clean the bowl. Knead 4 to 5 minutes on medium-low.

By food processor In a large measuring cup or bowl, sprinkle the yeast in the water to soften. Heat the reserved liquid to 100°F and add it to the yeast along with the honey. In the bowl of the food processor fitted with the dough blade, combine the salt, ginger, cinnamon, and 4 cups flour with 4 or 5 pulses. With the food processor running, add the liquid ingredients as fast as the dry ingredients will accept them. If you hear a sputtering sound, pour the liquid slower. As soon as all the liquid is added, turn the processor off. Check the liquid-to-flour ratio (see page 28). Pulse until the dough forms a ball, then process exactly 60 seconds. Turn the dough out onto a work surface and knead in the candied peels and the nuts.

By bread machine Put the reserved liquid, water, and honey in the bread pan. Add the salt, ginger, cinnamon, and 4 cups flour to the bread pan, then sprinkle with the yeast. If your machine has an Add Fruit cycle, add the candied peels and the nuts when prompted; if not, add them with the yeast. Select the Dough cycle and press Start. While the dough is mixing, check the liquid-to-flour ratio (see page 29). The machine stops after the kneading cycle. You may let the dough rise in the bread machine or a bowl.

First rise Put the dough in an oiled bowl and turn to coat the entire ball of dough with oil. Cover with a tightly woven towel and let rise about 1½ hours. The dough may not double in size.

Shape Turn the dough out onto a lightly oiled work surface and knead in the pears. Cover and let rest for 5 minutes. Divide the dough in half. Shape each half into a standard loaf: Roll the dough into a 10 by 14-inch rectangle. Roll the rectangle into a 10-inch cylinder and pinch the seam to the loaf. Fold each end of the loaf like a package by bringing the sides to meet at the center of the coiled end, then bringing the bottom layer of dough to the top and pinching it. Place pinched side down into well-greased 8½ by 4½-inch loaf pans.

Second rise Cover with a tightly woven towel and let rise for 55 minutes.

Preheat oven About 10 minutes before baking, preheat the oven to 375°F.

Bake and cool Bake for 40 minutes until the internal temperature of the bread reaches 190°F. Immediately remove the bread from the pans and place on a rack to cool. For a soft shiny crust, rub with soft butter.

NOTES: If you prefer to make your own candied peel, see page 326.

This bread freezes nicely for up to 6 months. To serve, first thaw the bread, then reheat on a baking sheet or directly on the oven rack in a 375° oven for 7 to 10 minutes.

Pretzels

Sometime about 1,500 years ago, a monk fashioned bread dough to resemble a person in prayer as a reward for children who learned their scriptures. The proper position for prayer was for people to cross their arms over their chests with their hands resting on their shoulders. The three holes in the pretzel shape represent the Holy Trinity—the Father, the Son, and the Holy Ghost.

Pretzels have since become an important custom in marriage ceremonies as a symbol of the binding love knot. The bride and groom each link a finger through a loop of the pretzel, make a wish, and pull the pretzel apart. The broken pieces are eaten to symbolize eternal unity.

IN GERMANY pretzels are dipped in *lauge* to give a slightly bitter coating that goes nicely with beer. Americans love these pretzels, but perhaps they wouldn't if they knew the translation of *lauge* is "lye." The amount of lye is very small, and the pretzels are quickly dipped into this solution, so very little adheres to the pretzels. There are two alternatives to using lye. One is to use sodium hydroxide (see Sources, page 331), which gives the same result as household lye but is safer for human consumption. The other is to use baking soda, which is safer than lye and more readily available than sodium hydroxide, but it doesn't deliver the characteristic bitterness.

MAKES 32 LARGE PRETZELS

For the Sponge

*1 scant tablespoon or 1 (¼-ounce) package
active dry yeast*

¼ cup warm water (about 110°F)

1 cup milk (about 110°F)

¼ cup granulated sugar

¼ cup vegetable shortening

2 cups unbleached all-purpose flour

For the Dough

1 teaspoon salt

1½ to 2½ cups unbleached all-purpose flour

For Poaching

2 quarts boiling water

*2 (500-gram) tablets sodium hydroxide
or 2 tablespoons baking soda*

For the Topping

Coarse salt or sesame seeds, optional

Prepare sponge In a large bowl, sprinkle
the yeast in the water to soften. Add the milk,
sugar, shortening, and flour and beat vigorously to combine. Cover with plastic wrap
and let rise for 30 minutes.

By hand Combine the sponge, salt, and
1 cup of the flour. Beat vigorously for
2 minutes. Gradually add the remaining
flour ¼ cup at a time until the dough begins
to pull away from the side of the bowl. Turn
the dough out onto a floured work surface.
Knead, adding flour a little at a time, until
the dough is smooth and elastic.

By mixer In the mixer bowl, combine the
sponge, salt, and 1 cup of the flour. Using the
mixer paddle, beat the mixture on medium-
low speed for 2 minutes. Gradually add the
remaining flour ¼ cup at a time until the
dough begins to pull away from the side of
the bowl. Change to the dough hook. Continue to add flour 1 tablespoon at a time until
the dough just begins to clean the bowl.
Knead 4 to 5 minutes on medium-low.

By food processor In the bowl of the food
processor fitted with the dough blade, combine the salt, 1½ cups flour, and the sponge
with 4 or 5 pulses. Pulse until the dough forms
a ball, check the liquid-to-flour ratio (see page
28), then process exactly 60 seconds.

By bread machine Put the sponge, salt, and 1½ cups flour in the bread pan. Select the Dough cycle and press Start. While the dough is mixing, check the liquid-to-flour ratio (see page 29). The machine stops after the kneading cycle. You may let the dough rise in the bread machine or a bowl.

First rise Put the dough in an oiled bowl and turn to coat the entire ball of dough with oil. Cover with a tightly woven towel and let rise until doubled, about one hour.

Shape Turn the dough out onto a lightly oiled work surface and divide into 32 equal pieces. Working with one piece at a time, roll each piece into a 24-inch-long rope and form into a U shape. About 2 inches from each end, cross the dough, then cross a second time. Picturing the dough as the face of a clock, bring the ends down and press them into the bottom of the U at 5 and 7 o'clock. Cover with a towel and let rest for 20 minutes on the work surface.

Preheat oven Preheat the oven to 400°F.

Poach Combine the boiling water and sodium hydroxide or baking soda over medium heat. Stir well. Drop the pretzels a few at a time into the boiling water for 10 seconds; remove with a slotted spoon or skimmer. Place on buttered waxed paper on baking sheets. Sprinkle with coarse salt or sesame seeds if desired.

Bake and cool Bake for 15 minutes until golden brown. Immediately remove from the baking sheets and place on a rack to cool.

NOTE: Pretzels freeze nicely for up to 6 months. To serve, first thaw, then reheat on a baking sheet in a 400°F oven for 5 minutes.

Speckbrot

Germans work exceptionally hard, and when work is over, they play just as hard. New Year's Eve is a time of great celebration; parties begin early in the evening and last until breakfast the next morning. In the town Rothenburg ob der Tauber, tasty Speckbrot, bacon bread, is always served. The rich dough with the addition of *speck,* or bacon, is said to ward off hangovers by coating the empty stomach with a healthy dose of fat before the celebrations begin.

THOUGH THIS is a New Year's Eve bread, I love to bake it in the summer for fresh tomato and lettuce sandwiches; it gives new life to a BLT. Should you have trouble finding slab bacon, thick-sliced bacon can be substituted, but the large chunks are much tastier. Coarse salt is a great addition if you use bacon, but not for the salt pork, which is salty enough by itself. This bread was a favorite of my recipe testers!

MAKES I ROUND LOAF

1 pound slab bacon or salt pork, cut into ½-inch dice

1 scant tablespoon or 1 (¼-ounce) package active dry yeast

¼ cup warm water

¾ cup milk

¼ cup (½ stick) unsalted butter, softened

1 large egg

1 teaspoon salt

4 to 5 cups unbleached all-purpose flour

Olive oil, optional

Coarse salt, optional

Cook bacon In a large skillet over medium heat, cook the bacon until most of the fat has been rendered and the meat is crisp, about 7 minutes. Drain on paper towels until cooled.

By hand In a large bowl, sprinkle the yeast in the water to soften. Heat the milk to 110°F and add it to the yeast along with the butter, egg, salt, and 2 cups of the flour. Beat vigorously for 2 minutes. Gradually add the remaining flour ¼ cup at a time until the dough begins to pull away from the side of the bowl. Turn the dough out onto a floured work surface. Knead, adding flour a little at a time, until the dough is smooth and elastic.

By mixer In the mixer bowl, sprinkle the yeast in the water to soften. Heat the milk to 110°F and add it to the yeast along with the butter, egg, salt, and 2 cups of the flour. Using the paddle, beat on medium-low speed for 2 minutes. Gradually add the remaining flour ¼ cup at a time until the dough begins to pull away from the side of the bowl. Change to the dough hook. Continue to add flour 1 tablespoon at a time until the dough just begins to clean the bowl. Knead 4 to 5 minutes on medium-low.

By food processor In a large measuring cup, sprinkle the yeast in water to soften. Heat the milk to 100°F and add it to the yeast along with the egg. In the bowl of the food processor fitted with the dough blade, combine the butter, salt, and 4 cups flour with 3 or 4 pulses. With the food processor running, add the liquid ingredients as fast as the dry ingredients will accept them. If you hear a sputtering sound, pour the liquid slower. As soon as all the liquid is added, turn the processor off. Check the liquid-to-flour ratio (see page 28). Pulse until the dough forms a ball, then process exactly 60 seconds.

By bread machine Put the water, milk, butter, egg, and salt in the bread pan. Add 4 cups flour and sprinkle with the yeast. Select the Dough cycle and press Start. While the dough is mixing, check the liquid-to-flour ratio (see page 29). The machine stops after the kneading cycle. You may let the dough rise in the bread machine or a bowl.

First rise Put the dough in an oiled bowl and turn to coat the entire ball of dough with oil. Cover with a tightly woven towel and let rise until doubled, about one hour.

Shape Turn the dough out onto a lightly oiled work surface. Knead the cooled bacon into the dough. Cover with a towel and let rest 5 minutes. Shape the dough into a 12-inch circle and place on a parchment-lined or well-greased baking sheet.

Second rise Cover with a tightly woven towel and let rise for 45 minutes.

Preheat oven About 10 minutes before baking, preheat the oven to 400°F.

Final preparation Brush the loaf with olive oil and sprinkle with coarse salt if desired. With a sharp serrated knife or razor blade, cut an X about ¼ inch deep into the top of the loaf.

Bake and cool Bake for 25 minutes until the internal temperature of the bread reaches 190°F. Immediately remove the bread from the baking sheet and place on a rack to cool.

NOTE: This bread is best served warm. If it's baked ahead of time, reheat it in a 375°F oven for 5 minutes. The bread can also be frozen once it has completely cooled; thaw completely before reheating.

Stollen

Historians have traced Christollen, Christ's stollen, back to about the year 1400 in Dresden, Germany. The first stollen consisted of only flour, oats, and water, as required by church doctrine.

Ernst of Saxony and his brother Albrecht requested of the pope that the ban on butter and milk during the Advent season be lifted. His Eminence replied, in the famous "Butter Letter," that milk and butter could be used to bake stollen with a clear conscience and God's blessing for a small fee.

Originally stollen was called *Striezel* or *Struzel,* which referred to a braided loaf. The three-stranded braid signified the Holy Trinity. The present-day shape—a large oval folded in half with tapered ends—is said to represent the Baby Jesus wrapped in swaddling clothing.

Around 1560 the bakers of Dresden gave the king of Saxony two 36-pound stollens as a Christmas gift. It took eight master bakers and eight journeymen to carry the bread to the palace safely.

In 1730 Augustus the Strong, electoral prince of Saxony and king of Poland, asked the Bakers' Guild of Dresden to bake a giant stollen for the farewell dinner of the Zeithain "campement." The 1.8-ton stollen fed more than 24,000 guests. To commemorate the event, a Stollenfest is held each December in Dresden.

The bread for the present-day Stollenfest weighs two tons and measures approximately four yards long. Each year the stollen is paraded through the market square, then sliced and sold to the public, with proceeds supporting local charities.

Although there is a basic recipe for making the original Dresden Christollen, each master baker, each village, and each home has its own secret recipe passed down from one generation to the next. The commercial production of Dresden stollen is carefully licensed and regulated to ensure quality and authenticity.

AUTHENTIC GERMAN STOLLEN is usually sprinkled heavily with confectioners' sugar prior to serving. I personally have never liked this topping and choose to drizzle the tops of my loaves lightly with a simple icing (confectioners' sugar mixed with enough heavy cream to reach the consistency of honey).

MAKES 1 LARGE LOAF OR 2 MEDIUM LOAVES

FOR THE FRUIT

1 cup mixed candied fruit (see Notes)

1 cup raisins

3 tablespoons dark rum or orange juice

FOR THE SPONGE

1 scant tablespoon or 1 (¼-ounce) package active dry yeast

¼ cup warm water (about 110°F)

⅔ cup milk

1 teaspoon honey

1 cup unbleached all-purpose flour

FOR THE DOUGH

¼ cup honey

1 large egg, beaten

½ cup (1 stick) unsalted butter, softened

1 tablespoon finely grated lemon zest

1 teaspoon salt

½ teaspoon ground mace

½ cup chopped almonds, toasted

3 to 4 cups unbleached all-purpose flour

FOR THE FILLING

2 tablespoons unsalted butter, melted

2 teaspoons ground cinnamon

3 tablespoons granulated sugar

FOR THE TOPPING

½ cup confectioners' sugar

Prepare fruit Combine the mixed fruit, raisins, and rum. Cover and set aside. Shake or stir the mixture every so often to coat the fruit with the rum.

Prepare sponge In a large bowl, sprinkle the yeast in the water to soften. Heat the milk to 110°F and add it to the yeast along with the honey and 1 cup flour. Cover the sponge with plastic wrap and let rise until light and full of bubbles, about 30 minutes.

By hand Add the fruit mixture, honey, egg, butter, zest, salt, mace, almonds, and 2 cups of the flour to the sponge. Beat vigorously for 2 minutes. Gradually add the remaining flour ¼ cup at a time until the dough begins to pull away from the side of the bowl. Turn the dough out onto a floured work surface. Knead, adding flour a little at a time, until the dough is smooth and elastic.

By mixer In the mixer bowl, add the fruit mixture, honey, egg, butter, zest, salt, mace, almonds, and 2 cups of the flour to the sponge. Using the mixer paddle, beat the mixture on medium-low speed for 2 minutes. Gradually add the remaining flour ¼ cup at a time until the dough begins to pull away from the side of the bowl. Change to the dough hook. Continue to add flour 1 tablespoon at a time until the dough just begins to clean the bowl. Knead 4 to 5 minutes on medium-low.

By food processor Add the honey and egg to the sponge and stir to combine. In the bowl of the food processor fitted with the dough blade, combine the butter, zest, salt, mace, and 3 cups flour with 4 or 5 pulses. With the food processor running, add the sponge mixture as fast as the dry ingredients will accept it. If you hear a sputtering sound, pour the liquid slower. As soon as all the liquid is added, turn the processor off. Check the liquid-to-flour ratio (see page 28). Pulse until the dough forms a ball, then process exactly 60 seconds. Turn the dough out onto a work surface and knead in the almonds and fruit mixture. You may need a little extra flour for kneading.

By bread machine Put the sponge, honey, egg, and butter in the bread pan. Add the zest, salt, mace, and 3 cups flour to the bread pan. If your machine has a fruit cycle, add the fruit and almonds then; if not, add them now. Select the Dough cycle and press Start. While the dough is mixing, check the liquid-to-flour ratio (see page 29). The machine stops after the kneading cycle. You may let the dough rise in the bread machine or a bowl.

First rise Put the dough in an oiled bowl and turn to coat the entire ball of dough with oil. Cover with a tightly woven towel and let rise until doubled, about one hour.

Shape and fill Turn the dough out onto a lightly oiled work surface. For one large loaf, roll the dough into a 9 by 13-inch oval. For 2 loaves, divide the dough in half and roll each half into a 7 by 9-inch oval. Brush the melted butter over the top of the oval(s). Combine the cinnamon and granulated sugar and sprinkle over one lengthwise half of the oval(s). Fold the dough in half lengthwise and carefully lift the bread(s) onto a parchment-lined or well-greased baking sheet. Press lightly on the folded side to help the loaf keep its shape during rising and baking.

Second rise Cover with a tightly woven towel and let rise for 45 minutes.

Preheat oven About 10 minutes before baking, preheat the oven to 375°F.

Bake and cool Bake for 25 minutes until the internal temperature of the bread reaches 190°F. Immediately remove from the baking sheet and place on a rack to cool.

To serve Sprinkle heavily with confectioners' sugar just before serving.

VARIATION: Between 2 pieces of waxed paper or plastic wrap, roll 3 ounces almond paste or marzipan into the lengthwise shape of half the oval. Omit the butter and cinnamon-sugar filling. Place the marzipan on half of the oval and fold the dough in half. Let rise and bake as directed.

NOTES: One cup coarsely chopped mixed dried fruits may be substituted for the candied fruit. Cover the dried fruit with boiling water and let sit at room temperature for 8 to 12 hours. Drain and use as you would candied fruit. You can also make your own candied fruit and peel (pages 325 and 326).

This bread freezes nicely for up to 6 months. If freezing it, do not sprinkle with confectioners' sugar. To serve, first thaw the bread, then reheat on a baking sheet in a 375°F oven for 7 to 10 minutes. Just before serving, sprinkle with confectioners' sugar.

Strietzel

In Germany, *Allerheiligen* (All Saints' Day) and *Allerseelen* (All Souls' Day) are important celebrations. All Saints' Day began in 835 as a celebration to honor all Christian martyrs and later included all saints who died defending the faith. Each martyr and saint had a day to honor his or her birth into eternal life. Over the years as more and more saints were added, it became evident that one day had to be designated to honor these worthy Christians. All Saints' Day is celebrated on November 1.

The feast for All Souls' Day began in 998 at the French Monastery of Cluny as a celebration of the departed, then expanded to other monasteries, orders, and dioceses. In the fourteenth century All Souls' Day began to commemorate the death of anyone's deceased relatives, not just the clergy, and is celebrated on November 2.

All Souls' Day was a time to pray for the poor souls still in purgatory. Requiem masses, cemetery processions, decorating graves with flowers and candles (for illumination to better see God), alms, and good deeds were all intended to shorten the time in purgatory and hasten their entry into heaven.

Families who have moved away all return home to visit the graves of deceased relatives. For some reason—maybe because the family was together during this time—the custom of godparents visiting their godchildren after the cemetery visits began. They always bring a gift of Strietzel or Spitz'l. These large braided loaves of sweet bread can measure up to 3 feet long and are made especially for All Souls' Day. Children being children and, of course, rarely little saints often compete to see who has received the longest and best braid.

STRIETZEL, OR Spitz'l, is a lovely braid made just over 3 feet long in commercial bakeries. Home bakers make them as large as their ovens allow.

When removing the skins from hazelnuts, I always seem to have little bits of skin still attached. If I make something in which I don't want the little bits of skin, I buy commercially blanched hazelnuts.

MAKES 1 LARGE LOAF

1½ cups hazelnuts

FOR THE FRUIT

½ cup dark rum

1 cup currants

FOR THE SPONGE

1 scant tablespoon or 1 (¼-ounce) package active dry yeast

¾ cup warm milk (about 110°F)

1 cup unbleached all-purpose flour

FOR THE DOUGH

¾ cup (1½ sticks) unsalted butter, softened

1 large egg, lightly beaten

1 teaspoon salt

3 to 4 cups unbleached all-purpose flour

FOR THE TOPPING

2 tablespoons butter, melted

Confectioners' sugar, optional

Prepare nuts Preheat the oven to 375°F. Place the nuts on an ungreased baking sheet. Bake for 20 minutes until the nuts under their skins are richly browned. Remove the pan from the oven and put the nuts in a coarse cloth (terrycloth is good). Rub the nuts with the cloth to remove as much of the skin as possible. Lift the nuts from the skins and coarsely chop.

Prepare fruit Heat the rum until hot but not boiling. Remove from the heat and add the currants. Cover and cool to room temperature.

Prepare sponge In a large bowl, sprinkle the yeast in the milk to soften. Add the flour and stir until the mixture is smooth. Cover with plastic wrap and let sit for 30 minutes.

By hand Combine the sponge with the butter, egg, salt, and 1 cup of the flour. Beat vigorously for 2 minutes. Add the hazelnuts and the currants with the rum. Gradually add the remaining flour ¼ cup at a time until the dough begins to pull away from the side of the bowl. Turn the dough out onto a floured work surface. Knead, adding flour a little at a time, until the dough is smooth and elastic.

By mixer In the mixer bowl, combine the sponge with the butter, egg, salt, and 1 cup of the flour. Using the mixer paddle, beat the mixture on medium-low speed for 2 minutes. Gradually add the remaining flour ¼ cup at a time until the dough begins to pull away from the side of the bowl. Change to the dough hook. Add the hazelnuts and the currants, with the rum. Continue to add the flour 1 tablespoon at a time until the dough just begins to clean the bowl. Knead 4 to 5 minutes on medium-low.

By food processor Drain the currants, reserving the rum. Add the rum and egg to the sponge. In the bowl of the food processor fitted with the dough blade, combine the salt, nuts, and 3 cups flour. Add the butter and currants. Pulse 4 or 5 times to combine. With the food processor running, add the liquid ingredients as fast as the dry ingredients will accept them. If you hear a sputtering sound, pour the liquid slower. As soon as all the liquid is added, turn the processor off. Check the liquid-to-flour ratio (see page 28). Pulse until the dough forms a ball, then process exactly 60 seconds.

By bread machine Drain the currants, reserving the rum. Combine the rum, sponge, butter, and egg in the bread pan. Add the salt and 3 cups flour. If your machine has an Add Fruit cycle, add the currants and nuts when prompted; if not, add them with the flour. Select the Dough cycle and press Start. While the dough is mixing, check the liquid-to-flour ratio (see page 29). The machine stops after the kneading cycle. You may let the dough rise in the bread machine or a bowl.

First rise Put the dough in an oiled bowl and turn to coat the entire ball of dough with oil. Cover with a tightly woven towel and let rise until doubled, about one hour.

Shape Turn the dough out onto a lightly oiled work surface and divide into thirds. Shape each piece into a 24-inch-long rope. Lay the ropes side by side. Starting in the center of the ropes, place the right rope over the middle rope (note that the right rope has now become the middle rope), then place the left rope over the middle, the right over the middle, left over the middle, and so on. Continue this process until the ropes are too short to braid. Pinch the ends together and tuck them under.

For the other end of the loaf, place the middle rope over the right rope, then the rope that is now in the middle over the left, middle over the right, middle over the left, and so on, until the ends are too short to braid. Pinch the ends together and tuck them under. Carefully lift and place the braid on a parchment-lined or well-greased baking sheet.

Second rise Cover with a tightly woven towel and let rise for 45 minutes.

Preheat oven About 10 minutes before baking, preheat the oven to 375°F.

Bake and cool Bake for 30 minutes until the internal temperature of the bread reaches 190°F. Immediately remove the bread from the baking sheet and place on a rack to cool.

Finish While the loaf is still warm, brush it with melted butter. Just before serving, sprinkle the loaf heavily with confectioners' sugar.

NOTE: This bread freezes nicely for up to 6 months. To serve, first thaw the bread, then reheat on a baking sheet in a 375°F oven for 7 to 10 minutes.

Colomba di Pasqua

This beautiful bread in the shape of a dove is associated with two wonderful Italian legends. The first goes back to 1176, just prior to the battle of Legano. Frederick Barbarossa's goal was to capture Italy for the Holy Roman Empire. Two doves appeared and landed on the battle standards of the Milanese army. The men took this manifestation of the Holy Ghost as a sign of protection and favor, leading them to defeat Barbarossa and bringing peace to the country.

In the second legend, cruel King Albion conquered the city of Pavia in 572 after a three-year battle and confiscated various treasures from the city. He also demanded twelve young virgins. Eleven of the girls wept and wailed, unable to accept their fate. The twelfth young girl baked a large sweet bread in the shape of the dove of peace. When the king called her to him, she presented him with her gift. The king was so pleased that he allowed her to go free and declared Pavia his capital, sparing it from destruction.

Colomba di Pasqua was served for many years to commemorate these victories. Today Italians serve it for dessert following Easter dinner.

This striking loaf is made in the shape of a dove. There are two schools of thought on the dough—one has the almond paste included in the dough (which I prefer), while the other uses small bits of almond paste to decorate the loaf.

MAKES 1 LARGE LOAF

FOR THE DOUGH

1 scant tablespoon or 1 (¼-ounce) package active dry yeast

¼ cup warm water (about 110°F)

1½ cups milk

¼ cup (½ stick) unsalted butter, softened

½ cup almond paste, crumbled

1 teaspoon vanilla extract

3 large eggs, lightly beaten

1 large egg yolk

1 tablespoon finely grated lemon zest

¼ cup granulated sugar

½ teaspoon salt

4 to 5 cups unbleached all-purpose flour

FOR THE TOPPING

1 large egg white

1 cup thinly sliced almonds

1 tablespoon granulated sugar

By hand In a large bowl, sprinkle the yeast in the water to soften. Heat the milk to 110°F and add it to the yeast along with the butter, almond paste, vanilla, eggs, egg yolk, lemon zest, sugar, salt, and 2 cups of the flour. Beat vigorously for 2 minutes. Gradually add the remaining flour ¼ cup at a time until the dough begins to pull away from the side of the bowl. Turn the dough out onto a floured work surface. Knead, adding flour a little at a time, until the dough is smooth and elastic.

By mixer In the mixer bowl, sprinkle the yeast in the water to soften. Heat the milk to 110°F and add it to the yeast along with the butter, almond paste, vanilla, eggs, egg yolk, lemon zest, sugar, salt, and 2 cups of the flour. Using the mixer paddle, beat the mixture on medium-low speed for 2 minutes. Gradually add the remaining flour ¼ cup at a time until the dough begins to pull away from the side of the bowl. Change to the dough hook. Continue to add flour 1 tablespoon at a time until the dough just begins to clean the bowl. Knead 4 to 5 minutes on medium-low.

By food processor In a large measuring cup or bowl, sprinkle the yeast in the water to soften. Heat the milk to 100°F and add it to the yeast along with the almond paste, vanilla, eggs, and egg yolk. In the bowl of the food processor fitted with the dough blade, combine the butter, lemon zest, sugar, salt, and 4 cups flour with 4 or 5 pulses. With the food processor running, add the liquid ingredients as fast as the dry ingredients will accept them. If you hear a sputtering sound, pour the liquid slower. As soon as all the liquid is added, turn the processor off. Check the liquid-to-flour ratio (see page 28). Pulse until the dough forms a ball, then process exactly 60 seconds.

By bread machine Put the water, milk, butter, almond paste, vanilla, eggs, and egg yolk in the bread pan. Add the lemon zest, sugar, salt, and 4 cups flour to the bread pan, then sprinkle with the yeast. Select the Dough cycle and press Start. While the dough is mixing, check the liquid-to-flour ratio (see page 29). The machine stops after the kneading cycle. You may let the dough rise in the bread machine or a bowl.

First rise Put the dough in an oiled bowl and turn to coat the entire ball of dough with oil. Cover with a tightly woven towel and let rise about 1½ hours. Because of the almond paste, this dough will not double in size.

Shape Turn the dough out onto a lightly oiled work surface and divide in half. Shape each half into a smooth ball. Cover and let rest 5 minutes. Shape one ball of dough into a half oval 12 inches long and 4 inches wide at the center (for the wings). See the illustration on page 296. Place in the center of a parchment-lined baking sheet. Flatten the center slightly so that when the next piece of dough is laid across it, it won't be so thick. Shape the other ball of dough into a triangle with an 8-inch base and 16-inch sides (for the head and body). Keep the points of the triangle rounded rather than pointed. Center the triangle on the flattened part of the half oval with about 3 inches above the oval. Fold the narrow top over to the right to make the head. Pinch with your fingers to form a beak on the right side of the dough. Fold the other end in the opposite direction to form the tail. Using scissors, cut 2-inch slits along the bottom edge of the tail and wings. Fan them out as for feathers.

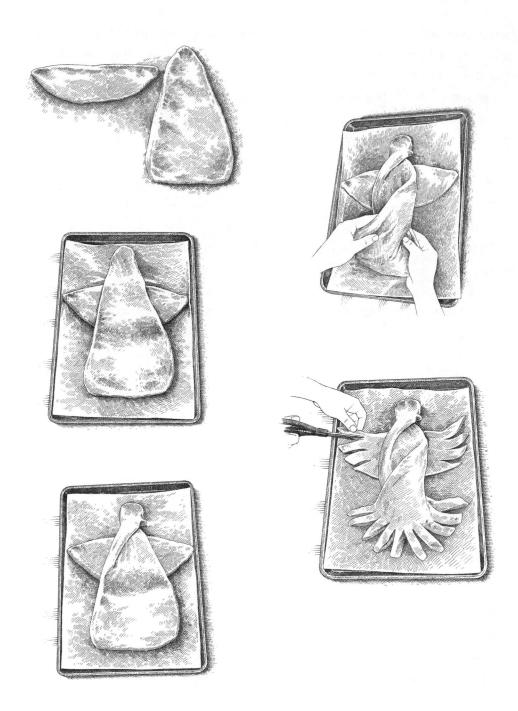

Second rise Cover with a tightly woven towel and let rise for 45 minutes.

Preheat oven About 10 minutes before baking, preheat the oven to 375°F.

Final preparation Just before baking, beat the egg white until frothy. Lightly brush the dove with the egg white. Arrange the thinly sliced almonds slightly overlapping on the tail and wings to simulate feathers. Use a small bit of an almond to make the dove's eye. Carefully brush the almond "feathers" with egg white, then sprinkle the entire dove with the sugar.

Bake and cool Bake for 25 minutes until the internal temperature of the bread reaches 190°F. Immediately remove the bread from the baking sheet and place on a rack to cool.

NOTE: This bread freezes nicely for up to 6 months. To serve, wrap the thawed bread in foil, then reheat in a 375°F oven for 10 to 15 minutes.

Crescia

Many of the folk customs and traditions associated with Easter began with pagan spring festivals. Spring and Easter (the day of resurrection) both represent rebirth. Families in Italy are ready to celebrate any occasion with a feast, but Easter is more eagerly awaited than most, since it follows the six-week Lenten fast.

Historically, Easter dinner includes multiple courses. In many areas of Italy, two foods are fundamental to the Easter dinner: a whole baby lamb, symbolizing the Lamb of God; and Crescia, a savory brioche-like bread made with a large quantity of eggs and Parmesan cheese. The loaf is often baked in clay or ceramic flowerpots to give it a unique shape and crispy crust; however, it is just as often coiled in large round pans. In other areas, Crescia is called pizza, though it shares no similarity to what we consider pizza in America.

BECAUSE OF THE LARGE AMOUNT of Parmesan cheese in this bread, it is very salty and goes especially well with thinly sliced Italian meats or sausages; salami is always a favorite of mine. This is wonderful picnic bread. Slice the loaf horizontally, fill with an assortment of meats, fresh basil, thinly sliced tomatoes, and drizzle all with oil. Put the top back on the loaf and cut into wedges.

MAKES 1 LARGE LOAF OR 2 SMALLER LOAVES

FOR THE DOUGH

1 scant tablespoon or 1 (¼-ounce) package active dry yeast

¼ cup warm water (about 110°F)

4 large eggs, beaten

1 large egg yolk, beaten

¼ cup olive oil

1 tablespoon granulated sugar

1 teaspoon salt

1 teaspoon coarsely cracked pepper

2 cups (8 ounces) shredded Parmesan cheese

4 to 5 cups unbleached all-purpose flour

FOR THE TOPPING

1 large egg white

By hand In a large bowl, sprinkle the yeast in the water to soften. Add the eggs, egg yolk, oil, sugar, salt, pepper, cheese, and 2 cups of the flour to the yeast. Beat vigorously for 2 minutes. Gradually add the remaining flour ¼ cup at a time until the dough begins to pull away from the side of the bowl. Turn the dough out onto a floured work surface. Knead, adding flour a little at a time, until the dough is smooth and elastic.

By mixer In the mixer bowl, sprinkle the yeast in the water to soften. Add the eggs, egg yolk, oil, sugar, salt, pepper, cheese, and 2 cups of the flour to the yeast. Using the mixer paddle, beat the mixture on medium-low speed for 2 minutes. Gradually add the remaining flour ¼ cup at a time until the dough begins to pull away from the side of the bowl. Change to the dough hook. Continue to add flour 1 tablespoon at a time until the dough just begins to clean the bowl. Knead 4 to 5 minutes on medium-low.

By food processor In a large measuring cup or bowl, sprinkle the yeast in the water to soften. Add the eggs, egg yolk, and oil. In the bowl of the food processor fitted with the dough blade, combine the sugar, salt, pepper, cheese, and 4 cups flour with 4 or 5 pulses. With the food processor running, add the liquid ingredients as fast as the dry ingredients will accept them. If you hear a sputtering sound, pour the liquid slower. As soon as all the liquid is added, turn the processor off. Check the liquid-to-flour ratio (see page 28). Pulse until the dough forms a ball, then process exactly 60 seconds.

By bread machine Put the water, eggs, egg yolk, and oil in the bread pan. Add the sugar, salt, pepper, cheese, and 4 cups flour to the bread pan, then sprinkle with the yeast. Select the Dough cycle and press Start. While the dough is mixing, check the liquid-to-flour ratio (see page 29). The machine stops after the kneading cycle. You may let the dough rise in the bread machine or a bowl.

First rise Put the dough in an oiled bowl and turn to coat the entire ball of dough with oil. Cover with a tightly woven towel and let rise until doubled, about 1½ hours.

Shape Turn the dough out onto a lightly oiled work surface and roll into a 48-inch-long rope. Coil the rope in a well-greased 12-inch round pan. The dough may also be divided in half and shaped into two 40-inch-long ropes. Coil each rope in a well-greased 8-inch round pan.

Second rise Cover with a tightly woven towel and let rise for 55 minutes.

Preheat oven About 10 minutes before baking, preheat the oven to 375°F.

Final preparation Beat the egg white until frothy and brush over the top of the loaf.

Bake and cool Bake for 25 minutes until the internal temperature of the bread reaches 190°F. Immediately remove the bread from the pan(s) and place on a rack to cool.

NOTE: This bread freezes nicely for up to 6 months. To serve, first thaw the bread, then reheat on a baking sheet or directly on the oven rack in a 375°F oven for 7 to 10 minutes.

Gubana

Gubana is the king of all celebration breads. It is served at all weddings and every festival or feast that takes place in the Natisone Valleys, a small area in northeast Italy that borders Austria and Slovenia. In the Friulian dialect, *gubana* means "good fortune" or "abundance," while the Slavic meaning of *guba* is "fold," which describes the coiled snail shape.

Gubana is mentioned as early as 1409 among the 72 courses served at the feast to honor Pope Gregory XII by the Commune of Cividale. The bread has evolved over the years from a bread made with what was available locally—several varieties of nuts, dried fruits, spices, and a sprinkling of liqueur—to one of the richest breads ever.

The filling for Gubana is equal to the weight of the sweetened dough. The dough is leavened several times to gain strength to stand up to such a large amount of filling. There are two versions of this celebration bread. The filling is the same for both, but one uses more of a puff-type pastry, while the other uses more of a bread-type dough. The latter is the more popular.

Until the 1960s, Gubana was made exclusively at home. Later, it was made commercially but was still little known in Italy outside the Friuli region. In 1965 for the Feast of San Pietro and San Paolo in San Pietro al Natisone, the first Gubana contest was held. This rich dessert bread has gained in popularity each year.

Although every family and village has its own secret recipe, Gubana is always made with an assortment of the nuts of the area, dried fruits, sometimes macaroons, a touch of chocolate, wines, and/or liqueurs. One such recipe used five different wines and liqueurs.

The filling is rolled in the dough to form a cylinder; then the cylinder is coiled in a round pan. The women of the Natisone Valleys still take immense pride in their Gubana, which has gained favor more as an Easter bread than for any other celebration.

I FIND THE FOOD PROCESSOR invaluable for making the filling for Gubana. First I grate the chocolate into the food processor bowl, add the nuts and finely chop them, then add the raisins. Once the raisins are finely chopped, I add the remaining ingredients and pulse until mixed. This is so much easier than doing it by hand. Toasting the nuts brings out their flavor; they can all be toasted together in a 350°F oven for 15 to 20 minutes.

I love to use Scandinavian *pärlsocker,* pearl sugar, in baking (this can be purchased in Scandinavian grocery stores; or see Sources, page 331). It is an unusual alternative to icing breads and gives much more satisfactory results than crushing sugar cubes, which is what the Italians do.

MAKES 1 LARGE LOAF

FOR THE SPONGE

1 scant tablespoon or 1 (¼-ounce) package active dry yeast

1 cup warm water (about 110°F)

½ cup unbleached all-purpose flour

FOR THE DOUGH

¼ cup granulated sugar

1 teaspoon salt

3 large eggs, beaten

¼ cup (½ stick) unsalted butter, softened

2 teaspoons vanilla extract

2½ to 3½ cups unbleached all-purpose flour

FOR THE FILLING

1 ounce unsweetened chocolate, finely grated

¼ cup toasted pine nuts, finely chopped

¼ cup toasted walnuts, finely chopped

½ cup toasted hazelnuts, finely chopped

¾ cup raisins, finely chopped

¼ cup brown sugar, firmly packed

2 teaspoons finely grated lemon zest

½ cup unflavored dry bread crumbs

¼ cup orange marmalade

¼ cup Marsala, grappa, rum, or sweet Italian dessert wine

FOR THE TOPPING

1 large egg

1 tablespoon cold water

Pärlsocker or coarsely crushed sugar cubes, optional

Prepare sponge In a large bowl, sprinkle the yeast in the water to soften. Add the flour and beat to combine. Cover with plastic wrap and let rise for 30 minutes.

By hand Add the sugar, salt, eggs, butter, vanilla, and 1 cup of the flour to the sponge and beat to combine. Gradually add the remaining flour ¼ cup at a time until the dough begins to pull away from the side of the bowl. Turn the dough out onto a floured work surface. Knead, adding flour a little at a time, until the dough is smooth and elastic.

By mixer In the mixer bowl, combine the sugar, salt, eggs, butter, vanilla, and 1 cup of the flour with the sponge. Using the mixer paddle, beat the mixture on medium-low speed until well mixed. Gradually add the remaining flour ¼ cup at a time until the dough begins to pull away from the side of the bowl. Change to the dough hook. Continue to add flour 1 tablespoon at a time until the dough just begins to clean the bowl. Knead 4 to 5 minutes on medium-low.

By food processor Combine the sponge, eggs, and vanilla until well mixed. In the bowl of the food processor fitted with the dough blade, combine the butter, sugar, salt, and 2½ cups flour with 4 or 5 pulses. Add the sponge mixture. Pulse until the dough forms a ball. Check the liquid-to-flour ratio (see page 28). Process exactly 60 seconds.

By bread machine Put the sponge, eggs, butter, and vanilla in the bread pan. Add the sugar, salt, and 2½ cups flour to the bread pan. Select the Dough cycle and press Start. While the dough is mixing, check the liquid-to-flour ratio (see page 29). The machine stops after the kneading cycle. You may let the dough rise in the bread machine or a bowl.

First rise Put the dough in an oiled bowl and turn to coat the entire ball of dough with oil. Cover with a tightly woven towel and let rise until doubled, about 1½ hours. Place your fist in the center of the dough and push to the bottom of the bowl. Fold in the sides of the dough to the center and push again to release all the air.

Second rise Cover with a tightly woven towel and let rise again until doubled, about one hour.

Prepare filling In a large bowl, combine the chocolate, pine nuts, walnuts, hazelnuts, raisins, brown sugar, zest, bread crumbs, marmalade, and Marsala and stir to mix well. Stir occasionally while the dough is rising.

Shape Turn the dough out onto a lightly oiled work surface and roll into a 14 by 18-inch rectangle. Spread the filling ingredients over the dough, leaving a ½-inch border on one 14-inch side. Roll the dough into a 14-inch cylinder starting at the edge opposite the border. Pinch the seam well to seal. Coil the dough with the seam side down in a well-greased 9-inch springform pan.

Third rise Cover with a tightly woven towel and let rise for 55 minutes. Because of the heavy filling, this dough will not double in size.

Preheat oven About 10 minutes before baking, preheat the oven to 375°F.

Final preparation Beat the egg and water together and brush over the top of the loaf. Sprinkle with the sugar if using.

Bake and cool Bake for 45 minutes until the internal temperature of the bread reaches 190°F. Immediately remove the bread from the pan and place on a rack to cool.

NOTE: This bread freezes nicely for up to 6 months. To serve, wrap the thawed bread in foil. Reheat in a 375°F oven on the center oven rack for 12 to 15 minutes. Let sit wrapped in the foil for 5 minutes before unwrapping and slicing.

Pandolce

Italians eat like royalty during the Christmas season, while the rest of the year meals are down-to-earth and unpretentious. During the holidays large platters of extravagant foods are consumed, and the ordinary simple breads of the country become rich and elaborate with the addition of lard, oil, butter, eggs, fruits, and nuts.

In the region of Montagnana, well known for its popular horse race and its delicate prosciutto, one of Italy's best Christmas breads was born—Pandolce. In the legend of this wonderful bread, the Emperor's vicar, Ezzelino III da Romano, saved the town from a terrible fire but in doing so was seriously injured. One of the women of the village made Pandolce; the sweet bread rich in fruits and nuts restored Ezzelino's health. In honor of the occasion, Pandolce is the favored sweet bread for Christmas.

THE TOASTED PINE NUTS are more modern than traditional; toasting them brings out their flavor, and it is well worth the additional effort. Don't be turned off by the number of ingredients in this bread; each one adds to its very special flavor and texture.

MAKES I LARGE LOAF

FOR THE SPONGE

1 scant tablespoon or 1 (¼-ounce) package active dry yeast

¼ cup warm water (about 110°F)

¼ cup honey

½ cup warm milk (about 110°F)

1 cup unbleached all-purpose flour

FOR THE DOUGH

2 large egg yolks, beaten

1 large egg white, beaten to soft peaks

½ cup Marsala

½ cup honey

6 tablespoons (¾ stick) unsalted butter, softened

1 teaspoon salt

1 teaspoon fennel seeds

3 to 4 cups unbleached all-purpose flour

½ cup pine nuts, toasted

½ cup pistachio nuts

1 cup golden raisins

½ cup currants

½ cup candied orange peel (see Notes)

½ cup candied lemon peel (see Notes)

FOR THE GLAZE

1 large egg white

1 tablespoon cold water

Prepare sponge Combine the yeast, water, honey, milk, and flour and mix until smooth. Cover with plastic wrap and let rise for 3 hours.

By hand In a large bowl, combine the sponge, egg yolks, egg white, Marsala, honey, butter, salt, and fennel seeds. Gradually add the flour ¼ cup at a time until the dough begins to pull away from the side of the bowl. Turn the dough out onto a floured work surface. Knead, adding flour a little at a time, until the dough is smooth and elastic.

By mixer In a large bowl, combine the sponge, egg yolks, egg white, Marsala, honey, butter, salt, and fennel seeds. Gradually add the flour ¼ cup at a time until the dough begins to pull away from the side of the bowl. Change to the dough hook. Continue to add flour 1 tablespoon at a time until the dough just begins to clean the bowl. Knead 4 to 5 minutes on medium-low.

By food processor To the bowl of the food processor fitted with the dough blade, add 3 cups flour. Combine the sponge, egg yolks, egg white, Marsala, honey, butter, salt, and fennel seeds and add to the processor bowl. Pulse until the dough begins to pull together. Check the liquid-to-flour ratio (see page 28). Pulse until the dough forms a ball, then process exactly 60 seconds.

By bread machine Put the sponge, egg yolks, egg white, Marsala, honey, and butter in the bread pan, then add the salt, fennel seeds, and 3 cups flour. Select the Dough cycle and press Start. While the dough is mixing, check the liquid-to-flour ratio (see page 29). The machine stops after the kneading cycle. You may let the dough rise in the bread machine or a bowl.

First rise Put the dough in an oiled bowl and turn to coat the entire ball of dough with oil. Cover with a tightly woven towel and let rise until doubled, about one hour.

Second kneading Turn the dough out onto a lightly oiled work surface and sprinkle with the pine nuts, pistachios, raisins, currants, and orange and lemon peels. Knead until the fruits and nuts are incorporated in the dough. Cover the dough with a tightly woven towel and let rise on the work surface for 30 minutes.

Shape Shape the dough into a ball and place on a parchment-lined or well-greased baking sheet. Lightly press the loaf to flatten it to about 2½ inches thick.

Second rise Cover with a tightly woven towel and let rise for one hour.

Preheat oven About 10 minutes before baking, preheat the oven to 375°F.

Final preparation Beat the egg white with the cold water and brush over the top and sides of the loaf. With a sharp serrated knife or razor blade, cut a cross about ½ inch deep in the top of the loaf.

Bake and cool Bake for 45 minutes until the internal temperature of the bread reaches 190°F. Watch the loaf carefully during the last 10 minutes of baking. If the loaf becomes too brown, cover it with foil, shiny side up. Immediately remove the bread from the baking sheet and place on a rack to cool.

NOTES: If you prefer to make your own candied peel, see page 326.

This bread freezes nicely for up to 6 months. To serve, first thaw the bread, then reheat on a baking sheet or directly on the oven rack in a 375°F oven for 7 to 10 minutes.

Panettone

No matter the disputed origins of Panettone, it has definitely become the national Christmas bread of Italy. Of the numerous tales attached to this bread, two are worthy of note.

The first tale begins with the Lord of Milan, Ludovico il Moro, hosting the largest banquet ever seen. As the feast begins, waiters bustle about the superbly laid tables, serving the finest foods and wines.

In the kitchen, however, the head cook is in a panic as he watches the beautiful cake he had so lovingly prepared and decorated collapse right before his eyes. A young kitchen helper sees that the head cook is in complete despair. He rolls up his sleeves and mixes flour, yeast, butter, sugar, spices, raisins, candied fruit, and anything else he can find in the kitchen.

The loaves rise and he begins to bake them. The sweet exotic smell spreads from the kitchen into the dining room. The head cook goes to see what the smell and excitement in the kitchen are and finds the young helper with his makeshift dessert. Since there is nothing else to do, the strange dessert is served.

After tasting the new treat, people enthusiastically praise the cake. Ludovico il Moro calls for the creator of the dessert, and the young helper finds himself shoved into the center of the room. He is greeted by loud, spontaneous applause. When Ludovico il Moro asks the young helper's name, he replies, "My name is Toni," and the bread has held the name *pan de Toni,* or Toni's bread, since then.

The other tale is much more romantic. A young Milanese noble falls in love with the daughter of a baker named Toni. The family of the young man opposes the marriage because of the young girl's humble beginnings. Knowing that his family values wealth above all, the nobleman makes it possible for Toni to purchase the finest ingredients and encourages him to bake a bread like none before. Toni creates a masterpiece that makes his reputation and fortune, and the young noble wins the hand of the baker's daughter.

ORIGINALLY THIS BREAD was baked in 6- to 10-pound loaves; today the size has been scaled down to 1 to 3 pounds. Due to the richness of the dough, the crust tends to turn too dark before the center of the loaves is done. Watch the bread carefully during the last 10 minutes of baking; if necessary, cover the loaves with foil, shiny side up.

MAKES 2 LARGE LOAVES

FOR THE SPONGE

1 scant tablespoon or 1 (¼-ounce) package active dry yeast

½ cup warm water (about 110°F)

½ cup unbleached all-purpose flour

FOR THE DOUGH

¼ cup honey

¼ cup granulated sugar

½ cup (1 stick) unsalted butter, melted

1 teaspoon salt

2 large eggs, beaten

6 large egg yolks, beaten

1 teaspoon vanilla extract

3½ to 4½ cups unbleached all-purpose flour

¾ cup golden raisins

½ cup chopped candied citron

¼ cup chopped candied lemon peel (see Notes)

¼ cup chopped candied orange peel (see Notes)

1 tablespoon finely grated lemon zest

1 tablespoon finely grated orange zest

FOR THE TOPPING

Confectioners' sugar

Prepare sponge Combine the yeast, water, and flour and mix until smooth. Cover with plastic wrap and let rise for 30 minutes.

By hand Add the honey, sugar, butter, salt, eggs, yolks, vanilla, and 2 cups of the flour to the sponge. Beat vigorously for 2 minutes. Gradually add the remaining flour ¼ cup at a time until the dough begins to pull away from the side of the bowl. Turn the dough out onto a floured work surface. Knead, adding flour a little at a time, until the dough is smooth and elastic. Keep the dough as light as possible.

By mixer Add the honey, sugar, butter, salt, eggs, yolks, vanilla, and 2 cups of the flour to the sponge. Using the mixer paddle, beat the mixture on medium-low speed for 2 minutes. Gradually add the remaining flour ¼ cup at a time until the dough begins to pull away from the side of the bowl. Change to the dough hook. Continue to add flour 1 tablespoon at a time until the dough just begins to clean the bowl. Knead 4 to 5 minutes on medium-low. Keep the dough as light as possible.

By food processor Add the honey, sugar, eggs, yolks, and vanilla to the sponge. In the bowl of the food processor fitted with the dough blade, combine the butter, salt, and 3½ cups flour with 4 or 5 pulses. With the food processor running, add the liquid ingredients as fast as the dry ingredients will accept them. If you hear a sputtering sound, pour the liquid slower. As soon as all the liquid is added, turn the processor off. Check the liquid-to-flour ratio (see page 28). Keep the dough as light as possible. Pulse until the dough forms a ball, then process exactly 60 seconds.

By bread machine Put the sponge, honey, sugar, butter, eggs, yolks, and vanilla in the bread pan. Add the salt and 3½ cups flour. Select the Dough cycle and press Start. While the dough is mixing, check the liquid-to-flour ratio (see page 29). The machine stops after the kneading cycle. You may let the dough rise in the bread machine or a bowl.

First rise Put the dough in an oiled bowl and turn to coat the entire ball of dough with oil. Cover with a tightly woven towel and let rise until doubled, about 1½ hours.

Add fruit Turn the dough out on a lightly oiled work surface and knead in the raisins, citron, candied lemon and orange peels, and lemon and orange zests. Cover the dough on the work surface and let rest for 5 minutes.

Shape Divide the dough in half and shape each half into a ball. Place in either two 7- or 8-inch well-greased round pans, in two well-greased 1-pound coffee cans, or on a parchment-lined or well-greased baking sheet. If the loaves are placed on a baking sheet, gently flatten the center of each loaf, remembering that the bread should have a rounded top and that the center of the loaf rises the highest.

Second rise Cover with a tightly woven towel and let rise for one hour.

Preheat oven About 10 minutes before baking, preheat the oven to 375°F.

Final preparation With a sharp serrated knife or razor blade, cut a ¼-inch-deep cross in the top of each loaf.

Bake and cool Bake for 30 minutes until the internal temperature of the bread reaches 190°F. Immediately remove the bread from the pans and place on a rack to cool.

Finish Just before serving, sprinkle the top of each loaf liberally with confectioners' sugar.

NOTES: If you prefer to make your own candied peel, see page 326.

This bread freezes nicely for up to 6 months. To serve, first thaw the bread, then reheat on a baking sheet or directly on the oven rack in a 375°F oven for 7 to 10 minutes.

Saint Joseph's Bread

PANE DE SAN GIUSEPPE

During the Middle Ages a severe drought struck Sicily. The people petitioned their patron saint, Joseph, to intervene on their behalf. They promised that if he would help, they would prepare a great feast in his honor each year. Rain soon fell; to fulfill their vow, a huge feast is held in the saint's honor each year on March 19. All are welcome; no one is turned away. To this day the whole town of Salemi, Italy, participates in the Feast of Saint Joseph.

There is very little mention of Joseph in the Bible other than that he was the husband of Mary, the earthly father of Jesus, and a carpenter. Nonetheless, he was held in such high esteem that he became the patron saint of many places and trades, including pastry cooks. He is the protector of the family and of the poor, orphans, unwed mothers, and the homeless; and the guardian of the spiritual home of Christians.

For the Feast of Saint Joseph, the people of Salemi create ornate altars in their homes. In the town a chapel-like structure is built, containing a three-tiered altar inside an overhanging canopy. The canopy is covered with myrtle and laurel and thickly hung with lemons, oranges, and thousands of small, exquisitely designed breads.

On the altar there are candles, crosses, religious objects, flowers, food, wine, and three large ornate breads. One of the breads is in the shape of a date palm to symbolize Mary. Legend states that when she traveled to Egypt, God made the date palms blossom with fruit. When she saw this miracle, she exclaimed, "Oh!" There is a small dot inside every date pit to represent the shape of her mouth. Joseph's loaf is in the shape of a staff, which is said to have burst into bloom when he was chosen to be Mary's husband. The loaf for Jesus is a large elaborate wreath with a star-shaped center to represent the light of truth.

The small breads hanging on the canopy are a sign of abundance and are shaped in intricate designs. There are images of fish representing Christ, love, and charity; Easter lambs symbolizing Christ's resurrection; roses representing Mary and virginity; Saint Joseph's staff adorned with a lily to symbolize loyalty and purity; broad beans representing fertility; horses signifying intelligence; peacocks for beauty and immortality; and eagles for strength and justice. There are flowers in all kinds of shapes, fruits, moons, stars, birds, baskets, canes, heads and beards to depict Saint Joseph, carpenter's tools, braids, crowns, crosses, wreaths, roosters, angels, sheaves of wheat—almost anything that could possibly have touched the life of Joseph.

It takes about fifteen women working ten full days to make all the ornamental breads used for the celebration. Today the dough is made in a mixer using flour made from local durum wheat, water, and small amounts of salt and yeast. The dough is very stiff and kneaded for up to two hours to make it soft and malleable.

Once the dough reaches the proper consistency, it is fed through pasta machines to produce long, thin strips to be cut and shaped. The tools the women use are simple—a fluted-edge ravioli cutter, an ultrathin sharp paring knife, a thimble, a comb used in looming cloth, scissors, needles, and thin dowels. The dough rises for three hours under blankets in a cool room. Before baking, the bread is brushed with a wash made from eggs beaten with lemon juice.

It is very expensive to purchase all the ingredients for the breads and the 101 courses served at the ritual feast. The people of the town donate food and money to cover the costs for the meal. It is also difficult to find more than a hundred different ways to prepare foods, especially when no meat or dairy is allowed, but these ingenious women do, and it is an astonishing spread.

Traditionally, three poor children were chosen to partake in this extravagant meal. However, today the people of Salemi claim it is hard to find poor children, so three children are chosen at random for this honor. These "little saints" are treated with extreme respect.

Once the three children are seated at the table in front of the altar, the priest blesses the altar and then the food. There is quite a ceremony made of washing the hands with holy water poured from a basin. The first plate served is always orange sections sprinkled with sugar, and the last plate is pasta tossed with olive oil, garlic, sugar, cinnamon, and bread crumbs. The three children must take at least one bite of every plate served—all 101 of them!

Once the ceremonial tasting from each dish is completed, the remaining food is passed to the spectators, who represent the poor. Saint Joseph's Bread, most often shaped like the patriarch's beard, is blessed by the priest and shared with everyone. Each guest receives a small bit of bread and a lucky fava bean to take home.

The Feast of Saint Joseph began in Sicily, but as southern Italians immigrated, it spread all over the world. Generosity marks this day, as it did the character of Joseph himself. Today Catholic Italian families who have received special blessings during the year may host a Saint Joseph's table in their home. The feast is always free and open to families, friends, neighbors, and even strangers—no one is ever turned away. A bonfire is built in front of the home to announce the feast.

IF USING a ¼-ounce package of active dry yeast, use 1 teaspoon for the sponge and the rest of the package for the bread. The sponge must be prepared 8 to 24 hours before making the bread. The longer the sponge sits, the more the flavors develop.

MAKES 1 LARGE LOAF

FOR THE SPONGE

1 teaspoon active dry yeast

¼ cup warm water (about 110°F)

¾ cup unbleached all-purpose flour

FOR THE BREAD

1 cup water, at room temperature

1½ teaspoons active dry yeast

1 teaspoon salt

1 tablespoon granulated sugar

1 cup semolina flour

2¼ to 3¼ cups unbleached all-purpose flour

FOR THE GLAZE

1 large egg

1 tablespoon fresh lemon juice

Prepare sponge In a medium bowl, sprinkle the yeast into the water to soften. Add the flour and stir to form a stiff dough. Turn out onto a work surface and knead until smooth, about 5 minutes. Put the dough in a large ungreased glass or pottery bowl. Cover the bowl first with plastic wrap, then a tightly woven towel. Let the dough sit at room temperature for 8 to 24 hours. The dough will rise but eventually fall.

By hand Add the water to the sponge and let sit 5 minutes. Squeeze the sponge through your fingers until it dissolves in the water. Sprinkle the yeast over the sponge mixture and let sit until each granule of yeast is moistened. Add the salt, sugar, semolina, and ½ cup of the all-purpose flour to the yeast mixture. Beat vigorously for 2 minutes. Gradually add the remaining flour ¼ cup at a time until the dough begins to pull away from the side of the bowl. Turn the dough out onto a floured work surface. Knead, adding flour a little at a time, until the dough is smooth and elastic.

By mixer In the mixer bowl, add the water to the sponge and let sit 5 minutes. Squeeze the sponge through your fingers until it dissolves in the water; do not beat with the mixer—the water will simply slosh out of the bowl. Sprinkle the yeast over the sponge mixture and let sit until each granule of yeast is

moistened. Add the salt, sugar, semolina, and ½ cup of the all-purpose flour to the yeast mixture. Using the mixer paddle, beat the mixture on medium-low speed for 2 minutes. Gradually add the remaining flour ¼ cup at a time until the dough begins to pull away from the side of the bowl. Change to the dough hook. Continue to add flour 1 tablespoon at a time until the dough just begins to clean the bowl. Knead 4 to 5 minutes on medium-low.

By food processor Add the water to the sponge and let sit 5 minutes. Squeeze the sponge through your fingers until it dissolves in the water. Sprinkle the yeast over the sponge mixture and let sit until each granule of yeast is moistened. In the bowl of the food processor fitted with the dough blade, combine the salt, sugar, semolina, and 2¼ cups all-purpose flour with 4 or 5 pulses. With the food processor running, add the liquid ingredients as fast as the dry ingredients will accept them. If you hear a sputtering sound, pour the liquid slower. As soon as all the liquid is added, turn the processor off. Check the liquid-to-flour ratio (see page 28). Pulse until the dough forms a ball, then process exactly 60 seconds.

By bread machine Add the water to the sponge and let sit 5 minutes. Squeeze the sponge through your fingers until it dissolves in the water. Sprinkle the yeast over the sponge mixture and let sit until each granule of yeast is moistened. Transfer to the bread pan, then add the salt, sugar, semolina, and 2¼ cups all-purpose flour. Select the Dough cycle and press Start. While the dough is mixing, check the liquid-to-flour ratio (see page 29). The machine stops after the kneading cycle. You may let the dough rise in the bread machine or a bowl.

First rise Put the dough in an oiled bowl and turn to coat the entire ball of dough with oil. Cover with a tightly woven towel and let rise until doubled, about 1½ hours.

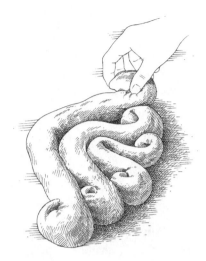

Shape Turn the dough out onto a lightly oiled work surface and divide into 3 pieces—one small, one medium, and one large. Refer to the illustration for an idea of the approximate sizes for these dough pieces. Roll the small piece into a 10-inch rope, the medium piece into a 15-inch rope, and the large piece into a 20-inch rope. Shape the dough into a stylized beard: On a parchment-lined or well-greased baking sheet, take one piece of dough and fold it in half with the ends facing the short sides of the baking sheet. Curl the ends to the outside. Place the second rope over the first rope, making certain that the rope keeps the ends of the first piece of dough from unrolling. Curl the ends of the second rope to the outside. Repeat with the third rope.

Second rise Cover with a tightly woven towel and let rise for 45 minutes.

Preheat oven About 10 minutes before baking, preheat the oven to 375°F.

Final preparation Beat the egg with the lemon juice and brush over the top and sides of the bread. Wait 5 minutes and brush again. Do not let the glaze puddle in the crevices of the loaf.

Bake and cool Bake for 30 minutes until the internal temperature of the bread reaches 190°F. Let the loaf cool for 10 minutes on the baking sheet before transferring to a rack to cool.

NOTE: This bread freezes nicely for up to 6 months. To serve, first thaw the bread, then reheat on a baking sheet or directly on the oven rack in a 375°F oven for 7 to 10 minutes.

Massa Sovada

Festa dos Tabuleiros, one of the most gorgeous harvest celebrations, takes place in the small town of Tomar, just north of Lisbon, Portugal. Four to five hundred young girls dressed in white take part in a procession through town. There are musicians, soldiers, standard bearers, oxen with gilded horns, and ornate wine carts, but what makes this parade truly spectacular are the girls' crowns, made of bread and decorated with brightly colored paper flowers, doves, and wheat. These elaborate handmade crowns are as tall as the girls wearing them. A male family member—father, brother, or fiancé—usually walks with the young woman to steady the crown and make sure the weight doesn't topple it over.

Festa dos Tabuleiros is held on the first Sunday in July on alternate years. It dates back to pagan times when the local farmers gave thanks to Ceres for a good harvest, and young women had to prove they were strong enough to bear children. The young women participating in this procession were all virgins ready to be chosen for marriage.

Prior to the procession, young virgins joined with other female family members to bake Massa Sovada, sweet bread. The bread is baked with raw eggs, still in the shell, placed at intervals in the round loaf to signify fertility. There should be at least one egg per person to be served.

The crowns, called *tabuleiros,* meaning "tray," contain about 30 pounds of bread plus the weight of the other decorations. Walking through the town with the awkward tall heavy weight on one's head is no easy feat. At the end of the procession, the young women gather in front of the church of Saint John the Baptist, where the seventeen most beautiful *tabuleiros* are chosen. The local priest blesses the breads and other feast items. (The next day the poor of the town are given gifts of bread from the crowns.) After the blessing, the day is filled with exciting festivities such as bullfights (Portuguese style, in which the bull is allowed to live), donkey cart races, dancing, eating, drinking, and, finally, fireworks to end the day.

THIS PORTUGUESE SWEET BREAD contains fresh lemon juice to relax the gluten and give the dough an unusual texture. Raw eggs are added to the top of the bread before baking—not dyed eggs, just regular well-washed eggs—then crossed with dough. During baking the eggs cook slightly. I personally don't like soft-cooked eggs, so I hard-boil my eggs before adding them.

MAKES TWO 9-INCH LOAVES

1 scant tablespoon or 1(¼-ounce) package active dry yeast

¼ cup warm water (about 110°F)

½ cup milk

½ cup (1 stick) unsalted butter, melted

3 large eggs, lightly beaten

2 tablespoons fresh lemon juice

1 tablespoon finely grated lemon zest

¾ cup granulated sugar

1 teaspoon salt

4 to 5 cups unbleached all-purpose flour

Raw eggs in the shell, washed

Milk to brush on loaves

By hand In a large bowl, sprinkle the yeast in the water to soften. Heat the milk to 110°F and add it to the yeast along with the butter, eggs, juice, zest, sugar, salt, and 2 cups of the flour. Beat vigorously for 2 minutes. Gradually add the remaining flour ¼ cup at a time until the dough begins to pull away from the side of the bowl. Turn the dough out onto a floured work surface. Knead, adding flour a little at a time, until the dough is smooth and elastic.

By mixer In the mixer bowl, sprinkle the yeast in the water to soften. Heat the milk to 110°F and add it to the yeast along with the butter, eggs, juice, zest, sugar, salt, and 2 cups of the flour. Using the mixer paddle, beat the mixture on medium-low speed for 2 minutes. Gradually add the remaining flour ¼ cup at a time until the dough begins to pull away from the side of the bowl. Change to the dough hook. Continue to add flour 1 tablespoon at a time until the dough just begins to clean the bowl. Knead 4 to 5 minutes on medium-low.

By food processor In a large measuring cup or bowl, sprinkle the yeast in the water to soften. Heat the milk to 100°F and add it to the yeast along with the butter, eggs, and lemon juice. In the bowl of the food processor fitted with the dough blade, combine the zest, sugar, salt, and 4 cups flour with 4 or 5 pulses. With the food processor running, add the liquid ingredients as fast as the dry ingredients will accept them. If you hear a sputtering sound, pour the liquid slower. As soon as all the liquid is added, turn the processor off. Check the liquid-to-flour ratio (see page 28). Pulse until the dough forms a ball, then process exactly 60 seconds.

By bread machine Put the water, milk, butter, eggs, and lemon juice in the bread pan. Add the zest, sugar, salt, and 4 cups flour, then sprinkle with the yeast. Select the Dough cycle and press Start. While the dough is mixing, check the liquid-to-flour ratio (see page 29). The machine stops after the kneading cycle. You may let the dough rise in the bread machine or a bowl.

First rise Put the dough in an oiled bowl and turn to coat the entire ball of dough with oil. Cover with a tightly woven towel and let rise until doubled, about one hour.

Shape Turn the dough out onto a lightly oiled work surface and divide in half. Round each half into a ball and place in well-greased 9-inch round pans about 1½ to 2 inches deep. Flatten the loaves. For each egg (at least 1 per person) pinch out a golf-ball-size piece of dough; space the holes at equal intervals. Place an egg in each hole. Divide each pinch of dough in half and roll into pencil-thin ropes about 4 inches long. Cross 2 ropes over each egg.

Second rise Cover with a tightly woven towel and let rise for 45 minutes.

Preheat oven About 10 minutes before baking, preheat the oven to 375°F.

Final preparation Brush the loaves with milk.

Bake and cool Bake for 25 minutes until the internal temperature of the bread reaches 190°F. Immediately remove the loaves from the pans and place on a rack to cool.

NOTE: Because of the eggs, this bread does not freeze well.

Rosca de Reyes

THREE KINGS' BREAD

Rosca de Reyes is the celebration bread of the Epiphany, when the Three Wise Men, Three Kings, or Magi (all terms used to describe the three astronomers) traveled a great distance to recognize and honor the Christ child. This celebration takes place on January 6.

Twelve days after the birth of Jesus in the town of Bethlehem, the Three Wise Men saw a bright star in the East. Understanding that the star told of a savior born, they traveled to Bethlehem. Along their way they met King Herod and told him of the birth of the new king. Herod ordered them to find the baby and return to give the news of the place where the Messiah had been born.

The Three Wise Men found the baby in a manger and offered him gifts of gold, representing the spiritual wealth of the child; frankincense, signifying the earth and sky; and myrrh, the oil used for medicinal and spiritual purposes. As they were leaving Bethlehem, the Three Kings were warned by an angel that they should return home by a different route, because Herod intended to kill the baby.

In Spain and many Latin American countries, children leave straw out for the Three Kings' camels, and the Kings leave candies and gifts for the children on Epiphany. This is when the children actually receive their Christmas gifts, rather than on the night the Christ child was born.

Rosca de Reyes is always served with hot chocolate. This sweet bread has a small doll or bean hidden inside the bread to symbolize the baby Jesus. The person who receives the piece of bread with the doll is obligated to give a party on Candlemas Day (February 2), the church festival in honor of the presentation of Jesus in the Temple and the purification of the Virgin Mary.

A bean or tiny ceramic doll should be added to the filling so that it is hidden. This symbolizes the hiding of the infant Christ from King Herod's troops. Note that the first rise takes place overnight.

Makes 1 large loaf

For the Dough

1 scant tablespoon or 1 (¼-ounce) package active dry yeast

1 tablespoon warm water (about 110°F)

½ cup milk

½ cup (1 stick) unsalted butter, softened

½ cup granulated sugar

2 tablespoons finely grated orange zest

1 teaspoon salt

3 cups unbleached all-purpose flour

3 large eggs

2 tablespoons brandy or 1 tablespoon vanilla extract

For the Filling

½ cup granulated sugar

2 cups ground almonds

¼ cup fresh orange juice

½ teaspoon almond extract

Large bean or tiny ceramic doll

For the Glaze

1 large egg

1 tablespoon cold water

Sliced almonds for garnish

By hand In a large bowl, sprinkle the yeast in the water to soften. Heat the milk to 110°F and add it to the yeast along with the butter, sugar, zest, salt, and 2 cups of the flour. In a small bowl, beat the eggs with the brandy and add to the yeast mixture. Beat vigorously for 2 minutes. Gradually add the remaining flour ¼ cup at a time until incorporated. The dough will be very soft.

By mixer In the mixer bowl, sprinkle the yeast in the water to soften. Heat the milk to 110°F and add it to the yeast along with the butter, sugar, zest, salt, and 2 cups of the flour. In a small bowl, beat the eggs with the brandy and add to the yeast mixture. Using the mixer paddle, beat the mixture on medium-low speed for 2 minutes. Gradually add the remaining flour ¼ cup at a time until incorporated. The dough will be very soft.

By food processor In a large measuring cup or bowl, sprinkle the yeast in the water to soften. Heat the milk to 100°F and add it to the yeast along with the eggs and brandy. In the bowl of the food processor fitted with the dough blade, combine the butter, sugar, zest, salt, and 3 cups flour with 4 or 5 pulses. With the food processor running, add the liquid ingredients as fast as the dry ingredients will accept them. If you hear a sputtering sound, pour the liquid slower. As soon as all the liquid is added, turn the processor off. The dough will be very soft.

By bread machine Put the water, milk, butter, eggs, and brandy in the bread pan. Add the sugar, zest, salt, and 3 cups flour to the bread pan, then sprinkle with the yeast. Select the Dough cycle and press Start. Note that this is a very soft dough and it will mix, but not knead, in the bread machine. The machine stops after the kneading cycle. You may let the dough rise in the bread machine or a bowl.

First rise Put the dough in an oiled bowl and turn to coat the entire ball of dough with oil. Cover with plastic wrap and then a tightly woven towel. Let rise in the refrigerator for 8 to 12 hours.

Prepare filling Combine the sugar, ground almonds, orange juice, and almond extract.

Shape Turn the dough out onto a lightly oiled work surface and roll into a 20 by 10-inch rectangle. Sprinkle the filling over the upper two-thirds of the rectangle, leaving a ½-inch border at the top. Add the bean or doll. Fold up the bottom third of dough, then fold the upper third over to within ½ inch of the bottom edge. Pinch the seam to seal. Bring the ends of the roll together and carefully place on a parchment-lined or well-greased baking sheet. Reshape if necessary. Grease an ovenproof bowl and place it in the center of the loaf to help the loaf keep its shape.

Second rise Cover with a tightly woven towel and let rise for one hour.

Preheat oven About 10 minutes before baking, preheat the oven to 375°F.

Final preparation Beat the egg with the cold water and brush over the loaf. Sprinkle liberally with sliced almonds.

Bake and cool Bake for 25 minutes until the internal temperature of the bread reaches 190°F. Immediately remove the bread from the baking sheet and place on a rack to cool.

NOTE: This bread freezes nicely for up to 6 months. To serve, first thaw the bread, then reheat on a baking sheet or directly on the oven rack in a 375°F oven for 7 to 10 minutes.

Birnenbrot

In the Canton Glarus in the eastern part of Switzerland, farmers dry pears and other fruits to preserve them. These home-preserved fruits are the basis for Birnenbrot, a heavily fruited pear bread, made early in December so the bread has plenty of time to mellow.

On December 6, the feast of Saint Nicholas, schoolchildren in Glarnerland parade through the village, ringing and jingling bells of all sizes, sometimes in rhythmic unison and sometimes in wild abandon. The bells signal the villagers that a gift is expected from each household along the way. The gifts are usually good things to eat or drink—fruit, candy, sweet breads, and cakes.

Santa Claus plays only a small part during Christmas in Switzerland. The *Christkind* or *le petit Jésus* (Christ child), a beautiful, radiant, angel-like being with wings, dressed in white with a shining crown and a magic wand, is the main focus of the celebration. Children are told that the Christ child brings their tree and gifts on Christmas Eve.

Usually the parents and grandparents decorate the family tree on Christmas Eve. At the foot of the decorated tree, often a crèche is arranged with figures representing the baby Jesus, Mary and Joseph, shepherds, angels, sheep, cows, donkeys, and the Three Magi or Wise Men. After dinner on Christmas Eve, the whole family, usually several generations, gathers around the tree. They sing songs, read the Christmas story, and then attend a festive midnight mass.

Birnenbrot is eaten throughout the holiday season and is often given as gifts to friends and family.

TRADITIONALLY, KIRSCH (cherry brandy) is used with the fruit, but you can use orange juice with a teaspoon of rum extract added as a substitute.

MAKES 2 LOAVES

FOR THE FILLING

2 cups finely chopped dried pears

1 cup finely chopped pitted prunes

1 cup golden raisins

1 tablespoon lemon juice

¾ cup water

½ cup brown sugar, packed

½ cup finely chopped walnuts

½ teaspoon ground cinnamon

½ cup kirschwasser or light rum

FOR THE DOUGH

1 scant tablespoon or 1 (¼-ounce) package active dry yeast

¼ cup warm water (about 110°F)

1 cup milk

¼ cup (½ stick) unsalted butter, softened

1 teaspoon finely grated lemon zest

1 teaspoon salt

½ cup granulated sugar

4 to 5 cups unbleached all-purpose flour

FOR THE TOPPING

Soft butter, optional

Prepare fruit In a large saucepan over medium heat, combine the pears, prunes, raisins, juice, water, and brown sugar. Cook, stirring often, until the mixture is very thick, 7 to 10 minutes. Remove from the heat. Add the walnuts, cinnamon, and kirsch and stir to combine. Set aside to cool.

By hand In a large bowl, sprinkle the yeast in the water to soften. Heat the milk to 110°F and add it to the yeast along with the butter, zest, salt, sugar, and 2 cups of the flour. Beat vigorously for 2 minutes. Gradually add the remaining flour ¼ cup at a time until the dough begins to pull away from the side of the bowl. Turn the dough out onto a floured work surface. Knead, adding flour a little at a time, until the dough is smooth and elastic.

By mixer In the mixer bowl, sprinkle the yeast in the water to soften. Heat the milk to 110°F and add it to the yeast along with the butter, zest, salt, sugar, and 2 cups of the flour. Using the mixer paddle, beat the mixture on medium-low speed for 2 minutes. Gradually add the remaining flour ¼ cup at a time until the dough begins to pull away from the side of the bowl. Change to the dough hook. Continue to add flour 1 tablespoon at a time until the dough just begins to clean the bowl. Knead 4 to 5 minutes on medium-low.

By food processor In a medium measuring cup or bowl, sprinkle the yeast in the water to soften. Heat the milk to 100°F and add it to the yeast. In the bowl of the food processor fitted with the dough blade, combine the butter, zest, salt, sugar, and 4 cups flour with 4 or 5 pulses. With the food processor running, add the liquid ingredients as fast as the dry ingredients will accept them. If you hear a sputtering sound, pour the liquid slower. As soon as all the liquid is added, turn the processor off. Check the liquid-to-flour ratio (see page 28). Pulse until the dough forms a ball, then process exactly 60 seconds.

By bread machine Put the water, milk, and butter in the bread pan. Add the zest, salt, sugar, and 4 cups flour to the bread pan, then sprinkle with the yeast. Select the Dough cycle and press Start. While the dough is mixing, check the liquid-to-flour ratio (see page 29). The machine stops after the kneading cycle. You may let the dough rise in the bread machine or a bowl.

First rise Put the dough in an oiled bowl and turn to coat the entire ball of dough with oil. Cover with a tightly woven towel and let rise until doubled, about one hour.

Shape Turn the dough out onto a lightly oiled work surface and divide in half. Roll each half into an 8 by 12-inch rectangle. Spread the cooled fruit evenly over the dough, leaving a ½-inch border along one 8-inch side. Roll up each dough rectangle into an 8-inch cylinder, ending at the border. Place each loaf, seam side down, in a well-greased 8½ by 4½-inch loaf pan or on a parchment-lined or well-greased baking sheet.

Second rise Cover with a tightly woven towel and let rise for one hour.

Preheat oven About 10 minutes before baking, preheat the oven to 375°F.

Bake and cool Bake for 35 minutes until the internal temperature of the bread reaches 190°F. Immediately remove the bread from the pans and place on a rack to cool. For a soft, shiny crust, rub the tops of the loaves with butter.

NOTE: This bread freezes nicely for up to 6 months. To serve, first thaw the bread, then reheat on a baking sheet in a 375°F oven for 7 to 10 minutes.

Candied Fruit

USING HOMEMADE CANDIED FRUIT for baking provides an intense fruit flavor without the strong, too sweet taste of commercially prepared fruit. The color of homemade candied fruit isn't as bright as the store-bought because no artificial colors are added. To liven the color and flavor, I add cranberries. The cranberries may split open during cooking, but they look lovely in the mixture. I also add fresh ginger to perk up the flavor. Limes can be used with lemons or in place of them, but their green color fades during cooking. Citron can also be added (if you can find it). You do not need to cover the pan during any of the following steps.

MAKES ABOUT 6 CUPS (2½ POUNDS)

*3 pieces fresh ginger, each about the size of
a wine cork*

1 large fresh pineapple

2 to 3 large thick-skinned lemons

2 to 3 large thick-skinned oranges

2 cups fresh or frozen cranberries, rinsed

1 cup sour cherries, rinsed and pitted

6 cups granulated sugar

¼ cup light corn syrup

Prepare ginger Peel the ginger and cut into ¼-inch cubes. Put in a saucepan, cover with water, and bring to a boil over medium-high heat. Reduce the heat and cook for 15 minutes. Drain the ginger and discard the water.

Prepare fruit Peel and core the pineapple. Cut into ¼-inch-thick slices, then cut the slices into ½-inch wedges. Measure 2 cups. Use the remaining pineapple for something else. Place the pineapple in a heavy pan with 4 cups water. Bring to a full boil over medium-high heat. Reduce the heat and simmer for 10 minutes. Remove the pineapple from the water with a slotted spoon or skimmer and set aside. Reserve the pineapple water.

While the pineapple is cooking, scrub the lemons and oranges with soap and water unless you know where they are grown. (Most commercial growers use a waxy coating to help them last longer and resist damage.) Cut the fruit into ¼-inch-thick slices, then cut the slices into ½-inch wedges. Measure the fruit. You need about 3 cups— a little more or a little less will not matter.

Put the lemons, oranges, cranberries, and cherries into a saucepan, cover with water, and bring to a full boil over medium-high heat. Reduce the heat and simmer for 10 minutes. Drain the fruit and discard the water.

Candy fruit Add 4 cups of the sugar, the corn syrup, and ginger into the pan with the pineapple water. Place over medium-high heat and bring the mixture to a full boil. Reduce the heat and cook at a slow boil for 10 minutes. Add the pineapple and citrus mixture and return to a rolling boil. Reduce the heat and simmer for 15 minutes, stirring the mixture often but gently.

Remove the fruit from the syrup and drain. I use large pizza screens to drain the fruit, but you can also shake the mixture gently in a colander. I save the syrup to sweeten tea or as a base for a holiday punch.

Dry fruit Preheat the oven to 200°F. Spread the fruit onto parchment-lined baking sheets (you really do need parchment paper for this job). If the fruit is sticky and clumps together, separate it with 2 forks. Dry the fruit in the oven for 2 hours.

Sugar mixture Pour the remaining 2 cups sugar into a large, sturdy plastic bag. Add the fruit and shake the bag to completely coat the fruit with sugar. Spread the fruit on parchment paper and let air-dry for 6 to 8 hours. Store in an airtight container for up to 6 weeks.

Candied Fruit Peel

IN MANY AREAS candied fruit peel can be bought only during the Thanksgiving and Christmas season. Making your own candied peel is easy, and it has much more flavor than the store-bought variety. Rough-skinned citrus fruits—the ones with larger pores— have a thicker peel and more white pith, while smooth-skinned fruit has more pulp and less pith. The thicker peel will candy easier because it can be cut into larger pieces. The ideal size for the peel is ¼ inch (that includes both the peel and pith together). If there is more than that, trim the pith slightly with a knife. You can make a mixture of peels if you like.

MAKES ABOUT 4 CUPS (1½ POUNDS)

4 large grapefruit, or 6 large navel oranges, or 10 tangerines, or 12 large lemons

3½ cups granulated sugar

2 tablespoons light corn syrup

Prepare fruit: Scrub the fruit with soap and water and rinse thoroughly to remove the waxy coating.

Remove the peel from the fruit. There are gadgets available in cookware stores that remove just the peel. If you don't have one of these gadgets, cut the fruit from end to end into fourths and separate the peel from the pulp by sliding your thumb or finger between the fruit and the peel. Cut the peel into ¼-inch dice.

Remove acid Put the peel in a pan and cover with water. Bring to a boil over medium-high heat. Reduce the heat and simmer for 5 minutes. Pour the peel into a strainer and discard the water. Cover the peel with fresh water and bring to a boil. Reduce the heat and simmer for 5 minutes more. Pour the peel into the strainer again and discard the water. This removes much of the acid and bitterness from the peel.

Candy peel Place 2½ cups of the sugar, the corn syrup, and 1½ cups water in a large pan and bring to a boil over medium-high heat. Stir the mixture constantly until the sugar dissolves completely. Add the peel to the sugar mixture and return to a boil. Reduce the heat and simmer uncovered for 45 minutes.

Pour the peel into a strainer. Reserve the syrup to sweeten drinks such as tea, lemonade, or mixed drinks that call for simple syrup when you might want a sharp citrus flavor.

Dry peel Preheat the oven to 200°F. Spread the peel on parchment-lined baking sheets. If the peel sticks together, separate it with 2 forks. Dry the fruit in the oven for 2 hours.

Sugar peel Pour the remaining 1 cup sugar into a large, sturdy plastic bag. Add the peel and shake the bag until the peel is completely coated with sugar. If the peel sticks together, separate it.

Spread the peel on parchment paper and allow to air-dry for 6 to 8 hours. Store in an airtight container for up to 6 weeks.

Liquid and Dry Measure Equivalencies

CUSTOMARY	METRIC
¼ teaspoon	1.25 milliliters
½ teaspoon	2.5 milliliters
1 teaspoon	5 milliliters
1 tablespoon	15 milliliters
1 fluid ounce	30 milliliters
¼ cup	60 milliliters
⅓ cup	80 milliliters
½ cup	120 milliliters
1 cup	240 milliliters
1 pint (2 cups)	480 milliliters
1 quart (4 cups; 32 ounces)	960 milliliters (.96 liter)
1 gallon (4 quarts)	3.84 liters
1 ounce (by weight)	28 grams
¼ pound (4 ounces)	114 grams
1 pound (16 ounces)	454 grams
2.2 pounds	1 kilogram (1,000 grams)

Oven Temperature Equivalents

DESCRIPTION	FAHRENHEIT	CELSIUS
Cool	200	90
Very slow	250	120
Slow	300–325	150–160
Moderately slow	325–350	160–180
Moderate	350–375	180–190
Moderately hot	375–400	190–200
Hot	400–450	200–230
Very hot	450–500	230–260

Sources

THE BAKER'S CATALOGUE is a wonderful resource for all types of baking supplies and high-quality baking equipment, as well as *pärlsocker* and pumpernickel (dark rye) flour. This is the catalog that I started for home bread bakers and sold to the King Arthur Flour Company in 1990. P. J. Hammel does a remarkable job writing and editing their newsletter, *The Baking Sheet,* which is filled with all types of information and recipes to keep home bakers well informed and happy. Call 800-827-6836; write P.O. Box 876, Norwich, VT 05055 for a catalog; or visit online at www.bakerscatalogue.com

BOB'S RED MILL sells a wide assortment of exceptional grains, mixes, and high-quality freshly milled flours, plus a complete line of good baking equipment. They grind all their flours on site and ship them out immediately, which guarantees exceptionally fresh products. Call 503-654-3215; write 5201 SE International Way, Milwaukie, OR 97222 for a catalog; or visit online at www.bobsredmill.com

THE BREADWORKS, INC., carries outstanding necessities for bread baking such as pizza peels and heavy-duty roux whisks, not to mention Betsy's videos *Perfect Bread: How to Conquer Bread Baking* and *Perfect Bread: Fun with Creative Shapes.* Call 603-632-9171 for a brochure; write 333 Choate Road, Enfield, NH 03748; or visit online at www.breadworksinc.com

NORA MILL GRANARY is located in the Sautee-Nacoochee Valley in north Georgia, where I was raised. They sell an assortment of flours and mixes and the best freshly ground white self-rising cornmeal in the country! This is also where I buy my speckled grits. Call 800-927-2375; write 7107 South Main Street, Helen, GA 30545; or visit online at www.noramill.com

PENZEYS SPICES is a catalog of herbs and spices. This is a good source for fenugreek, mahlab, and other hard-to-find herbs and spices. Call 800-741-7787; write P.O. Box 924, Brookfield, WI 53008-0924 for a catalog; or visit online at www.penzeys.com

SULTAN'S DELIGHT is a great source for some of those hard-to-find items like fenugreek, ground anise and caraway seeds, or orange and rose flower water. Call 800-852-5046; write P.O. Box 090302, Brooklyn, NY 11209; or visit online at www.sultansdelight.com

VOIGT GLOBAL DISTRIBUTION, LLC, is the only source I've found that carries sodium hydroxide for pretzel making. Call 816-471-9500; write P.O. Box 412762, Kansas City, MO 64141-2762; or visit online at www.vgdllc.com

Bibliography

Books and Periodicals

Alford, Jeffrey, and Naomi Duguid, *Flatbreads & Flavors*. New York: William Morrow, 1995.

Baily, Adrian Morrow, *The Blessings of Bread*. New York: Paddington Press, 1975.

Bateman, Michael, and Heather Maisner, *The Sunday Times Book of Real Bread*. Aylesbury, England: Rodale Press, 1982.

Bennett, Paula Pogany, and Velma R. Clark, *The Art of Hungarian Cooking*. Garden City, N.Y.: Doubleday, 1954.

Berk, Edi, Janez Bogataj, and Janez Pukšič, *Traditional Arts and Crafts in Slovenia*. Ljubljana, Slovenia: Domus, 1993.

Burton, Katherine, and Helmut Ripperger, *Feast Day Cookbook*. New York: David McKay, 1951.

Casella, Delores, *A World of Breads*. New York: David White, 1966.

Cutler, Kathy, *The Festive Bread Book*. New York: Barron's, 1982.

David, Elizabeth, *English Bread & Yeast Cookery, American Edition*. New York: Penguin Books, 1980.

Davidson, Alan, *The Oxford Companion to Food*. Oxford, England: Oxford University Press, 1999.

Duff, Gail, *A Loaf of Bread*. Edison, N.J.: Chartwell Books, 1998.

——, *Bread*. New York: Macmillan, 1993.

Dupaigne, Bernard, *The History of Bread*. New York: Harry N. Abrams, 1999.

Ecumenical Review, April 1997 v49 n2 p282(2).

Farley, Marta Pisetska, *Festive Ukrainian Cooking*. Pittsburgh, Pa.: University of Pittsburgh Press, 1990.

Feingold, Helen, and Mary Lee Grasanti, *The Joy of Christmas*. New York: Barron's, 1988.

Field, Carol, *Celebrating Italy*. New York: William Morrow, 1990.

——, *The Italian Baker*. New York: Harper & Row, 1985.

Gay, Kathlyn, and Martin K. Gay, *Encyclopedia of North American Eating and Drinking*. Santa Barbara, Calif.: ABC-CLLO, 1996.

Goldman, Marcy, *Jewish Holiday Baking*. New York: Doubleday, 1998.

Gubser, Mary, *America's Bread Book*. New York: William Morrow, 1985.

Hahn, Emily, *Time Life: The Cooking of China*. New York: Time, 1968.

Herbst, Sharon Tyler, *Food Lover's Companion*. Hauppauge, N.Y.: Barron's, 1995.

Honig, Mariana, *Breads of the World*. New York: Chelsea House, 1977.

Iaia, Sara Kelly, *Festive Baking*. Garden City, N.Y.: Doubleday, 1988.

Imbrasiené, Biruté, Giedré Ambrazaitiené, and Baltos Iankos, *Lithuanian Traditional Foods*. Vilnius, Lithuania: Baltos Lankos, 1998.

Ingram, Christine, and Jennie Shapter, *The World Encyclopedia of Bread and Bread Making.* London: Hermes House, 2001.

Kasper, Lynne Rossetto, *The Italian Country Table.* New York: Scribner, 1999.

Koehler, Margaret H., *Recipes from the Portuguese of Provincetown.* Riverside, Conn.: Chatham Press, 1973.

Moore, Marilyn M., *The Wooden Spoon Bread Book.* New York: Atlantic Monthly Press, 1987.

Nathan, Joan, *The Jewish Holiday Baker.* New York: Schocken Books, 1997.

Ojakangas, Beatrice, *The Finnish Cookbook.* New York: Crown Publishers, 1964.

——, *The Great Scandinavian Baking Book.* Boston: Little Brown & Company, 1988.

Ortiz, Elisabeth Lambert, *The Food of Spain and Portugal.* New York: Atheneum, 1989.

"Paczki Day," *Polish American Journal.* February 1995.

Polanie Club, *Treasured Polish Recipes for Americans.* Minneapolis: Polanie Publishing, 1948.

Reider, Freda, *The Hallah Book.* Hoboken, N.J.: Ktav, 1987.

Schwarcz, Joe, "The Secret Life of Bagels: Why the Montreal variety still ranks as the best in the world," *Montreal Gazette,* May 27, 2001.

Sheppard, Ronald, and Edward Newton, *The Story of Bread.* London: Routledge & Kegan Paul, 1957.

Slovenian Women's Union of America, *More Pots and Pans.* Joliet, Ill.: Slovenian Women's Union of America, 1998.

Spicer, Dorothy Gladys, *From an English Oven.* New York: The Women's Press, 1948.

Sunset Magazine, April 1984.

Swahn, Jan-Öjvind, The Swedish Institute, *Maypoles, Crayfish and Lucia—Swedish Holidays and Traditions.* Stockholm: Swedish Institute, 1999.

Torres, Marimar, *The Spanish Table.* Garden City, N.Y.: Doubleday, 1986.

Treuille, Eric, and Ursula Ferrigno, *Ultimate Bread.* New York: DK Publishing, 1998.

Volokh, Anne, with Mavis Manus, *The Art of Russian Cuisine.* New York: Macmillan, 1983.

Voth, Norma Jost, *Festive Breads of Christmas.* Scottdale, Pa.: Herald Press, 1983.

——, *Mennonite Foods & Folkways from South Russia, Volume I.* Intercourse, Pa.: Good Books, 1990.

Wilson, C. Anne, *Food & Drink in Britain from the Stone Age to Recent Times.* London: Constable and Company, 1973.

INTERNET*

Alexian Brothers Health System—Mission and Spiritual Services, www.alexianhealthsystems.org/mission/culture/germans.html

Alexian Brothers Health System—Mission and Spiritual Services, www.alexianhealthsystems.org/mission/culture/finns.html

---

* Some of these websites may no longer be available.

Alexian Brothers Health System—Mission and Spiritual Services, www.alexianhealthsystems.org/mission/culture/Iceland.html

Alexian Brothers Health System—Mission and Spiritual Services, www.alexianhealthsystems.org/mission/culture/swedish.html

Baker's Toolbox Progressive Baker Profiles, www.progressivebaker.com/toolbox/profiles/goulast/goulart1.html

Birnbrot, www.glanderland.ch

Bonnets & Bunnies, www.web-holidays.com/easter/recipes/paasis.htm

Boston Globe, www.boston.com/dining/recipes/m/Moroccan_anise_bread.html

Bulgarian Christmas Customs, www.eat-online.net/english/habits/christmas/beliefs_bulgaria.htm

Bulgarian Easter Traditions, b-info.com/places/Bulgaria/Easter/

Caldwell Kolache Festival, www.rtis.com/reg/caldwell/ent/claudia.htm

Children's Jewish Holiday Kitchen, www.blueskypie.com

Christmas in Finland, virtual.finland.fi/finfo/English/joulueng.html

Christmas Time Together, www.imagitek.com/xmas/recipes/kolach.html

Clague, John: Manx Reminiscences, Chapter X—Superstitions and Sorcery, www.mcb.net/manxrem/mrch10.htm

Control Signs, etext.lib.virginia.edu/railton/projects/riedy/list1.html

Cooking Around the World—Finnish Cooking, members.tripod.com/~WrightPlace/caw-Finland10.html

Cultural Overview, slis.cua.edu/ihy/sp2000/cuisines/Culture.htm

Cultures and Cuisine of Eastern Europe, www.unc.edu/depts/slavic/publications/brochure2.html

Cyprus Government, www.pio.gov.cy/cyprus_today/jul_dec98/feast.htm

Day of the Dead, www.nacnet.org/assunta/dead.htm

Desert Living Messages, forums.about.com

Digest, afsnet.org/sections/foodways/93toc.htm

Edibilia. Peter's Mum's Soda Bread Wisdom, www.ibmpcug.co.uk/~owls/sodabred.htm

Egypt—Food of the Gods, Part 1: Wine in Ancient Egypt, www.egyptmonth.com/mag01012001/magf2.htm

Everyday Superstitions coordinated by the project group of Bela III Grammar School, Baja, Hungary, www.bajabela.sulinet.hu/tubi/iearn/superst/newyear.htm

Finland Bread: A Firm Favorite, www.globalgourmet.com/destinations/finland/finbread.html

Finnish Bread, members.spree.com/ojoronen/leipa.htm

Flour Advisory Board, www.wheatintolerance.co.uk/superstitions.asp

Grains: Bread to Borek,
    www.about-Turkey.com/cuisine/
    grains.htm
Happy Holiday happenings 2001–2002,
    members.aol.com/Momosarebad/
    holiday.html
History of Christmas, www.birthdayexpress.com/
    bexpress/planning/Christmas.asp
Home and Garden, www.nwnews.com/
    vvissues/v9n48/home1.html
Jubilee days, the Jubilee Easter,
    www.giubileo.rai.it/eng/schede/
    15/001567.htm
Kahk, www.touregypt.net/recipes/kahk2.htm
Kazakh Culture, www.kazalliance.com/
    page/clt.html
Leipatiedotus Finnish Bread,
    www.leipatiedotus.fi/fried.htm
Life & Leisure story, www.smc.edu/corsair/
    Archive/fall98/issue14/issue14_pages/life
    _leisure/life_leisure_s07/15/2001
Loukoumades, www.geocities.com/
    NapaValley/4722/loukoumades.html
Lucyfest/The Queen of Lights/Festival of Lights,
    www.serve.com/shea/germusa/lucia.htm
Mexico Hot . . . or Not!—Mexican Cooking Rosca
    de Reyes, www.mexconnect.com/
    mex_/recipes/puebla/kgreyesbread.html
Oliebollen, www.dnc.net/users/king/recipe/
    olie.htm
Omens, Tamaria Young,
    www.savetamariayoung.com/
    omens-mar98.htm

Peru, www.li.gatech.edu/~student/
    magazine/GAPAGE/festival.htm
Recipes.alastra.com/breads-yeast/pulla03.txt
Sankt Barbara, www.serve.com/shea/germusa/
    barbara.htm
SHOWCOOK Cook's Class,
    www.showcook.co.za/simnel.htm
Sickness, Disease—The superstitions
    and folklore you need to make life
    magnificent or miserable,
    www.sandiego-books.com/sickness.htm
Story Behind a Loaf of Bread, The Botham
    Company, www.botham.co.uk/
    bread/supersti.htm
Strat's Place—Daniel Rogov—Israel—
    numerous articles, www.stratsplace.com/
    rogov/Israel
Superstitions and Traditions, www.breannas.com
Superstitions, Jenny Brahney, www.orbitca_com/
    jennybrahney/intro.html
Swedish Institute, www.swedish-embassy.org
Taste of Culture, Elizabeth Andoh,
    www.bento.com/taste/tc-anpan.html
Taste of Jordan, www.jibdc.org/jordan4kids/
    culture_cuisine.html
Tribes: Berber festival of the Moussem of
    Imilchil in Morocco, www.tribes.co.uk/
    Mor_T_Moussem.htm
Virtual Purim, www.chabadonline.com/
    scripts/tgij/paper/indexpurim.asp?Article
    ID=1463
Yom Kippur, www.infoplease.com/spot/
    yomkippur1.html

Index

topping:

    sugar, 149

towels, tightly woven, 18

Treize Desserts, Les, 273

Tsoureki, 180–84

Twelfth Night, 98

U

Ukraine:

    Kalyra, 163–65

    Korovai (Wedding Bread), 153–59

    Mandryky, 160–62

    Pampushky, 163, 166–67

    Paska, 168–71

unbleached flour, 7

V

Vanocka, 124–28

Vasilopita (Saint Basil's Bread), 185–87

vegetable shortening, 11

Vortbrøt (Doppbrød), 254–56

W

Wales, Barmbrack, 102–5

War Between the States, 61

water, 10

Weddings:

    Gubana, 301–4

    Irish Soda Bread, 95–97

    Kneeldown Bread, 55–56

    Korovai (Ukrainian Wedding Bread), 153–59

    Pretzels, 279–81

    Zwieback, 223–25

Western Europe, *see* Europe

wheat flour, 7–8

whisks, 19

whole-wheat flour, 8

Wiggs (Wigs, Wygges, Wigges, Whigs), 92–94

Wisconsin, Kringle, 232–35

witches, 241

wrap, plastic, 18

Y

yeast, 6–7

    activating, 22–23

    active dry, 6

    compressed, 6

    fast-rising, 6

    fresh, 6

    heat as damaging to, 37

    proofing method for, 22–23, 27

    quick method for, 23

    quick-rising, 6

    rising and, 30

    standard method for, 23

Yemen, Kubaneh, 198–200

Yom Kippur:

    Montreal Bagels, 63–65

    Sephardi Bread, 48–51

Z

Zalabya, 42–44

zatar herb topping, 193–94

zest:

    graters for removal of, 15

    pomeransskal, 255

Zwieback, 223–25